Web Browsing
with
The Microsoft®
Network

D1616052

Other Prima Computer Books Available Now!

Access From the Ground Up, 2nd Edition
ACT! 2.0 for Windows: The Visual Learning Guide
Build a Web Site: The Programmer's Guide to Creating, Building, and Maintaining a Web Presence
The CD-ROM Revolution
CompuServe Information Manager for Windows: The Complete Membership Kit & Handbook
      (with two 3½" disks)
Computer's Don't Byte
Computer Gamer's Survival Guide
CorelDRAW! 5 Revealed!
Create Wealth with Quicken, Second Edition
Cruising America Online: The Visual Learning Guide
DOS 6.2: Everything You Need to Know
Excel 5 for Windows: The Visual Learning Guide
IBM Smalltalk Programming for Windows & OS/2
Internet After Hours
Internet for Windows–America Online Edition: The Visual Learning Guide
KidWare: The Parent's Guide to Software for Children
Lotus Notes 3 Revealed!
Mac Tips and Tricks
Macintosh Design to Production: The Definitive Guide
Making Movies with Your PC
Making Music with Your PC
Migrating to Windows 95
OS/2 Warp: Easy Installation Guide
PageMaker 5.0 for the Mac: Everything You Need to Know
PageMaker 5.0 for Windows: Everything You Need to Know
Paradox 4.5 for DOS Revealed! (with 3½" disk)
Paradox for Windows Essential Power Programming (with 3½" disk)
PowerPoint: The Visual Learning Guide
PROCOMM PLUS for Windows: The Visual Learning Guide
Quicken 3 for Windows: The Visual Learning Guide
QuickTime: Making Movies with Your Macintosh, Second Edition
The Slightly Skewed Computer Dictionary
Smalltalk Programming for Windows (with 3½" disk)
The Software Developer's Complete Legal Companion (with 3½" disk)
Software: What's Hot! What's Not!
Think THINK C! (with two 3½" disks)
Thom Duncan's Guide to NetWare Shareware (with 3½" disk)
UnInstaller 3 Uncluttering Your PC
The Usenet Navigator Kit (with 3½" disk)
Visual Basic for Applications Revealed!
The Warp Book: Your Definitive Guide to Installing and Using OS/2 v3
WinComm PRO: The Visual Learning Guide
Windows 3.1: The Visual Learning Guide
WinFax PRO 4: The Visual Learning Guide
Word 6 for the Mac: The Visual Learning Guide
Word for Windows 2: The Visual Learning Guide
Word for Windows 6: The Visual Learning Guide
WordPerfect 6.1 for Windows: The Visual Learning Guide

How to Order:

For information on quantity discounts contact the publisher: Prima Publishing, P.O. Box 1260BK, Rocklin, CA 95677-1260; (916) 632-4400. On your letterhead include information concerning the intended use of the books and the number of books you wish to purchase. For individual orders, turn to the back of this book for more information.

Web Browsing with The Microsoft® Network

Jeff Bankston

PRIMA PUBLISHING

Senior Project Editor: Dan J. Foster

ISBN: 0-7615-0288-2
Library of Congress Catalog Card Number: 95-70829
Printed in the United States of America
95 96 97 98 AA 10 9 8 7 6 5 4 3 2

Contents

FOREWORD

Over the years, Microsoft has vowed to deliver on its promise to empower personal-computer users with technology that promotes new ways of thinking and communicating. Along with that promise, Microsoft committed itself to its vision of making technology accessible, useful, personal, and fun for all computer users. They call this vision "Information at Your Fingertips," and with the release of the long-awaited Windows 95, Microsoft comes close to realizing that vision by putting "Information at Your Desktop."

Information at your desktop comes via an electronic connection between your Windows 95 computer and The Microsoft Network. The Microsoft Network is an online service that reaches beyond your Windows-based desktop to a worldwide community of people, ideas, and information. It sets the stage for a worldwide electronic marketplace of products and services, and can serve as your gateway to the Internet.

So just what is the Internet? The Internet is a massive network of computers spanning continents around the globe. You've no doubt heard it referred to as the "Information Super Highway," and that description is dead on. Depending on how you get on the highway and the tools you use to navigate, your trip can be a joy ride or a long ride over bumpy roads.

Jeff Bankston is a knowledgeable guide who takes you through all the stops and roadways to the Internet via The Microsoft Network. Jeff takes the bumps out of cruising the "Net" by showing you everything you need to know—from preparing to go online to the sights you see along the way, and what to do when you get there.

If you're looking for safe passage on to MSN and the Internet, then *Web Browsing with The Microsoft Network* is your passport. Inside this book you learn what the Internet is, how it came to be, what you need to access it, and how to explore it safely. With your competent tour guide, feel free to go forth and explore!

Valda Hilley
President, Convergent Press Literary Group

ACKNOWLEDGMENTS

Throughout my professional computing life I have dedicated myself to the premise of empowering a user of a computer, a reader of a book, or a new programmer, with the skills and knowledge that I've accumulated over time. My learning experiences frequently brought on sleepless nights, significant expenses of computing resources, and more. To the end of it all, I've strived tirelessly to teach others what I've learned, and I've loved every step of that beaten path.

With this book I had the pristine opportunity to share that wealth of experience, and for that I owe many fine folks a debt of gratitude. I'd like to thank Bob Mullen for his unselfish efforts and for understanding what it's like to be an author. If it were not for him believing in me, this book would not have been possible. To Dan Foster, a heartfelt handshake for his role in keeping me in-line. Behind the scenes was the staff of Prima Publishing, who quietly keep the production rolling—a grateful thank you.

There's a special lady in Michelle who unselfishly gave of her time, listening to me at the office. And of all the folks I've been around during this project, it was my loving and devoted wife Anja who stuck with me through the sleepless nights and long days required to write this book. She was my first proofreader, and she let me know when I was about to do something really bone-headed. I couldn't have done this without her at my side.

Above all, and above us, is the recognition that a higher authority in God Almighty gave me the heart, soul, and wisdom to plan and execute the complicated steps necessary to produce this work. It is truly mysterious how He works at times.

CHAPTER 1

The Microsoft Network Meets the World Wide Web

In the world of online information services, users have seen a wide range of functionality and resources evolve and mature into a seemingly never ending pool of things to do, places to go, and things to see. This informational flow has been growing at exponential rates over the past few years to the point that the average computer users who are experienced offline becomes overloaded when they first meet the online world. Where the offline user has a vast list of utilities and tools to help find data on the local computer, the online user finds himself in an awkward position—knowledge of computers but unsure of how he should, or could, apply it to a brave new world online.

The Microsoft Network is perhaps the first online information service that addresses the user's needs right from the start. MSN, as it's abbreviated, uses the point-and-shoot methodology to ease these and other concerns that routinely perplex the user. Microsoft Corporation musters its vast resources to expose a style of computing that promises to enhance the way we use our computers, and reshape our thoughts of how an online service should be viewed.

Right from the start, the Microsoft Internet Explorer (the MSN Web browser) provides us with a way to become active and productive Web surfers with the use of gopher, a web browser, FTP access, and much more. All of this functionality is provided by the ease of point-and-shoot mentioned earlier in which the user's concerns about the complexity of the Web are eased.

What Is MSN?

I can see it now. You're wondering what's this book about, right?—browsing something called the World Wide Web using something called "the Microsoft Network"? (or MSN for short)—some Microsoft product that's part of Windows 95. Exploring a bit further, you find out it's an online service! Oh, no, not another one! There's CompuServe, America Online, Prodigy, and Genie, to name the main players. So what's Microsoft got to offer the others don't already have?

Plenty. MSN was designed to be an online community of international proportions. It spans 23 nations across the globe from the outset, and it is expected to connect as many as 5 million people by the year 1998 and as many as 20 million by the year 2005. MSN has multilingual tree structures for German, French, and many other languages, as Figure 1-1 shows.

This book will take you on a journey through the Microsoft Network and show you how it gets you onto the online world commonly referred to as the World Wide Web, the Web for short. Along the way, we'll tell you about the Microsoft Network itself and a bit about how Windows 95 can get you there with the greatest of ease. MSN provides a mix of the two predominant modes of online operation, graphical and command line, but it leans heavily to the GUI side of life. The point-and-shoot mode of computing makes MSN and Windows 95 perhaps the easiest of the online services to navigate. Everything that can be done on MSN can be done via point and shoot. No keywords to memorize, no forum names to

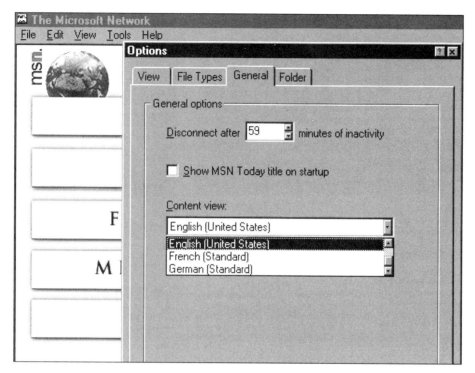

Figure 1-1
**Basic MSN
settings for
language
support**

remember, no special codes. The old saying that a picture is worth a thousand words has never been truer!

Many online services, if not all of them, have come to reflect how the graphical user interface (or GUI) has taken over the computing world. If it's not GUI, it isn't worth anything, it seems. That's not exactly true because each interface has its good points and bad points. Users of various backgrounds prefer the method that best suits their online needs, but most aren't willing to give up the level of ease that a GUI provides.

MSN has compounded the command line and GUI interfaces in a way well calculated to offer the best of both worlds. The power user will appreciate the flexibility of command line functions, whereas the novice will enjoy the point-and-shoot style of operation. As we travel together from cover to cover, I'll point the differences out at the correct places.

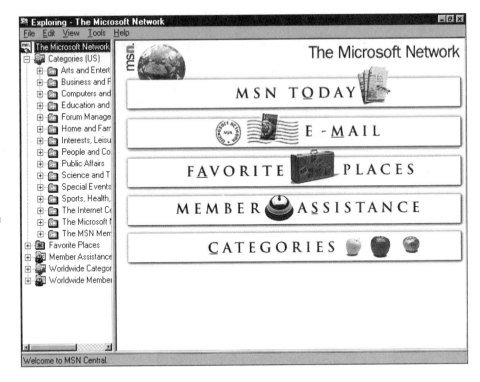

Figure 1-2
Microsoft
Network's
opening screen

The Rationale

But why another online service? Haven't we got enough now? It depends on how you look at it, as well as on what you want to get out of the service itself. Microsoft has addressed questions of the overall spirit and intent of online services. What can MSN provide for your dollar? How will it change your attitude toward computing online from home, from your business, or in any other sphere?

Microsoft firmly believes that the key to success with this service is building community, and quite frankly I believe them—wholeheartedly, in fact. Go online, browse through a few of the forums and chat rooms on your way to the Web, and you'll see what I mean. It's not just another service, it's a community! In the rest of this chapter, I'll tell you what you need to know to get comfortable with these environments called Windows 95 and MSN.

The Microsoft Network itself is composed of PCs running the Windows NT Advanced Server operating system. These systems are linked together to form a network powerful enough to handle large numbers of users' computers doing a good many things. To get to these servers, you use your personal computer running Windows 95 and connected to a modem to dial into a point of presence (POP for short) that connects you to the server. As of this writing, Microsoft has over 40,000 POPs all across the globe in 23 countries. In later sections, you'll learn in detail how to make this connection. Once connected to MSN over a modem, you can cruise through MSN to your heart's content. In this book, we'll be using MSN as the conduit to browse an equally fun and diverse place called the World Wide Web.

What's So Special about One More Service?

Some may find "Why MSN?" A tough question to answer, whereas others may find it easy. You may find it enlightening to understand the goals of the service:

- ◆ Build the online community spirit.
- ◆ Provide a fun, entertaining, and educational experience.
- ◆ Give users more value for their online dollar.
- ◆ Give users a compelling reason to come back.

Okay, so MSN's developers have a vision of what they want the network to do, or be, as it becomes an active online service. When it goes live upon release of Windows 95, MSN will be one of the most heavily tested projects that was ever in beta. Windows 95 itself will have had nearly 250,000 testers, and early statistics placed about 40,000 of those on MSN itself in the network's early days. That's quite a test!

In addition to seeing that the product has been rigorously tested and beaten upon, MSN's developers have striven to provide a wide quantity of resources for all ages and lifestyles in a quality setting. They have accomplished this feat through several novel approaches. One of these is to empower the forum managers of the service with the authority, the ability, and the tool sets to change forum designs to match the ever-changing conditions of the online world. Although this may not seem vastly important, it is a revolution in the way massive systems like MSN have traditionally operated. Forum managers on CompuServe have to work with their sponsors or management to discuss the whys and wherefores of desired changes. Forum managers rarely prevail on their management to negotiate with the service provider, such as CompuServe, to make actual changes in a forum's structure.

Microsoft, by contrast, has departed from what MIS managers would call the normal way to conduct business: Empower the forum manager to handle broad issues affecting users. In normal online settings, letting forum managers make direct changes to forum structures is strictly taboo, but MSN allows it. In fact, MSN encourages forum managers to review forum structures often to see if they meet the needs of the users.

For instance, forum managers are free to respond to breaking news events by creating new sections or areas such as chat rooms within their forums in which to hold community discussions about the events. When interest in an event wanes, a forum manager can delete the extra room or section as required. If interest in an event exceeds anticipations, a forum manager can create yet more chat rooms or sections to fulfill the need. Figure 1-3 shows what such a new section might look like.

In this manner, MSN has provided an avenue to meet users' evolving needs rapidly. Although such a policy may lead to performance hits to a system, it reflects one of Microsoft's core goals for MSN: Give the users a compelling reason to come back. Make MSN worth their time and worth their online dollar. Microsoft has carefully chosen the forum managers of MSN for their own individual abilities and ideas, their background and past or present online experience, and their reasons for wanting to be on MSN. Thus they hope to build a network of communities where users can

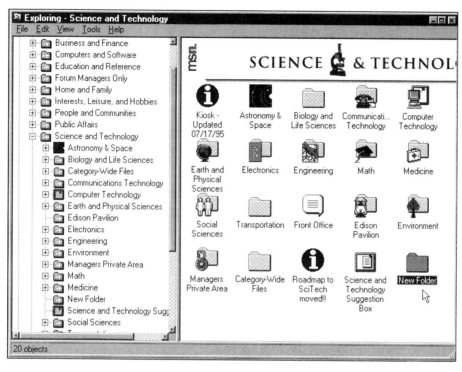

Figure 1-3
A newly added folder

be always assured of finding what they're looking for and what they need to meet their goals. Give the user a compelling reason to come back.

Requirements for MSN

Before you decide to dive into MSN and the Web, there are a few things you should ask yourself:

◆   What do you expect to get out of MSN?
◆   What do you want out of the Web?
◆   How old is your computer?
◆   How much money are you willing to spend to make it handle the complex requirements of Windows 95, MSN, and graphic-intensive online services?

I ask these questions because you need to understand that the days of using a DOS-based program to do your online computing are over if you want to cruise the Web and MSN alike. The enjoyment and fulfillment that these two services offer come accompanied by additional demands both on your computer system (hardware and software) and on your background with computers in general. In the next sections, I will detail these issues.

The Hardware

DOS itself is a single-tasking operating system that handles the hardware and coordinates the software's use of the hardware. As such, it does one task, and then it ends that task to start the next, and so on and so forth. Pretty straightforward. With the advent of MS Windows and OS/2, on the other hand, multiple tasks can be performed with the computer at once, a feat that was previously not possible. This added functionality has come with a price tag for more memory, more disk space, and a faster processor. Doing more things with a computer suddenly took a more expensive turn! This progression of more complicated operating systems led to further expenses in hardware. This was all necessary to keep up with the ever-expanding sizes of the software.

Around the time of Windows version 3.0 and OS/2 version 1.2, it was common to need a 386DX/20, 4MB RAM, and a 65MB hard disk to just do the basic things. As Windows and OS/2 matured and gained in functionality, the hardware required to run them kept pace. These days, a 486DX/33 and 8MB of RAM with a 340MB hard disk is considered to be the baseline for most users. There are still plenty of 386DX-based machines out there running 4MB of RAM and 120MB of disk space, and those users will have problems running MSN and the Web software on Windows 95. All of this new-fangled software, and all of the fun it brings to the party, comes with a price tag.

As I see it, here's the absolute bare minimum hardware that should be used to install and run Windows 95, MSN, or any Web browser:

- A 486DX/33 or 486DX/40 PC
- 8MB of RAM memory—12MB is better, 16MB is optimum
- A 340MB hard disk with 100MB free space
- A 14400 bps modem with error correction

The monitor resolution is up to you, but Super VGA mode at 800x600 and 256 colors looks really nice. Windows 95 will install with MSN in 35MB of disk space, but once you add a few applets and the other tools you're likely to install, the installation can easily go to 65MB of space. If you already have Windows version 3.1 installed, the space requirements will be a bit less. With modem prices dirt cheap now, you can get a 14.4K modem (internal flavor) for under $100 and the external variety for about $40 more. I recently purchased a 28.8K external fax/modem for $240 retail, and prices are falling again. MSN supports a maximum of 14.4K at the moment, but 28.8K nodes are planned at release time of Windows 95. The future may even bring ISDN connectivity to MSN!

The Software

Okay, so you've got the hardware to handle the task, but what about the software? Windows 95 is the base upon which all other operations are built, and it does not require DOS to be present. When you install Windows 95, in fact, "MSDOS v7" is installed for the sake of compatibility with other apps that demand or need DOS functions and utilities.

After installing Windows 95, you install MSN as an optional applet. You could have chosen to install MSN along with Windows 95, but we'll presume that you didn't choose to do so. With MSN installed and working, you'll need to log on with MSN, create an account, and perform some basic setups. That process, whose beginning is shown in Figure 1-4, will be covered in detail in Chapter 2.

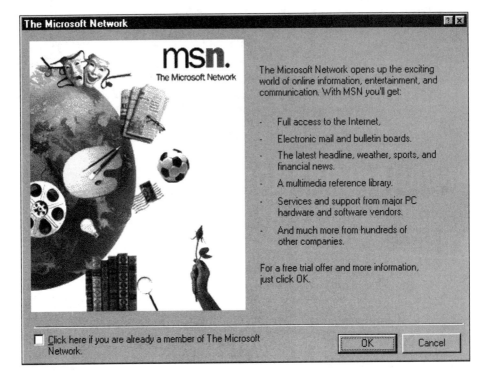

Figure 1-4
Creating an
MSN account

As you go through the installation of the software, notice a few things that have changed since Windows version 3.*x*. All the way through the installation, a *Wizard* is available to assist you through most of the steps to installing the software. The Wizard is a part of the program that gives you advice on what to do next and generally provides a guiding light to the process.

The Mind-Set

The question of mind-set is usually one of the hardest parts of the entire job as you install and first use the new operating system and MSN. Microsoft did an extraordinarily huge amount of user testing to find the optimal fit and finish for both Windows 95 and MSN. When you look for programs to run or attempt to find files on your computer, you'll inevitably run across things that represent approaches that are different, sometimes radically different, from how you used to compute.

"This is the way we always do it" points to perhaps the single most treacherous aspect of Windows 95 that I could find. Users were so ingrained as to past habits that they could not see the forest for the trees, as the saying goes. Keep an open mind about the changes, and the whole process will be a thrill.

Preparing for MSN

I've said that the minimum computer you should have is a 486DX/33 with 8MB of RAM and a large hard drive preferably with 100MB free after installing Windows 95 and MSN.

You've got to plan your Windows 95 installation out to some degree due to the differences between Windows 95 and Windows 3.*x*. One major problem I've found is that if you don't install Windows 95 over the top of your current Windows 3.*x* installation, you'll have to reinstall all of your applications that you expect to use in Windows 95 from within Windows 95. There are three primary reasons for this:

◆ Windows 95 registers each application as it's installed. Registering the application means that the application is made globally visible to other Windows apps that might use it in different ways.

◆ The necessary files such as DLLs or configuration files have to be established within Windows 95. While you might be able to copy these files from a Windows 3.*x* installation, don't try it, as this is not sufficient.

◆ If you install Windows 95 to a separate directory away from Windows 3.*x*, and you have to reinstall your apps, don't reinstall them to the original Windows 3.1 directory. Data corruption will occur.

To clarify on the third point, let's say you have Winword version 6 installed to C:\WINWORD. Windows 3.1 is at D:\WINDOWS, and you install Windows 95 to `E:\WIN400`. For Winword to work properly in Windows 95, you must reinstall Winword while running Windows 95. Simply creating a shortcut to Winword in `C:\WINWORD` will not work.

CAUTION

Installing a Windows 3.1 application to its original directory while Windows 95 is running will cause corruption and loss of data.

As you install these applications in Windows 95, each has its own set of operational parameters that function in Windows 95 in a slightly different fashion than in Windows 3.1. Should you decide to install Windows 95 to a separate directory and leave your Windows 3.*x* alone, disk space requirements will go up considerably. The benefit to this strategy is that, if something goes wrong while you're getting accustomed to Windows 95, you can always reboot into Windows 3.*x* and continue with your work. This can be particularly helpful if you're on a system such as NetWare™ or Vines™ where multiple networks may exist.

Requirements for the Web

Hmm. What can the Web possibly require? It's just software, right? Well, yes and no. The Web is a set of systems and services that provide a pipeline for data to be exchanged all across the globe. Just like the spider's web that connects many pieces for the spider, the World Wide Web provides the connection for computers.

What's This Web Business?

The Web is quite a sophisticated electronic machine whose name really doesn't adequately describe what it does or can do. In reality, it allows users to connect to databases, universities, research labs, and a host of other resources. While doing this, the Web provides for diverse communications between people and machines.

But, what exactly is the Web? The Web is a joint effort by a consortium of European research organizations and universities but is centered on CERN, the European Particle Physics Lab located near Geneva, Switzerland. The purpose of the Web is to provide effective communications between organizations through the use of a *hypertext* language in which a point-and-shoot style of selection could be made to transfer documents between locations. If you've ever used Windows before and had to consult with the online help system, you've undoubtedly seen the green highlighted text that caused the mouse cursor to change into a hand with a pointing finger. Clicking on the text takes you to another location in the help text.

The Web is much the same. Click on a *hypertext jump,* like the one in Figure 1-5, and it takes you half way across the world! How's that for instant communications? This is the premise behind the Web: rapid and effective communications among people, places, and things.

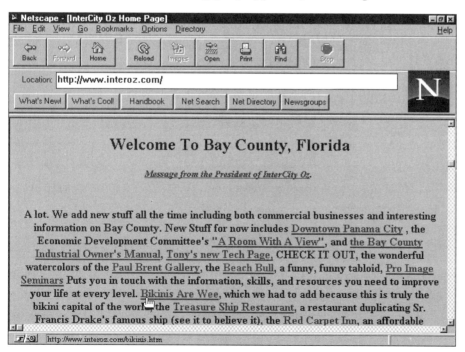

Figure 1-5
Example of a hypertext link

To connect all these sites, UNIX servers are installed at these sites. Most run UNIX in one form or another either on Sun™ workstations or on pure UNIX machines such as AT&T 3B series minicomputers or DEC™ minicomputers. In the early days of the Web back in 1988 and 1989, fewer than 100 servers existed on the Web. As of the latest data I could find, nearly 11,000 servers are in existence! Yow! How do you keep track of these servers and what they have to offer? The answer to that is in Chapters 5 and 6.

Is There Anything Special Here?

You bet there is something special to the Web! All across the Web you'll find interesting things like new books to buy, places to get utilities (free ones, too!) to enhance your Web carousing, and much more. This is part of what we'll be doing in Chapter 7 with Netscape. But, one of the most important things to keep in mind is how you connect to the Web. In doing it via MSN, you remove the need for a separate Internet provider and can drastically reduce your online costs. In my case, I have an MSN connection point, referred to as a MSN node, that's a local phone call away. In this way, one more cost is removed.

Your Navigator's License

As you prepare yourself to cruise cyberspace, think about driving a car cross-country. When you decided to do so, did you just hop in the car and hit the road? Not likely. I bet you planned the trip out for places to stay, to eat—perhaps you've made this trip before and have favorite rest stops or scenic areas. Of course, you could have just spontaneously begun the trip and taken it haphazardly.

On the Web, you can do much the same. Take either road, and get either result. If you're out for the evening doing the town, you may tend to do it rough and tumble, eh? Carefree, just out to see what can be seen. The Web allows this approach, no problem. If, on the other hand, you've certain goals for this online session, there are plenty of tools on the Web to assist you in getting around in an orderly manner. Not as orderly as MSN, perhaps, but fairly well organized. This aspect of the Web is covered in detail in Chapter 3.

Understanding a Few Terms

As you cross the highways and byways of the Web, you'll run across a number of acronyms that will drive a sane person right up the wall in nothing flat! In the back of this book, Appendix A to be exact, you'll find a list of commonly used terms. Some you may recognize; others may be completely Greek to you. Don't let that bother you. The terms are listed in alphabetical order with a brief description.

Here's a sample of acronyms that are common on the Web:

Name	Description
WWW	World Wide Web
HTTP	HyperText Transfer Protocol
FTP	File Transfer Protocol
SMTP	Simple Mail Transfer Protocol
FAQ	Frequently Asked Questions
URL	Uniform Resource Locator
WAIS	Wide Area Information Server

Getting around MSN

As you complete the setup of Windows 95 and initial setup of Exchange client and MSN, you'll probably wonder what you'll see when you first log on. Not a lot—your first logon is dedicated to signing on and creating an account. We'll do that in Chapter 2, but let's discuss how MSN will indeed look to you.

Terms of Endearment

Upon setting up and logging on, you'll create an account, in the process supplying quite a bit of information, including your real name, to MSN.

In return, you'll be asked to choose a nickname for yourself. Kind of like a CB handle from the 70s and 80s. Remember those? Nightrider. Spook Central. Sledgehammer. The list goes on forever, but the principle is the same. When you go online for the next and subsequent times, you will log on under this nickname, or alias, and that is how other MSN users will see you. You can look at the properties for any logged-on user, but only in a chat room, or via the MSN address book. We'll discuss these areas more in Chapter 8.

For now, it's important to realize that one term you'll see and that *you should never forget* is your logon name! Honestly, you wouldn't believe how many new users forget their logon name in the excitement of creating a new account. It can be the same as your real name, but most folks use a "handle," as it's called. Users frequently pick a pet nickname or a word chosen for sentimental reasons. Businesses often use an alias because several employees may use the same account. There's no real use in having 20 accounts when one will do, is there? Well, there may be.

When you create an account and are registered with the MSN address book, every single user on MSN sees that address book and can create his or her own offline address book. So, let's say that 250 MSN users get your address in their personal address book. Now, your company changes the name on the account, or the alias, to suit other business needs. What happens to the address books of those 250 users? Nothing! Nothing at all. They still have the same alias as before! Your listing isn't automatically updated in the users' personal address books, although it is changed on MSN's online address book.

TIP

If you or your business plan on having multiple users, it's best to create separate accounts for each user.

The Basic Structure of MSN

MSN can be thought of much like the subjects in a school—History, Physics, English—all of which can be broken down into more specialized areas of interest. There's Environmental Chemistry, Metallurgical Chemistry, Biomedical Chemistry—the list goes on from there. Similarly, each MSN category (Figure 1-6) is further broken down into more detailed areas: forums, suggestion boxes, auditoriums for conferences and chats, and other related matters of interest. You can use the mouse to point and click to any area. You can use the *go word* if one has been assigned to a subject, but the mouse will always work. What's more, the right mouse button works! How's that for progress? Appendix B will provide complete details on the structure of MSN as it exists at the time of this writing.

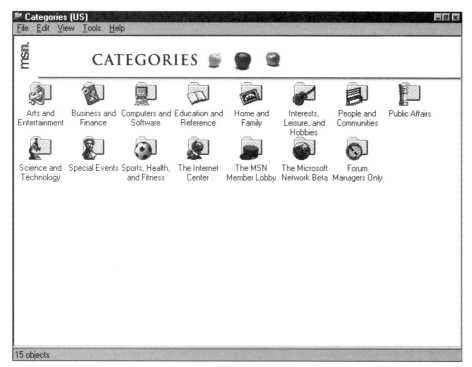

Figure 1-6
MSN's category screen

Of Categories and Forums

When you cruise through MSN for the first time, it's easy to forget where you are at, or how you got there, or even where you're going. MSN comes to your aid by keeping multiple windows open showing all of the places you've opened in the course of a session, as Figure 1-7 shows.

These multiple screens are actually one screen opened for each of the areas you've visited; you have to close a screen manually by leaving the associated activity. Again, Chapter 8 will present more on MSN-specific configurations.

Figure 1-7
MSN's multiple screens

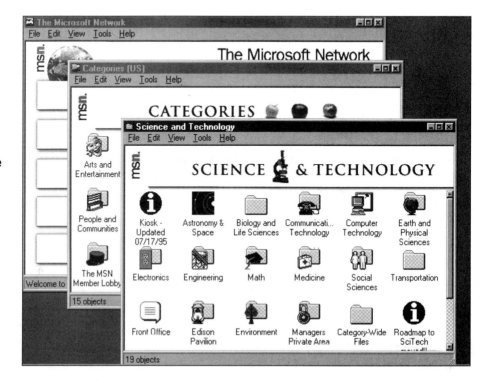

Basic Internet Services

The Internet is one of the most diverse systems of its type in the world, and it has a considerable number of services to offer. In the maze we call the Internet, there are three primary functions utilized by 90 percent of the Internet community:

◆   Electronic mail, e-mail for short
◆   Usenet newsgroups
◆   File transfers

In the next three sections, we'll introduce each of these topics to give you a better idea of what to expect in Chapter 5, when we go for a test drive of the Net.

E-mail

Of all the functions available on the Internet, or on any computer network, e-mail is perhaps the most popular and widely used. Almost every networking operating system around—including Novell NetWare, Microsoft NT Server, and UNIX, the best represented operating system on the Internet—has its native e-mail service.

So what exactly is e-mail? In its basic form, it's the act of writing and sending a letter using a computer and some form of communications device, usually a modem, to move the bits and bytes. Let's say that you and a friend—we'll call her Joyce—wish to meet for lunch the next time you fly into her town. So, you write her a letter detailing all the facts. Basically, here are the steps:

◆   Tell your Internet e-mail software to create a new message.
◆   Using your address book, label the message with the recipient's address.
◆   Compose the message (letter).
◆   Send it by electronic means.

In sending the message, we've apparently left out the return address! Most e-mail software will simply insert your Internet address into a "Reply To" field. When you send the message, you've done much what you would do with a letter—you've placed it in the hands of the mail carrier. In the case of e-mail, the carrier consists in the Internet servers and networking infrastructure; in the case of a letter, it's the U.S. Post Office. Most Internet service providers offer e-mail for free, but others charge for it. In any event, e-mail is very fast— your message generally gets to its destination in less than five minutes. Your mileage may vary. The P.O., on the other hand, always charges, and your letter may never get there!

Usenet Newsgroups

Okay, so what is a newsgroup? Think about the local gossip corner. Every small town, and a few big ones, has somewhere to go to learn all the latest news and happenings. Newsgroups are much the same. They're a part of the Internet that resides on servers; they are a lot like bulletin boards where you'd leave a 3x5 index card with advertisements or the like. Newsgroups allow you to read a message and then answer it while the original poster of the question is off elsewhere. That person comes back later, retrieves your reply to his or her message, and replies.

This process can go on for quite a series of related messages, which form a *thread*. Think of a thread in a coat. It weaves back and forth through the fabric, but it always stays together so that you could find your way back to the beginning of it. Newsgroups will be covered in more detail in Chapter 5 as we go for a spin on the Internet.

File Transfers

The last item of interest for this opening chapter is the File Transfer Protocol, commonly abbreviated to FTP. As you cruise the Internet and surf the Web, you'll get e-mail or see newsgroup postings informing you that file XYZ (that's the best thing since sliced bread) is located on server FTP.MICROSOFT.COM. Uh oh, more gobbledygook technobabble. As we look at this FTP address, though, all it means is this:

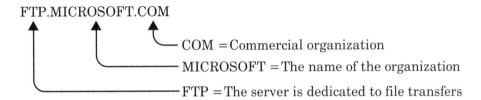

FTP.MICROSOFT.COM

COM = Commercial organization
MICROSOFT = The name of the organization
FTP = The server is dedicated to file transfers

There are MIL or military sites, ORG sites for nonprofit organizations, NET Internet providers, and EDU educational sites. Collectively, these names form what is called the *domain* of a server—domain as in a region of responsibility or authority, such as MICROSOFT.COM, in which only Microsoft Corporation has authority to handle the affairs of the server.

So what's all this got to do with getting that hot file? Well, you've got to know the name of the server that has the file, and how to access the server. Some servers require you to have a user account on it, but most allow *anonymous* logons. As such, instead of using your Internet name, you log on as "anonymous." After logging on, you'll navigate the server much as you do your own PC and retrieve the file.

Is FTP hard? Not at all. You can think of it as being much the same as moving files around on your own hard drive, where, using some utility program, you pick out the file to be moved or copied and tell the program where to move or copy it. The same principle holds on the Internet, but you're just making the move across a few miles via a modem! In Chapter 3, we'll get a bit more detailed about FTP, and we'll get even deeper in Chapter 5 when we process files downloaded across the Web.

Summary

This chapter has introduced quite a few aspects and of the Internet MSN. We've learned why Microsoft has decided to try it's hand at online services, and how service designers intend to access the Internet. We've learned the basics of MSN and a few terms that we'll meet as we peruse the Web. In the next chapter, we'll explore how to get connected to MSN and the Internet.

 Getting Connected

The next topic of interest to us is to make the connection to MSN. Chapter 1 introduced us to many new toys, and a brief way to use these, but we've got to *get connected* as the saying goes. Chapter 2 takes us into the world of connectivity by way of the UNIX ideology called TCP/IP, and dialup networking. If you've done this before, hang loose and bear with us. If you've never heard the word *network* before, have no fear. We'll guide you on the long and bumpy road of networking with modems.

TCP/IP and Connectivity

TCP/IP, which stands for Transmission Control Protocol/Internet Protocol, is the glue that binds disparate types of computer systems together so that one system doesn't have to know what the other one is by type or design. TCP/IP provides a common protocol, or language, that computer systems communicate with across telecommunications links. In essence, it is the heart of the networking system called the Internet. At the core of this protocol are some basic networking functions and features that we need to address before really diving into the Net or MSN. So, you say, you're not a networking person. In fact, you don't even know up from down or left from right in networking.

In reality, you don't have to know these things, but it helps to understand some basic concepts of what we'll be doing. This section, and the whole chapter in fact, will teach you the basics of TCP/IP, a few simple networking ideas and principles, and a small sprinkle of computer theory.

What's TCP/IP?

TCP/IP is a communications standard whose creation was founded, and funded, by the organization known as the Defense Advanced Research Projects Agency, or DARPA for short. DARPA evolved the project into a set of standards by which computer networks and systems could talk to one another across various communications channels and multiple networks.

At the beginning of the project, DARPA planners realized that they needed to allow many agencies working on similar projects to share data and exchange e-mail. The goal was a simple one, but the final result was problematic and difficult to reach. These scientists and computer experts were dealing with unknowns and black areas of science that had far reaching effects without knowing what the end result would be or when it would be reached. Many trying days and weeks were experienced as they strove for the ultimate solution.

The project evolved into a multiagency effort that lead to scores of small networks (of under a hundred users) being interconnected building to building as the tests progressed. As successes reached milestone after milestone, the researchers realized the potential of this new system of interconnections as they spread its work out between multiple agencies. The result was a series of tightly connected diverse networks in which each network was connected to the next by a common language, or protocol. This *language* was called TCP/IP, and a standard was born.

The viability of such a system became immediately clear as government agencies such as NASA, the Department of Defense, the

National Science Foundation, and others hooked into this evolving super-network that successfully linked their institutions. Networks were successively interconnected to form a growing web of internetworks between agencies. Research centers and major universities were connected, and the Internet was born.

At the heart of the Internet TCP/IP provides the ability of one computer to *converse* by removing the ambiguity of the underlying hardware. Because of this, applications can focus on their tasks, such as FTP or e-mail. In this manner, there are two sets of software that are needed to complete the desired operation. The first is the software that resides on the network *server* itself and performs the actual processing of the data at that end of the communications link. This software runs on top of the operating system. The second set consists of the software that is used on your PC, by which you initiate functions such as FTP. Since this software resides on the "workstation" computer, your PC, it is called the *client* software.

In order to initiate and complete the operation, both sets of software must be properly installed and running, providing a *client/server* setup. You may be familiar with this term if you do any programming or network operations. In essence, all it means is that there are two sides to the equation, in which each must operate in sync with one the other to get the job done. The problem here is that if the server-side software gets fouled up, it affects everyone using it. Client-side problems affect only the client PC—usually.

As work on the Internet progressed, the National Science Foundation (NSF) worked on the larger goal of the project, to connect as many universities and scientists as it possibly could to form a larger internetwork of computers. In 1985, they established six supercomputer centers across the United States that eventually tied in with the hundreds of smaller internetworks. These supercomputers were key in bringing it all together because of the power and the diversity they offered. As more networks were brought online, these centers became a repository for software that was distributed to other centers and the smaller networks. Eventually, the NSF's work to bring the scientific community together resulted in the largest network to date.

So You've Never Networked

By 1990, over 3500 servers were online, with some quarter million users attached to the Internet. What was once intended to be a scientific linkage to the Department of Defense and other U.S. government agencies was rapidly becoming a commercialized venture. The pure, open nature of the Internet lent itself to more servers and users being attached, and that propelled the growth of the Internet beyond anyone's dreams.

Where was this explosive growth leading? Many people thought it would never reach such a size. When it did, it became apparent that a logical scheme was needed to address the many computers attached to the Internet, both client and server. This need was met through the *Domain Name System*, or DNS for short. DNS is a huge database of all the assigned addresses provided so that, when one computer wanted to talk to another, it could look up the name of the destination system in this database.

The purpose of DNS was to ease the burden of having to remember so many addresses for these computers. In UNIX lingo, one part of the connectivity is provided through the IP address, which is represented by a 32-bit number commonly grouped into 4 sections. An IP address looks like *204.49.131.1* and can be broken down into subsections. A complete treatment of IP theory could fill another book. The basic idea is that each server has a unique IP address. Wouldn't it be quite a burden to remember dozens of IP addresses? Wouldn't it be much easier to remember the name of a server?

Sure it would! Accordingly, an IP numerical address can be assigned a "nickname" called its *alias*. DNS works by resolving the alias to a numerical address and providing the connectivity after resolution has occurred. This process is called *DNS resolution*. When a computer desires to connect to another, the destination's alias is resolved to locate the server. When you try to reach an FTP site, your client software performs a DNS resolution to locate that site before actually allowing the FTP to occur. The DNS database is so huge that it would be unwise to place it on one server, so the actual DNS function is spread out among several key servers in such a way that if DNS fails lookup on one server, another is tried.

Imagine the scope of such a system as DNS—think about looking up a phone number for someone in New York City. What a job that would be, yes? There may be 350 Smiths in good old NYC, so how do you find the right one? The address, maybe, but this particular Smith may live within a block of three other Smiths. The same search dilemma occurs with these thousands of servers and clients attached to the Internet. DNS was the solution.

You may wonder if any one server, even a supercomputer, could handle such a task. The answer is a firm no, and you'd not want to attempt this for several reasons.

◆ Having the entire DNS database on one computer would be an invitation to disaster. If the database corrupted, or the computer melted down, down would come the Internet with it.

◆ The sheer number of DNS lookups being performed on one system could not satisfy the needs of the thousands of users on the Internet. It would be prohibitively slow.

◆ Due to the volume of use, such a single point of contact would require massive amounts of communications links and services to handle the workload. This would be quite expensive.

These and other issues were among the many that had to be solved by the first internetworking pioneers. They never dreamed that a little science project would turn into such an affair, but it did! As it did, a whole

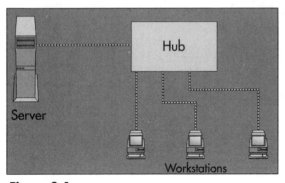

Figure 2-1
A sample network system

new set of rules and guidelines evolved into what is known as TCP/IP.

If you've never networked a system together, don't despair. It's not that bad, and you'll see that as we progress onward. When you get online with MSN and the Web, you're actually networking! (See Figure 2-1.) The way we'll connect is called *dialup networking* (illustrated in Figure 2-2) and is the subject of our discussion very soon in this chapter.

If You're Not Networked, You're Not Connected!

It has often been thought that sometime in the future, connecting to other computers will be just as easy as turning on our TVs or picking up our telephones. Current computer systems have become so inexpensive, in fact, that it is estimated that some 20 million homes in the U.S. have a computer of some sort, and this number is expected to triple by the year 2000. To get connected to the Internet from one of these PCs, all you need is a modem, TCP/IP communications software, an Internet provider, and a little patience.

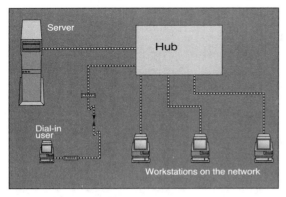

Figure 2-2
A sample network system using dialup method

With Windows 95 dialup networking, the dialup aspect comes into play when your PC uses the standard style of modem connectivity to make the connection itself, and then TCP/IP takes over for the rest of your journey through the Web. When you terminate a session online and are ready to quit, TCP/IP ends and hands over the task of breaking the connection back to the dialup software.

Windows 95 comes with its own version of dialup networking in addition to the

connectivity within MSN itself. When you connect to MSN to access the
Web, you've in fact connected with the Internet itself via MSN. When
you use Windows 95's dialup networking connectivity (illustrated in
Figure 2-3), you'll dial directly into an Internet provider of your choice.

Although Windows 95 provides you with Internet connectivity from
two aspects (you can use dialup networking or the MSN) to the Web, you
don't have to use it if you have a favorite Internet software package. An
old favorite of many is Trumpet Winsock shareware TCP/IP connectivity
for PCs. Our Macintosh-user friends enjoy TCP/IP with the MAC
System 7 and MacTCP using Mosaic or similar browsers. Trumpet can
be obtained from several sites across the Internet, and finding this and
other files will be the subject of one section in Chapter 5.

My longtime favorite Internet tools are the suite called Internet
Chameleon by Netmanage, shown in Figure 2-4. Below is an example of
direct dialing to my local Internet provider to access the Web.

As we said earlier, a few TCP/IP basics came into play here in making

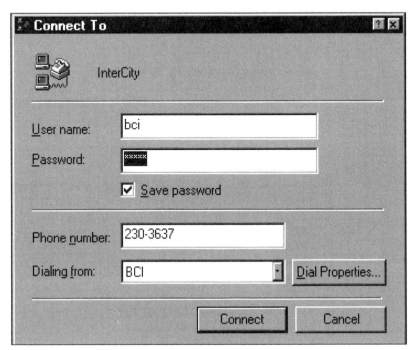

Figure 2-3
**Windows 95
dialup network
connectivity**

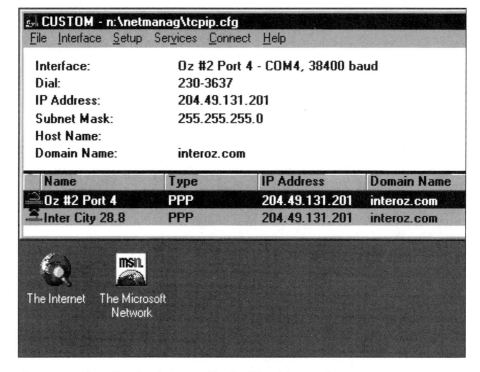

Figure 2-4
Using
Chameleon to
connect to the
Internet

the connection. I've had to specify the IP address of my Internet provider, my own IP address, the domain I am using, the phone number to call, and a few settings for my modem. After making the connection, I minimize the connection to the icon level, and I'm ready to go, as you can see from Figure 2-5. I can now FTP, get my e-mail, or engage in any number of other Internet activities like surfing the Web. Before we can take up this last activity, we've got a few more issues to cover.

How to Tell If You're Connected

Okay, so we made the connection, or would like to believe we did, anyhow. But did we? Computers are wonderful devices and bring us lots to do and see, but they also bring a few headaches along the way. In TCP/IP connectivity, one of these headaches is determining when we've made it from point A to point B, including making the actual connection. Just when we believe we're there, we're not.

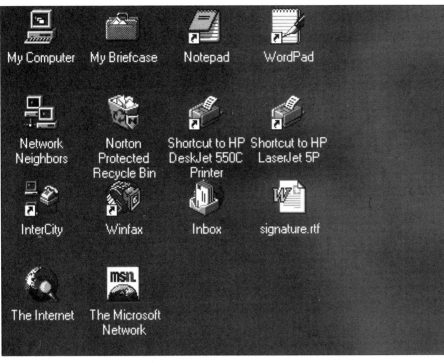

Figure 2-5
**Fully connected,
and ready to
go!**

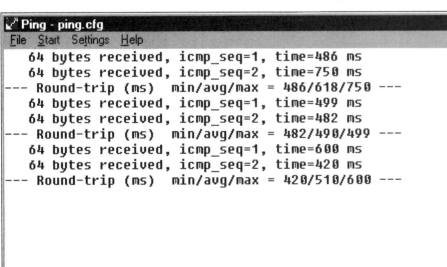

Figure 2-6
**PINGing our
way to success**

Perhaps of the most seldom used, but highly important tools available on UNIX systems is called PING. PING works like the sonar on a ship, which sends out a signal that strikes some object. Part of the signal is returned to the sending device, enabling the sender to see if the destination exists, or (in the case of PING) is online. If no signal is returned, then the destination may not exist anymore, or it may not be online at this time. If the destination exists and can respond, PING will tell you how long it took the signal to go there and return. The times you'll see are in seconds and parts of a second called *milliseconds*. One millisecond is one thousandth of a second. Typically, PING returns are in the 300- to 500-millisecond range. PING will also tell you what the actual IP address of the destination is if you told it the alias of the destination.

Native MSN Links

Thus far, we've talked a lot about generic connectivity and the Internet. This section will tell you all about connecting to MSN via Windows 95 and using your modem to make the connection with standard telephone lines.

The Link Itself

Let's take a minute to chat about the bare-bones telephone link that you'll be using to make this connection. So, what's so special about a phone line, you may ask? Unfortunately, more than lots of folks know or realize. A phone line is what is called an *analog* type of line—one designed to carry continuously varying audio signals, such as voices, not digitized data.

Analog phone lines are inherently noisy. If you've ever been using the phone and heard scratchy noises or static, it's due to interference on the line. This problem is natural on analog lines, but it is deadly to digital communications between computer systems. *Digital* communications are the native method used by computers to talk between themselves. Digital means that the data are in binary format, either a binary 1 or a binary 0. 1s and 0s are the only thing computers understand. No voltages, no noise, nothing else but 1s and 0s. Anything in between is useless to a computer.

What this means is that when you connect your computer, a digital device, across an analog phone line to another digital device (the destination computer), the data must be converted from digital format to analog format and then back to digital format. Oh, boy, what a headache! Fortunately for us, the modem handles all the problems for us. Well, almost all of them. *Modem* stands for *modulator/demodulator*, the term for the little device attached to the serial port on your computer. It modulates, or changes, the digital signal into an analog equivalent and merges it with the electrical signal already on the phone line. When this signal gets to the destination, the receiver demodulates it, or separates the digital signal from the electrical carrier (Figure 2-7).

That done, the digital signal is then routed to the destination computer. From this, you can see that one main problem exists that is outside of your control—your local phone company! The main problem is noise on the line. As your data scream along, the carrier is subjected to all sorts of noises and interference that degrade the quality of the line and ultimately the data traversing it as well.

What can be done about it? Frequently, nothing. It largely depends on how interested your local phone company is in customer service and in pleasing you. Many rural areas still have phone systems from back in the stone ages. These lines are seldom reliable enough to operate a dialup link, but if that's all you have, that's all you have, so it's time to spend some money. In the next section, we'll deal with creating an account on MSN, along with all of the parameters needed to create this account.

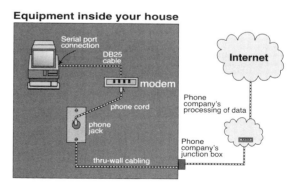

Figure 2-7

How a modem works to get you connected

One of the issues taken up will be error correcting modems that handle noisy or bad lines much better than other modems.

The Whys and Wherefores of MSN Connectivity

Okay, so now we understand more about what we're going to do, and be doing, when we create the dialup link. MSN largely uses SprintNet to provide you with the dialup connectivity. Sprint has *nodes*, or points of presence (POPs), all over the U.S. and the world where you can connect. In most cases, you'll find a local connection. First you have to create a MSN account. To do so, you'll dial an 800 phone number and follow a few steps.

To create this account, you'll need several pieces of information:

♦ Method of payment—VISA, Mastercard, American Express, or other.

♦ A nickname you'd like to be known as on MSN. It can be your real name, your business name, or something else like *Midnight_Raider_of_the_Fridge*. Up to 256 characters are allowed to form your alias.

♦ The area code and number that you'll be dialing from.

♦ General billing information.

There are three ways to create the account. The first way applies when you install Windows 95 and are given the chance to install and configure MSN. If you decline at that time, the second way is to run the sign-up process manually. I'll concentrate on this manual approach, since the first method is well covered by Windows 95 setup. The third way is to install MSN and Exchange via the Control Panel by selecting Add/Install New Software.

To create your MSN account manually, start up Explorer. Navigate to the home drive where Windows 95 is installed, and find the directory called The Microsoft Network, which resides under the Program Files

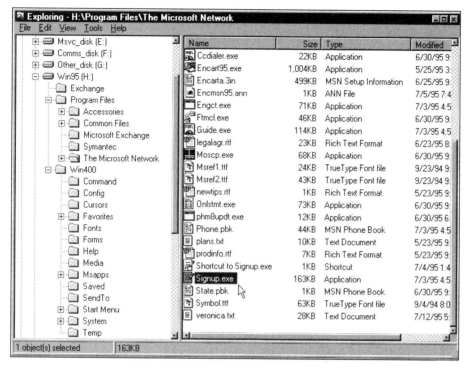

Figure 2-8
**Finding the
sign-up
program**

directory. Inside that directory is a file called SIGNUP.EXE, as you can
see in Figure 2-8.

The preceding description represents the old-fashioned way of
locating files, much like using the Windows 3.*x* File Manager. Windows
95 gives you a considerably more powerful tool called *FIND*. To use
FIND, start the Explorer, choose Tools, choose Find (as in Figure 2-9),
and then click on Files or Folders on your computer.

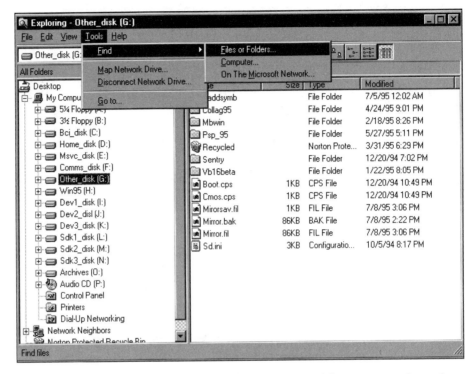

Figure 2-9
**Starting FIND
to find
programs**

When you start FIND, you'll be presented with a screen that gives you all the options necessary to find files or folders on your computer or on MSN (as in Figure 2-10). When we play around with MSN in Chapter 9, we'll use FIND much more. It's a superb tool and a welcome enhancement to the Windows operating system utility suite.

Feed FIND the pertinent data and let it do all the work for you! (See Figure 2-11.) What if you forgot where the Microsoft Network folder is located? I have 14 partitions on my system, including one for the CD-ROM, and it can be rather difficult locating data at times.

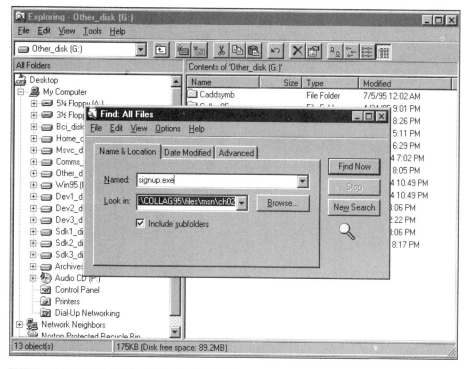

Figure 2-10
Using FIND to locate programs

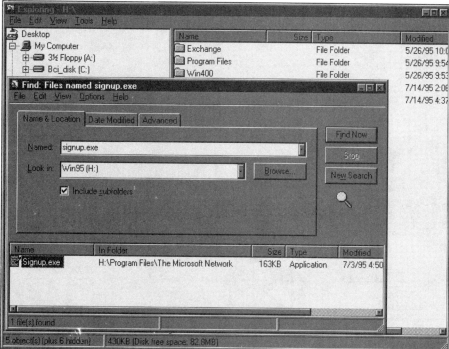

Figure 2-11
The results of a FIND operation

When FIND has completed its search operation, only one copy of SIGNUP.EXE should have been found. Now, all you have to do is double-click in SIGNUP, and away you go! (See Figure 2-12.)

Getting Hooked Up with MSN

CAUTION

You must have a modem already installed and configured in Windows 95 before beginning your MSN sign-up process! Failure to do so will cause the process to abort.

After starting SIGNUP, you'll get a screen like the one in Figure 2-13.

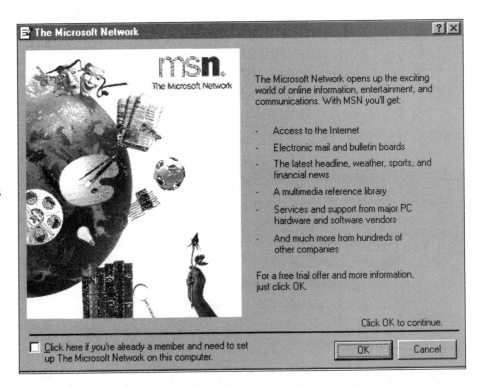

Figure 2-12
Starting the sign-up process for MSN after FINDing SIGNUP.EXE

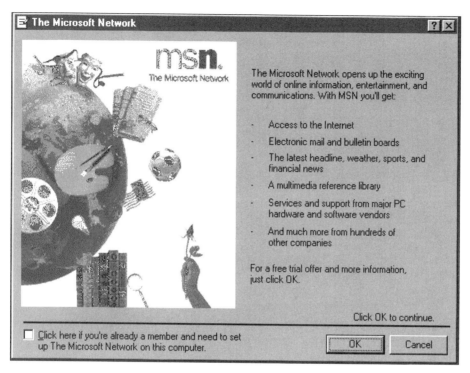

Figure 2-13
**The opening
screen for
signing up with
MSN**

This screen welcomes you to the world of MSN and lets you know some of the benefits you'll enjoy as a member. There's a block in the lower-left corner of this screen to check if you're a current member of MSN. This is for when you have problems with the MSN software, or for some reason have to reinstall Windows 95. Checking this box enables a portion of the MSN software so you can recreate only the parts required to get you back online. No need to sign up again and create a new account, is there? As of this writing, the MSN Customer Service phone number to assist you with recovery of an account is 800-386-5550.

After pressing on past this screen, you'll be presented with a screen to enter the area code and prefix you'll be calling from. These will be used to automatically find the closest point of presence.

Figure 2-14
Entering the
calling area
code and prefix

CAUTION

Entering incorrect data may cause your default calling POP to be long distance. It is advisable to double-check the returned settings after creating the account.

Okay, you've got the basics down, so now tell the sign-up process to press onward. You'll be given the opportunity to change any of the calling options in this screen. If you have two modems and prefer to use one, click the Settings box to make that selection, as shown in Figure 2-15.

With that settled, click on the Connect box from the Calling screen to make the initial call. You'll now connect to MSN and create the new account. Data will be transferred after a period of time in which nothing seems to happen. Be patient! Allow the process to complete, and you'll be presented with The Microsoft Network sign-up screen shown in Figure 2-16. Click on each of the buttons in order from top to bottom, and fill in the appropriate information.

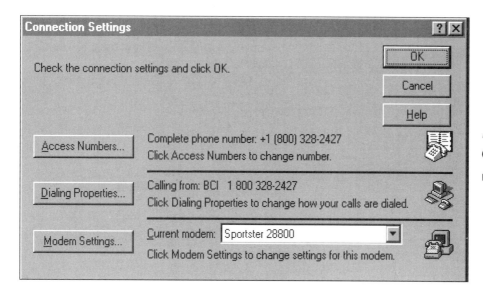

Figure 2-15
Changing modem settings

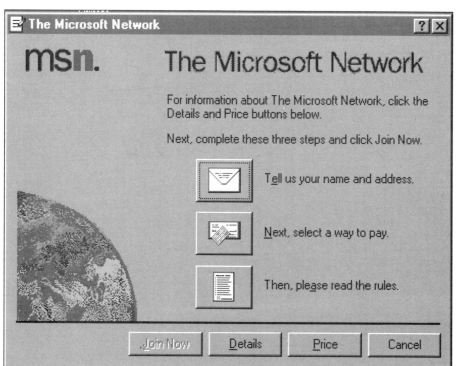

Figure 2-16
Filling in the new account information

With all the required data completed, you'll see a check mark beside each of the completed items (Figure 2-17). With everything done, click on the Join Now button to complete the final actions.

The next screen shows you the number that sign-up will use to complete the process. This is the number that you will use now and forever unless you physically change it (Figure 2-18). I'll show you how to do that in a later section of this chapter. Click Connect to join and then provide the information asked of you. Here, give whatever descriptive nickname you want, up to 256 characters.

After the MSN process completes, congratulations! You're a new member and can start the next part of the journey (Figure 2-19).

Figure 2-17
All done, ready to complete sign-up

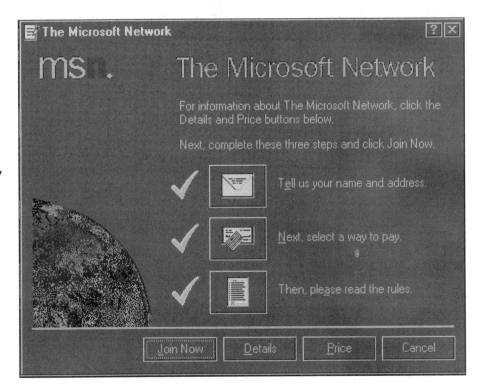

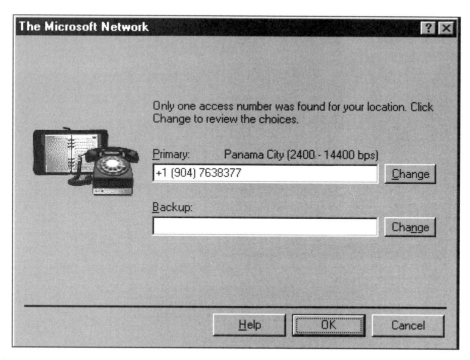

Figure 2-18
Returning the final call

Figure 2-19
The final screen signaling completion of the process

Dialup Connections

In previous sections, we've discussed various aspects of networking including TCP/IP connectivity as it relates to dedicated networks. MSN provides the user with a clean and effortless way to get connected via dialup lines (Figure 2-20). The next three sections will discuss in more depth the pros and cons of dialup networking. As you peruse these data, keep in mind that not all nodes provide the same speed of access to MSN, nor do all Internet providers provide the same types of connections. The last section in this chapter will talk about what are called *dedicated leased lines*, in which you get a guaranteed speed of connectivity, but at a considerably larger fee.

Modems, Modems Everywhere!

You know that a modem is a modulator/demodulator that converts your computer's digital data to analog to send it to the destination, where it is returned to digital. That's the simple version of telecommunications. The complete version would take up a whole book, so I'll not bedevil you just yet with many more technical facts. There are a few more terms and topics to touch on relating to access. One of these is the speed at which you connect to the destination, whether it be one of MSN's SprintNet nodes or your own Internet provider.

You may have heard the term *baud rate* or *bits per second (bps)* in relation to modems. Well, bits per second is not the same as baud rate except at the rate of 300. In the earlier days, back when a mainframe computer with the power of a 486DX/33 took up 500 square feet of air-conditioned computer room, communications links of 300 bits per second were the norm. Also, there were rates of 75 and 150 bits per second. In days gone by, I used

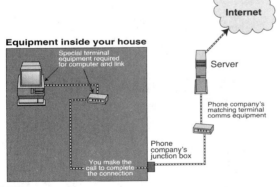

Figure 2-20

Basic concept of a dialup leased line

to repair this equipment! I thought it was amazing to see this stuff, and then we got 1200-baud and 2400-baud modems. So, naturally I thought we were operating at 1200 and 2400 bits per second. Not really, because in order to get higher transmission speeds, the data are multiplexed and discombobulated into a form suitable for these new speeds.

What resulted was a form of data transfer called Manchester-encoded transmissions, giving us higher speeds on the same phone lines with equal protection for the safety of our data. As a result of the new form and higher speeds, existing phone lines were presenting the modem makers with more challenges due to problems on the wire. Information getting corrupted on the way isn't much good to anyone. What's worse is that you wouldn't know that the data were corrupted until you tried to use them—not fun if you're retrieving 10MB files across a 1200-baud link. That takes hours to complete and wears on your patience.

The resulting standards included error detecting and correcting protocols and were called v.42 and v.42bis. *Bis* is the French word for change or update, so v.42 is the original error detection scheme and v.42bis is the update to the original scheme. Virtually all modems produced today come with this function, but be careful and ask when you purchase a modem.

The next topic about modems that is of interest to us includes the actual speed of the modem and related issues. The standards associated with these speeds are listed below. There are 16 common speeds at which you can or once could expect to connect using a modem:

50, 75, 150, 300, and 600	All from older days
1200 and 2400	Still in use, but fading(v.22 is the 1200 baud standard; v.22bis for 2400)
4800,7200, and 9600	Common for modem and fax use (v.32)
12000, 14400, 19200	v.32bis connections
21600, 26400, 28800	v.34 speeds—currently the highest possible rate

These are the raw speeds at which modems can communicate with each other. Beyond this, *data compression* results in higher throughput—usually. I say "usually" because this standard allows the modems and software driving them to decide when to use compression and when not to. Normal text files, graphics, and the like are highly compressible, to ratios of up to 10:1. Graphics files like JPEG and MPEG are compressible up to 50:1, greatly speeding up overall transmission time. The net effect of compression is that you can achieve throughput of over 57,000 baud on a 28.8K link! How's that for progress? Nice, but these increased speeds tend to be affected more and more by noisy phone lines, and they lead to more data retries with each error.

However—and you know there's always one "however" somewhere— files such as ZIP archives and self-extracting archives called EXEs are already compressed. Further attempts to compress these files frequently result in an *increase* in file sizes and transmission time! Compression can slow down connections because it allows more data to be packed into the stream and if errors occur, more data has to be resent during subsequent retries. Compression can also decrease throughput if you're moving a lot of compressed files. This is strange enough, but with the client software computing the relative compression of the file, this phenomenon is bad to networks and the Internet. For this reason and a few others, the use of compression is taboo on MSN and the Internet, whether you're on the Web or using FTP or doing any other thing.

Okay, so we've got some more modem issues out of the way. What next? How about the actual modem itself? Which one is right for you? What standard should you use, and with which modem? While there's no perfect solution that applies to everyone, I believe there's a baseline for everything. I recently purchased a new 28.8K v.34 external fax/modem for $239 (plus the governor's share) with which I can send or receive faxes or connect with my favorite BBS or Internet provider at 28,800 baud. That said, my recommendation is to purchase a 28.8K v.34 modem if you can squeeze it out of your budget. My Internet provider operates at that speed, and it's a joy to use.

In addition, I save money. With large files and frequent use, I can save a lot of money! Table 2-1 below illustrates a few facts and figures about the relative costs. Let's assume the file to be transferred is 5MB in size, and that your connect rate is $5 per hour. We'll also assume that we are making a local call, so this is not a factor in the cost. At this rate, the cost is 8⅓ cents per minute.

Table 2-1 Relative Costs of Data Transmission

Speed	Time (minutes)	Cost
1200	4369	$363
2400	2184	$182
9600	546	$46
14400	364	$30
28000	182	$15

This example clearly illustrates the benefits of a fast modem. If you process more than 5MB of files in one month, you've paid your provider the cost of a new modem in one month alone. A side issue to this is if the link gets chopped off for any reason, you get to start over. No refunds, no explanations or "I'm sorry, Mr. Internet User"—you get to start over. Give your hard-earned money to them, or keep it. Your choice. If you're serious about the Web and MSN, then you owe it to yourself to get the fastest modem possible. At the present, MSN's fastest speed is 14.4K, but there are 28.8K links in testing as this is being written. These higher-speed links should be operational and very widespread by the time you read this. The alternative to the fastest dialup link is a dedicated leased line.

Dialup versus Dedicated Links

You've been modemized beyond what you may have wanted, so we'll give you a break and discuss one aspect of communications links that most

Web surfers are unfamiliar with—dedicated leased lines.

Such lines function quite differently than dialups. We've noted that modems convert the digital signal to analog and then back again. We've also said that this process is not without its faults or errors, but it's relatively cheap to acquire. Leased lines are almost exclusively digital in nature from source to destination, eliminating this conversion process. Dialup lines have the problem of nonavailability as well. When you dial the modem, you'll never know if the connection can be made until you actually connect. Leased lines are always available because they're always connected—but at a price. An alternative called Switched 56 leased lines will be discussed later in this section.

Dedicated leased lines offer the user up to 128K baud transmission rates, but the most common is the 56K link (Figure 2-21). In this scenario, your computer has an extra circuit card installed in it connected to a special junction box right beside your computer. The junction box, often referred to as the *termination* device, is used to convert the digital data into a form usable across the link. They're still digital going across the link, but the data have to be adapted to the type of line employed. The receiver has a similar device to reconvert the digital data stream back into the destination computer's digital form. I want to emphasize that the entire process is digital from start to finish! In addition to the added security of the dedicated line, most leased line providers guarantee that your link, if it is a 56K link, will always provide 56K of throughput. In dialup links, the actual throughput is subject to the conditions of the lines themselves. You may start at 28.8K but wind down to 7200 as the link deteriorates. Pay for 28.8K, get 7200. What a concept!

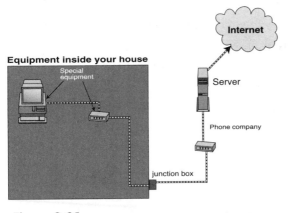

Figure 2-21

The Basic concept of a dedicated leased line

The benefits of leased lines?

◆   Guaranteed throughput
◆   Error-free transmissions
◆   Always available, always connected

The detriments of leased lines?

◆   Quite expensive to operate
◆   Require specialized hardware to use
◆   May not be available in your area

I explored the possibility of leased lines in my area when I moved here recently, and I got the reply I thought I would. "What's a leased line?" was the answer I got from my local carrier. Right. I dug and dug into the carrier until I found someone who understood what I was talking about, and this person was the VP of Operations for this carrier. This clearly demonstrates where some regions of the U.S. are in terms of what has been commonly called "The Information SuperHighway," or the Internet. Most of the network professionals I work with have been dealing with this topic for 10 or more years, but some parts of our data processing society are still at 1200 baud and proud of it.

Returning to my story, it took three weeks just to find this person and another week to discuss business arrangements. Much to my dismay, establishing a dedicated leased line to my residence was a six-month effort costing $4500 in initial costs and $1600 per month minimum connection fees. For this, I get a 56K link always online, always ready, and guaranteed to be available. Should the link go down, they'd automatically reroute me to a working circuit until mine got fixed at no additional charge. The terminal equipment was another $2000 if I wanted to purchase it instead of including the rental fee in the monthly costs.

By contrast, my local Internet provider charges me $50 to establish the account, $20 for 20 hours of online time, and $1.25 for each hour beyond the initial 20 hours. I have found that I can always get at least 21.6K throughput, and that usually I'll get the full 28.8K link speed. In Windows 95, I routinely get 4K throughput, versus 2.4K in Windows 3.1 with the same provider. If I really needed 56K of throughput for short periods of time, I could use two accounts with my provider each on a 28.8K modem. I have tested such a setup under Windows 95, and Windows 95 handled the effective throughput of 56K with ease. It took two lines to do it, but it worked! Far cheaper than a leased line, right?

The bottom line is that you will have to decide how serious you are about your online wants, needs, and desires. Some questions you can ask yourself each time you think you need more online capabilities are:

- How much time do I spend online each week?
- Out of that online time, what is the volume of files that I transfer across the link?
- How much time do I have to devote to maintenance or other operational needs of the leased line?
- What is my budget for the link?
- Can I really justify the link?

Switched 56 Services

Leased lines are certainly not for everyone. If your time is so valuable that you can't wait for anything, then such a connection may be what you need. If not, then ask your local phone carrier if they offer Switched 56 services. This is the same kind of link as the dedicated leased line, but it is a dialup like the modem line. You have the same equipment as the dedicated line, but you activate this line much like you do with a modem line. You have to place a call from your equipment to the destination equipment, and establish the link using available bandwidth. This means that a portion of the link's bandwidth may or may not be available for you at that time. If it's available, then you're online. If not, you wait until it becomes available. It's still more expensive than the modem dialup, but it's cheaper than the dedicated leased line by about 40 percent.

Horsepower to Spare

Thus far, this section has concentrated upon the various services offered for telecommunications, but the impact upon the data processing equipment has not been considered. Let's consider dialup modems for node ABC. Node ABC is a bank of 36 modems, each 28.8K in capacity. A bit of math reveals that if all 36 of these devices were active at the same time, then the processing equipment directly attached to these 36 modems would have to be capable of handling 1036.8K aggregate throughput. That's a lot of data in anyone's calculator! Now, consider that there are six banks of 36 modems in the node ABC's processing center, and the processing equipment rapidly turns into the class of minicomputers or small mainframes. Yes? Not exactly.

As the world of computing has evolved faster hardware, faster processors, and more complicated software, so have the overall capabilities of these systems grown when integrated fully into a client/server network. By comparison, the DEC™ VAX minicomputer 11/780 that I worked on in the past is now easily surpassed by a Pentium 90 MHz processor running Windows NT Advanced Server!—and at about 1/20th the cost. How's that for progress?

It's progress, but the networking world is coming full circle to the way things were done 20 years ago. PC networks are getting faster and more capable, and they are doing more each year with better operating systems. These same PC networks are just now handling the volume of users that minicomputers were handling 20 years ago, but more cheaply. With this decrease in equipment costs, however, have come increased training needs and increased hardware needs as we've asked more of less. In line with these considerations, it has become the standard that the slowest computer that you should use for online work is a 486DX/33 with a 14.4K modem. With the advent of OS/2 and Windows 95, that minimum has been pushed to a 486DX2/66 with 16MB of RAM and a 28.8K modem, to be completely realistic.

We've covered a lot of ground in the last three paragraphs, but what does it all mean? With the increased demands that online services (such as MSN/Windows 95 and the Internet/Web) place on computers, it is wise to get the fastest hardware that you can afford. With prices dropping (as it seems) monthly, each and every component of your computer can be upgraded or purchased new very cheaply. While I certainly don't advocate making the computer vendors any richer than is necessary, the trend to more complex and demanding software and services warrants the fastest and best hardware that you can afford. You may be able to get by with what you have now, but if you're serious about being online, the demands will catch up with you sooner than you think.

Summary

This chapter has touched several topics of online life, and it paves the way for Chapter 3, where we'll jump right into the Internet and treat a few needed preliminaries before we finalize our plans to hop into the Web using MSN in Chapter 4. We've discussed dialup modem lines versus dedicated leased lines into the Internet and through MSN. We've defined the use of modems, modem terms, and transmission speeds along with associated terminology. We'll begin pulling this all together into a more useful picture soon, so turn the page and let's go!

 What Is This Internet Thing?

In Chapter 2, we talked about the Internet in more technical terms of TCP/IP and hosts and configurations. But, what really is the Internet composed of? What is the nature of the beast, as the saying goes?

In this chapter, we'll talk about the Internet from more of a user's perspective: the hows and whys of the Internet in terms of what do you do with it, or what can it do for you. More specifically, you'll understand:

◆   The Internet's place in history
◆   The user's view of the client/server model
◆   The File Transfer Protocol with examples
◆   E-mail and examples
◆   A rodent called Gopher
◆   Finding files with Archie
◆   Common sense and the Internet

The Beginning of Time

If you think about the word *network* and apply it to things all around you, you'll see that there are all kinds of networks. Ants have a network of tunnels to get them through their busy day. Cities have networks of telephone systems interconnecting friends and families across town. To be serious, the word *network* can be applied to a vast number of items that are linked together by some medium or structure.

Computers are no different, as we'll see in this chapter. But first, let's talk a little more generically about computers and networks.

What Exactly Is the Internet?

The Internet is a collection of computers linked by a physical medium, usually cable of some sort such as thin copper wire or even thinner fiber optics cable. These links form the spider-like connections that we're accustomed to calling a *Web*, like the spider web in the morning dew. Remember those? Neat how the spider manages to do all of that and not get her feet stuck in it. The core principle of the Internet is in reality much the same as the spider's web.

Points all across the fabric of the web are used to make one connection at a time, one computer at a time, one user at a time. It's amazing and mind-boggling how all of this works without clogging the communications channels, but TCP/IP makes it happen. It does this in part by using its capability to reroute information from one Web site to another to another. Think back to the spider's web—aren't there lots of connections? Many paths by which one web thread connects to another at the other side of the web?

The same is true for the World Wide Web. One server is connected to another, which in turn is connected to one more, and so on. Let's take a hypothetical example of four Web servers called A, B, C, and D (Figure 3-1).

In this example, you can see that there are many different paths to get data moved from Server A to Server B. What if the direct link from A to B were inoperative (Figure 3-2)? No problem, just reroute the data from A to C to D to B. One shorter step would be from A to D to B. One step saved, and a bit faster. Or is it? This recovery mechanism is a fine point in favor of TCP/IP and the Internet, but what if Server D is busier than all of the other servers combined? The data may never reach Server B at all!

On days when you're traveling home, have you ever wished you had an extra pair of eyes down the street to see how congested it was so you could take that alternate path? TCP/IP routers use such an associated function called a *spanning tree algorithm*, in which the routing device checks for the shortest possible path between the source and destination points. I won't bore you with the details, but it's your extra set of eyes. If you're really interested in reaching deeper levels of understanding of TCP/IP and the Internet, I highly recommend Douglas E. Comer's *Internetworking with TCP/IP, Second Edition*.

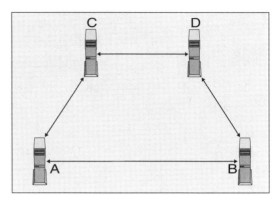

Figure 3-1
Routing of data across the Web

This rerouting system is the basic premise of the Internet that allows it to function as a huge number of smaller networks connected together to form a Web; thousands of network servers and millions of Internet users are doing this work every day of the year.

History Repeats Itself

At the dawn of the computer age, it was not unheard of for a mainframe computer system that supported a dozen users to physically take up several hundred square

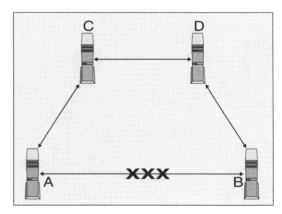

Figure 3-2
Rerouting of data across the Web with a broken link

feet of a room that was heavily air conditioned. These computers were the most powerful in their day, but they now are relics of the computer boneyard. Typically, they had only a megabyte of memory installed in them that was called *core memory* because it held the *core*, or heart, of the computer programs.

In time, the computers evolved into faster systems with more functionality than their predecessors. They also became smaller in size, took up less physical space, and required less cooling. This was a natural advance in science and technology, but the costs of running such beasts never got cheaper, it seemed! As the computers got smaller and smaller, faster and faster, one day the computing world woke up and decided it no longer wanted to pay the costs associated with Big Iron, as it was once called. What computer managers wanted were even smaller machines capable of ten times the processing ability of their Big Iron, but these machines were still in their infancy. Intel Corporation released the first of the 80x86 series of microprocessors around 1984, but these were used in what were little more than smart terminals. Current day MIS (Management of Information Services) types, the folks that ran the entire corporation's computers and held the keys to the kingdom, saw little use for these toys! Some computer, right?

Right. So what came next was an evolutionary period of the smaller systems called *minicomputers* because they were smaller than Big Iron but larger than these new-fangled PCs. Actually, the earliest minicomputers were operating in the mid to late 1960s and early 1970s. Digital Equipment Corporation, Data General, Hewlett-Packard, and Sun Microsystems were among the big names in minicomputers in those days, and today as well. All through the 70s and 80s, these machines matured into enterprise computing solutions easily capable of supporting a thousand users simultaneously on a single server. With this awesome power came the maintenance and programming expenses commonly seen with Big Iron.

With the increased push to smaller systems with more power, and ever-tightening budgets squeezing businesses, MIS groups around the world were looking for a solution—one that provided equal processing power serving the same volume of users for less money. The end result was an increase in the processing power of Intel-based computers running networked operating systems. Many of these new operating systems appeared as early as 1985 in a viable form for the new Intel 80286 processor, or the 286 as it is commonly called. At its heyday, the 286 and six megabytes of RAM could handle about 10 users, but typical storage capacity back then was only about 20MB.

These parallel trends of Intel processors increasing in performance and minicomputers decreasing in popularity had continued for several more years when a new set of rules called *Client/Server* began finding wide application. Another term called *downsizing* made its debut to signify the installation of more and more PC-based network servers with fewer and fewer minicomputers or mainframes left on the scene. The expenses were coming down, true, but a larger demon was hiding in the background—a monster called the Internet that demanded more power and *bandwidth* than the average PC server could provide. Bandwidth represents the device's full capability to process data. Think of a water pipe four inches wide. It can handle a greater volume of water than can a two-inch pipe. The larger pipe could be said to have greater bandwidth than the smaller one. This increased bandwidth helped minicomputers hang around longer, and they seemed to have their niche carved solidly on the Web. Table 3-1 shows a few relative statistics that should give you an idea of how computing power and costs have evolved.

Table 3-1 Expenses versus Power over Time

Name	Relative Processing Power	Cost to Operate	Date of Mfg.
Mainframe	100	$10M	1975
Mainframe	125	$14M	1984
Minicomputer	75	$3M	1980
Minicomputer	90	$250,000	1988
Workstation	40	$75,000	1985
Workstation	65	$135,000	1990
PC	2	$5,000	1985
PC	8	$7,000	1988
PC	15	$9,000	1990
PC	30	$20,000	1993
PC	65	$65,000	1995

Table 3-1 suggests how relative costs for systems have changed over the years. Most significant is the very last line, which shows a PC priced comparably to a workstation such as a Sun UNIX machine. This PC is really a high-powered Pentium™ network server capable of running two Pentium™ processors and holding about 20GB of storage and 128MB of RAM; such a machine would be used as an enterprise network server. This server would take the place of one of the low-end minicomputers costing three times as much. One of the many hidden costs not represented here, however, is the training to operate, program, and maintain such a PC server.

Both minicomputers and mainframes have their places in computing life, but the trend is clearly towards PC-based servers for networks. The flip side of the coin is that PC-based servers and workstations running modern operating systems are leading the way into the future of the Internet and the Web. What is happening is that PC-based servers are finally maturing along with their kindred operating systems to the point of being able to support the volume and type of users on the Internet that minicomputers have excelled at supporting for years.

The motivating factor in this trend has been financial savings due to the simplicity of the PCs, but they've advanced to the degree that it can now require a programmer or systems integrator of minicomputer caliber to maintain such equipment. Costs have been going up on PC-based servers in recent years, as these once simple computers now outperform their Big Iron counterparts of old. What has happened is that PCs have become powerful enough to operate as servers for large numbers of users just as minicomputers have been doing, and their once low costs are marching upward to match. This has been much the same circle that the early computer systems went through 20 or 30 years ago.

Quite a Little Network

So, we've talked about how computers have evolved over the years, but what does this have to do with the Internet in general or the Web specifically? The difference is that where you once could count on having only one or two types of computers running the show, now there are perhaps a dozen or more operating systems that'll get you from Server A to Server B, as shown in Figure 3-3.

Network Infrastructures and the Internet

One look at Figure 3-3 is enough to let you know some of the obstacles you're bound to face as you surf the Web. It's enough to know that each of these types of servers has its own idiosyncrasies, but TCP/IP comes to the rescue to keep you from having to know all of this. That's part of the glory of TCP/IP, but you're not out of the woods yet!

Internet tools like FTP want to know what kind of server you're connecting to, and how to talk to it. By "talk to it" I mean is this a UNIX server connected to another UNIX server, or to a Windows NT™ server? NT speaks TCP/IP, but if the client FTP program you use is Windows-based instead if UNIX-based, the server and client programs need to know this. With the tone of the conversation set, so to speak, the operation will proceed along smoothly and simply. If the client software has to take time to figure out some problem, you'll experience slight delays in processing of your request.

One more matter of interest is the link itself. Referring back to our Figure 3-3, let's add in one more part of the equation called a *router*, shown in Figure 3-4.

This nifty device is used to connect both similar and disparate hardware platforms to each other by converting the

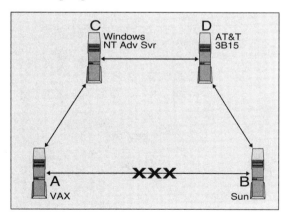

Figure 3-3

Routing of data across the Web via different server types

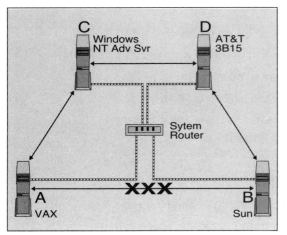

Figure 3-4

Moving data across the Web with a router and server-to-server direct connections

language they speak, or protocol, from one type to another, just as a translator would do for English to German or French. These devices perform another useful function we mentioned earlier called the *spanning tree algorithm*, which enables the most efficient movement of data possible between several destinations and sources.

Your Place in the Sun

So we've cemented in place one more part of the road to the Web, but where do you fit in? Exactly what do you do here, or have to do with the Internet? We mere users of the Web are but one barnacle on the Internet hull, but collectively we're the Web! (See Figure 3-5.) Yes, all of the people that build, maintain, and share problems and solutions on the Internet are the real heart and soul of the Web—what makes it tick—what keeps it alive. It's your ideas and issues of computing or life in general that provide the fuel for the fire. It's a fire that can burn bright and provide a light for all to see, or it can mean the headlight on the train coming through the tunnel! Don't go online before considering the Netiquette issues taken up later in this chapter.

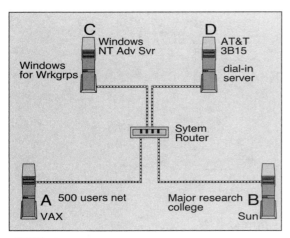

Figure 3-5

Where each user fits into the Internet

The Client/Server Paradigm

As we get closer to actually getting onto the Web, there are a few more things we need to discuss. These are primarily local concerns on your PC itself relating to configuration, system settings, and software you may be using that could possibly interfere with Web operations and just getting connected to the Internet.

How Client/Server Directly Affects You

To recap the client/server model, your PC will contain the software called the *client*, by which you instruct the software to do something on the Web or MSN. The server software receives the commands from the client and responds with the answer, hopefully the appropriate one. When it doesn't, there are any number of problems or errors that could come about, but the most frequent is the time-out condition. This occurs when the server is so busy or overwhelmed that it can't possibly handle your request. In many client applications, there may be a setting by which you tell the application to allow a specific amount of time for any action to complete regardless of what the action may be (Figure 3-6).

Such settings can be very important when it comes to busy sites like the University of Minnesota's or University of North Carolina's FTP site. These two are special locations on the Web and Internet because they contain files and storehouses of information pertinent to starting out on the Web and may be the first sites you turn to looking for files. At this time, I won't bore you with the site names and IP addresses because I want you to focus on the theory of the subject. In Chapter 4, when we fire up MSN and the Web, you'll see quite a few locations on the Web where you can start your collection of programs.

By now you should be settled down with the fundamentals of the Web and the Internet. A deeper discussion of MSN will take place in Chapters 8 and 9, so we'll restrict the remainder of this chapter to the Web.

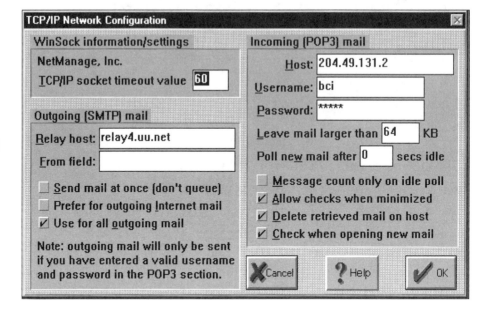

Figure 3-6
Special setting for time-out value in the Pegasus e-mailer

Web Browsing and Client/Server

For this section, let's turn our attention to the Web and how it works on the Internet and with your client software. The last major section is titled *FTP, E-mail, and Other Matters*; there we'll look at the Big Four Web tools that are the most commonly used Windows-based applications:

- ◆ An FTP client for downloading files
- ◆ An e-mail client for sending and receiving mail
- ◆ A gopher client used on information database servers
- ◆ Archie—a search tool used to hunt through the Internet for files and other archives of files

Archie wasn't mentioned much before this, so I'll take just a minute with it before pressing onward. There are a good many programs stored all across the Internet and all across the globe. How is the new user to find these files tucked away in these reservoirs of data?

This is where Archie really shines. There are two types of centralized data repositories where these and other files are kept. One is called a *mirrored server* in which one primary site is essentially copied to another site (Figure 3-7). One whole site is not an exact copy of the other, but the files deemed worthy to be mirrored, such as the most popular programs and archives, are copied. The basic theory of this configuration is that if one site went down, then either the other site could take over as a backup site, or users could go to the backup location on their own initiative.

The other reason for mirrored sites is that the most popular sites are always busy, and I do mean always! I've logged onto some sites at 3 A.M. only to be denied access because the site is at maximum capacity. The other most common reason for denied access is congested communications lines between you and the destination server. This congestion could, in fact, be in your own Internet provider if it is running at maximum

capabilities or is in some way incapable of supporting your needs. By yourself, you'll not cause the problem, but collectively with a hundred other users, you sure could! If Server A goes down or is overloaded with requests, then the mirrored site can take up the slack and continue the job. Depending on how the site is set up, this switching action may be automatic, or you may just have to know the address of this mirrored site to get to it.

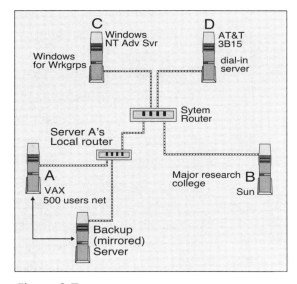

There's one last issue of delays and noncompleted actions, and that concerns how you get routed from your PC as the client to the destination server. It's nice to

Figure 3-7
Mirrored server sites

be able to start a program, initiate the desired action, and let TCP/IP and the Internet find their way for you to the destination. What you don't see—and this fact can be a blessing or a curse—are all of the paths used to get you from point A (you as the client) to point B (the destination). In UNIX lingo, the sum of the paths is called the *hop count*. At one location where I've worked with a highly complex network, FTP requests took 11 hops to get out to the Internet and then to the destination—11 hops! In a normal situation, if there is such a thing on the Web, 4 hops is a more acceptable level, with 7 or 8 usually the maximum that you'll encounter. The result of such excessive routing is delayed actions, or at worst terminated client sessions.

> ### TIP
> If you're experiencing lots of delays, try using PING to see what the return times are with the server you're working with, or connected to.

The computer technobabble term for this effect is *propagation delay*; it represents the time required for the data to travel from server to router to server across long-haul telecommunications lines to more routers and then to the destination. All the while that this is occurring, your client software has to sit idly waiting for the response. It normally can't do anything else during this period of time, and you usually don't want to be doing anything else, either.

But wait a minute! Aren't we running a multitasking operating system, Windows 95? Sure we are, but the client software that started this process is not multitasking! It is still waiting for the first action to complete, so asking your Internet provider to do another action such as e-mail will slow down the system somewhat. To what degree is really unknown due to variations in performance of the different PCs and how they're configured. PCs with a 486DX2/66 and 32MB RAM with a fast hard drive are more likely to be able to complete multiple transactions and handle delays well than are slower 386DX/40s or 486DX/33 computers.

One last factor is the operating system itself. In Windows 3.1, FTP downloads from my Internet provider average 1.8K to 2.4K characters per second (cps). When I tried similar tests in Windows 95, regardless of the stage of the beta software, I was getting up to 3.8K cps rates with the norm now being about 3.2K or so. Because the operating system can process the data more quickly, I can complete more transactions and handle more errors and sessions than I could with Windows 3.1. These increased transfer rates were not just on the Web, but on CompuServe as well along with some of my favorite bulletin boards.

FTP, E-mail, and Other Matters

This section is intended to enlarge on the four main Internet functions I mentioned in Chapter 1. MSN will provide your first Web browser and is a superb starting point. As time progresses, and as you use more Web clients, you're bound to have a favorite program. You may even decide to purchase one of the many commercial products that exist and feel that it suits your needs better.

That's well and good, but I'd like you to understand that Windows 95 and MSN provide all of the core functionality that you'll need to get started when Web browsing with the Microsoft Network. To this end, I will use NetManage's Internet Chameleon for the purposes below, and in Chapters 4 and 5 we'll peruse MSN's Web browser to give you a comparison of features and functions where applicable. Scattered throughout the Internet are similar tools that do the job just as well, but these are not in any kind of integrated set of programs. The commercial packages hold the edge here because when you purchase such a set, you get all of these tools together and don't have to hunt around for them. You also get technical support if something goes wrong. You will get support from many of the authors of Web programs, but it's not normally their prime focus.

What Is FTP?

File Transfer Protocol is what it's called, but there's a deeper meaning to this name. You're probably very accustomed to copying files on your PC from the hard drive to the floppy, or to other locations on the hard drive. Not much to it—just use the DOS COPY command, the File Manager in Windows, or the like. Under the hood, DOS handles all of the intricacies to file handling so that you don't have to worry about this. With FTP, this is true to a degree, but there are a few things to consider. Consider Figure 3-8 below, and notice the directory listings:

This text that you read is in ASCII format. American Standard Code for Information Interchange, ASCII for short, is plain text and numbers. It defines the character set that is used in computer processing for different languages. In transferring data across the Internet, you have to tell the FTP program which mode of transfer to use—ASCII or binary. Binary is the pure ones-and-zeros representation of the alphanumeric

Figure 3-8
An FTP client connected to a site

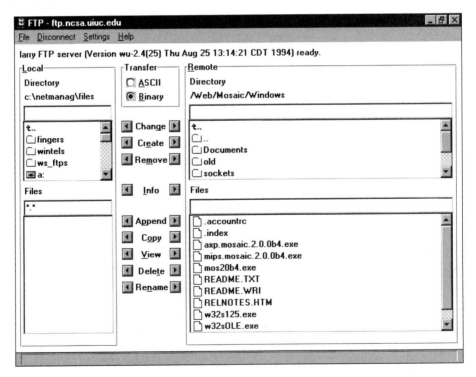

data you see in the screen. For instance, the letter 'A' is character 65 in the ASCII character set. The value 65 translates into *0110 0101* in binary format.

Do you remember a previous discussion where I said computers know only ones and zeros? That's still true, and ASCII transfers are interpreted by the contents of the value so that they can be copied from one format to another. Binary transfers do a bit-for-bit copy, no translations. When you FTP files, be sure to set the proper type of file transfer (Figure 3-9). For text files, use ASCII format, and for almost all others, use binary format.

You can download more than one file at a time if you want. It's as easy as pressing Ctrl and clicking the left mouse button to multiple select files (Figure 3-10). Once the transfer is started, it's on its way until completion or until an error causes abnormal termination.

If you visit sites on a regular basis, then consider setting up a

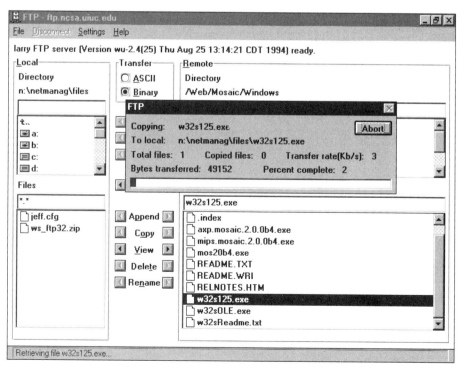

Figure 3-9
An FTP client downloading a file

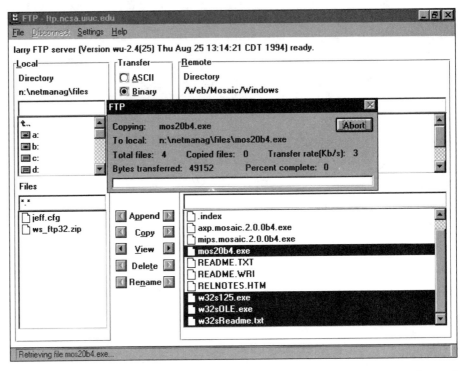

Figure 3-10
Multiple file
downloading

connection profile in which all of the necessary settings to get logged onto the site are kept in a special setup file within the FTP client (Figure 3-11). This setup file normally contains the site name, the connections parameters, your user name and password, and perhaps the default directory that you want to go to when the connection is made.

Now, whenever you want to go to that site, just use the profile to make it quick and simple (Figure 3-12).

The Basics of E-mail

E-mail is the second basic need that propelled the Internet into becoming what is today. It's a neat thing, but it has a dark secret. E-mail is a function that performs much like the U.S. Post Office in that it moves letters between two parties. It has a sender, a receiver, and a method of transportation. Both have levels of priorities in getting the message from here to there, and both can generate return receipts. But,

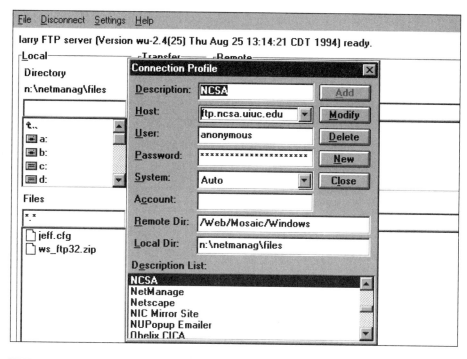

Figure 3-11
Creating a connection profile

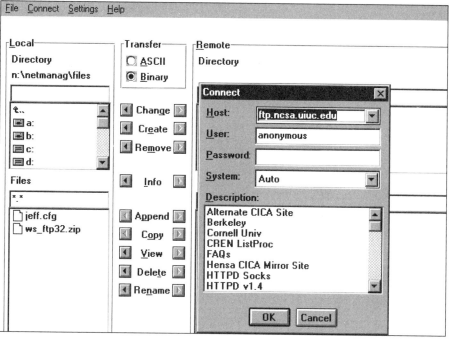

Figure 3-12
Using a connection profile

beyond this point, the similarities end rather quickly. E-mail generally gets to its destination within two minutes of being sent, although it can take up to four hours in some situations. E-mail has the distinction of generally being free or of costing at most a flat rate for a bulk of messages that your provider may allot. My provider charges me $20 a month for my account, and I get 20 hours of connectivity for that fee. It matters not if these hours are occupied by e-mail, chat, downloading files, or just staying connected. I pay for the connection, and that's it.

Other providers charge $20 a month for the account and then $5 an hour for connect time. They may also charge $10 or so for access to newsgroups and the like. There are as many schemes for connectivity as there are directions for the wind to blow. You'll have to find the one that suits your needs best or go with one of the popular service providers like MSN, CompuServe, AOL, or Prodigy. MSN has not announced pricing for the service, but rumor has it that the basic connectivity will be peanuts plus the cost of your phone call. If you call locally to attach to MSN, then you just may have a very cheap Internet provider in MSN! Imagine getting a swell Internet connection plus a service like MSN at the same time. What a concept!

Back to e-mail and the Internet. Taking the Post Office example to heart, let's look at the anatomy of an e-mail message (Figure 3-13):

Notice that you can do all of the same things that you can by paper, but faster. Oh, there's one other thing—the dark secret I mentioned. E-mail was created long ago under a standard called SMTP, which stands for Simple Mail Transport Protocol. As its name implies, it's for simple mail of few items. Well, that's what the original authors of the standard meant, but the ability to attach files to the mail message was allowed, and now e-mail is used for much more than simple mail and small files.

At my office where I'm a network administrator, one of the most aggravating problems we have is users attaching files of 300K or larger to an e-mail message (Figure 3-14). I've seen files in excess of 5MB attached to e-mail when it isn't meant to handle that volume of data. Simple mail is its name, but it gets complicated daily.

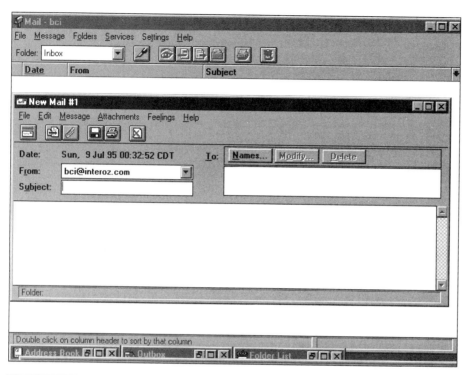

Figure 3-13
**Composing a
new e-mail
message**

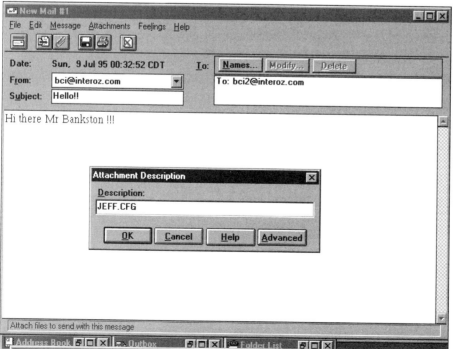

Figure 3-14
**E-mail with an
attached file**

Over time, e-mail programs have matured to the point that file transfers via e-mail have gotten easier to do and to manage. Leaving aside the Internet for just a minute, many mail systems used on internal networks within a business allow for file attachments. As an attachment, a file retains its form from source to destination. A document is attached as a document file and is received as a document file. However, when you are sending this kind of mail with attachments across the Internet, the file can't be sent as a pure binary file. By the way, files like WinWord documents are in reality binary files, not text files. File transfers using e-mail over the Internet *must* be performed with ASCII files. The Internet system does not know how to handle binary files in this manner.

So, what takes care of this? An ancillary function called *uuencoding* occurs in which the binary file is converted to an ASCII equivalent (Figure 3-15).

Figure 3-15
A uuencoded attachment

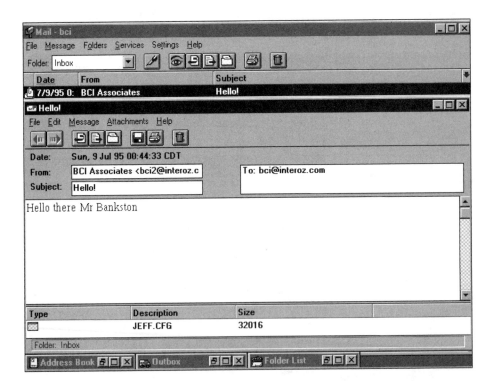

When the file reaches the destination, the receiving e-mail client will either have to convert the attachment back into its binary equivalent or at least let the recipient know that the attachment is a uuencoded file. The recipient will then have to convert the file using one of the many uucode converters that can be found on the Internet. In Figure 3.15, the process was fully automatic.

The Gopher

The Gopher is a sly little animal that helps you to find information stored in databases all over the Internet (Figure 3-16). The client is named "Gopher" because the first Gopher program was created by computer science students at the University of Minnesota, whose mascot is the gopher!

Gopher servers exist all over the world, and this client can help you find many if not all of them. It has search-and-retrieval functions that

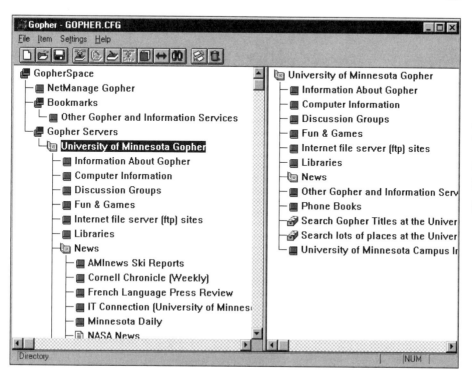

Figure 3-16
The Gopher client at the University of Minnesota

make finding topics a real breeze. Along with data searches, you can go to find newsgroups, FTP sites, archives such as the Library of Congress, other gopher servers, and more (Figure 3-17).

I included the previous figure to demonstrate that you can customize many gopher clients always to start up at a certain gopher site or topic that you last used. Gopher can be a great tool to catch up on world events by perusing many online magazines and news wire feeds (Figure 3-18).

Archie

The last Internet tool to describe is an excellent tool for finding files on the Internet. Archie provides the ability to search across the entire Internet, but its normal mode of operation is to key on several central sites that serve as the core databases for the Internet's file resources. These sites are located all across the globe in countries like the U.S., Germany, Israel, Finland, and Japan. There's plenty to choose from, but start with a database that you think is in the same country as the site you are looking for. The search will go faster as a result (Figure 3-19).

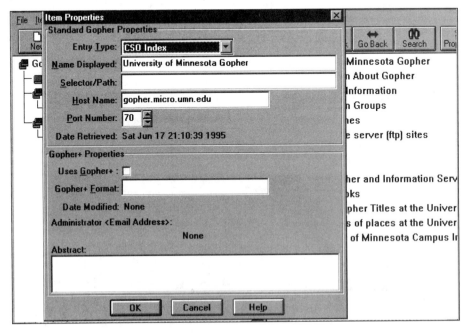

Figure 3-17
**Gopher
properties for
one site**

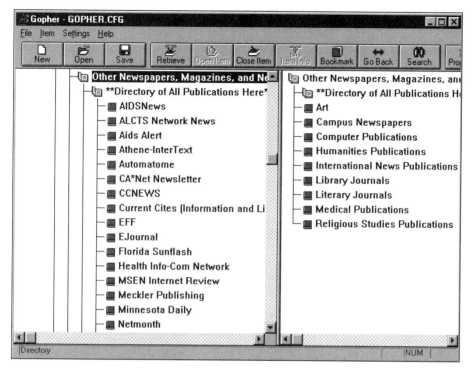

Figure 3-18
Newspapers,
magazines, and
other
periodicals

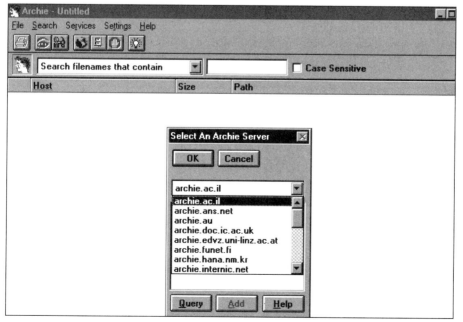

Figure 3-19
Choosing an
Archie server

When the search completes, you'll get a screen showing the results (Figure 3-20). From this screen, you can download any of the files that were found. Notice that one of the pieces of data returned is the server on which the file was found, and this is what gives Archie part of its power.

Instead of obliging you to write down this server name and use an FTP client to get the file, Archie lets you do it right on the spot by double-clicking on the file to be downloaded and confirming the download options (Figure 3-21).

Be Nice, or Be Bounced!

However wild and carefree the Internet may be viewed as, you still have to behave or face strange consequences. Just for an example, if you spend any amount of time with online services, you've undoubtedly heard of *flame mail*, or *flames* as they may be called for short.

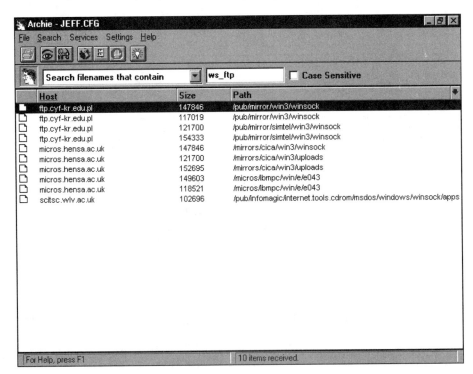

Figure 3-20
Results of an Archie search, ready for downloading

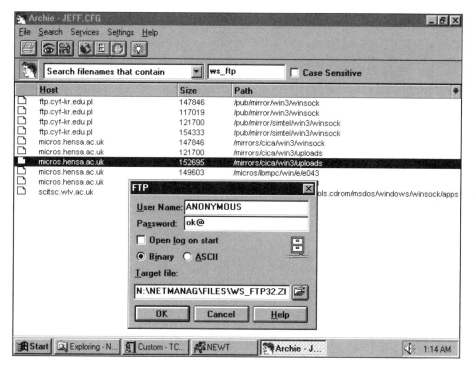

Figure 3-21
**Downloading
one of the
found files**

Basic Etiquette

As you surf the Web feeling good about yourself and get bolder about where you go and what you do, just keep in mind that there are various levels of attitude you'll run across. They'll range from the friendliest to the nastiest, and the gamut in between. By and large, treat people the way you do in real life, and you'll make a lot of new friends online.

> ### TIP
> Everyone likes a friendly face. Be nice and sociable, and you'll not get run off the Internet!

What a tip! What could that possibly mean? How could someone actually run me off of the Net? Laughing a hearty chuckle, I can personally cite three instances in which I know someone has been tossed off of the Net for various "offenses." One of the absolute worst booboos you could ever do is to mass-post an advertisement on the Internet. Baaaaaad mistake! Super bad! Why? For one thing, people are paying for their own e-mail for the most part, and such ads are nothing but junk to them and cost money.

So, how would this get you tossed like last week's sandwiches? Word travels like wildfire on the Internet by means of the newsgroups that we'll see in later chapters. When word gets around you're violating the basic rules of the playground, it's flame time! Yes, mass mailings in *your* direction that frequently flood your provider's mail server. Nothing ticks off a system administrator more than something that clogs up his or her server. In one incident, the person lost his membership with that Internet provider and was denied access for future accounts with that provider. Serious business, I assure you.

Language and the Net

This and the next section cover two topics that I've always felt strongly about. While maintaining my own professionalism and personal degree of moral standards prevents me from saying many things, or doing a variety of things, I can avoid unpleasantness by planning my trip wherever it may take me. On the Internet, once considered the last frontier of computing, keeping your thoughts clean and keeping out of unpleasant situations could prove to be a trial of patience. I'm not saying all of the Internet and the Web are bad, but you should prepare yourself for the eventuality of foul language and the occasional verbal abuse someone may dish out to another user.

The newsgroups are sometimes infiltrated by raunchy language or stories of immoral matters. No offense to the sailors of the world, but the old saying "language so bad a sailor would blush!" fits more often than not. If you're squeamish about foul language, you're just going to have to bear it while you find your desired topic or location.

On MSN, Microsoft is working on a scheme of adult tokens whereby individuals desiring access to an area of the Internet known to display less than pure behavior would be required to complete an electronic form requesting access to this area. Essentially, the form would state something to the effect that you attest that you're over 18, accept what you'll see, won't hold it against anyone, and won't otherwise be offended.

Graphical Graphics

The graphical aspect of the Web and the Internet as a whole has been getting more attention lately from both the media and our congressional body in Washington. Some folks had been roaming through the file libraries at some site and ran across some very explicit sexual pictures. While many adults may view such as normal or accepted on the Internet, the person looking at the pictures was a 13-year-old youngster on a first spin on the Web. Imagine the reaction of mom and dad when they saw that!

Well, that's just the reaction a few U.S. Senators had on the floor of the Capitol building! There are currently three bills pending in Congress (three that I know of) that regulate or intend to ban such X-rated types of graphics and hold owners of servers responsible for these and other sensitive material. In attempting to clean up a 25-year-old situation, Congress forgot to allocate more funds for the electronic police and hall monitors. I'm not condoning the pictures, far from it, but it goes back to a good many other matters in life where the parents need to exercise good solid control over where their children go, and what they do or see.

The moral of the story is if your morals are at risk, you can bet that the `alt.sex.animals` newsgroup is not for you! Most groups are named as close to the general topics inside them as possible. There are stray discussions in every newsgroup, but for the most part it's right on track. The file libraries, on the other hand, are a complete crap shoot as to whether or not you'll get a shot of moon graphics, or a shot of the moon!

Just the FAQs

The last topic in this discussion of Internet Etiquette, or Netiquette as it's sometimes called, involves FAQs—Frequently Asked Questions. So, you're a new user on the Net sounding the depths of your first server or newsgroup, or trying to figure out how e-mail works. Good for you! Keep at it! Work hard! And you just simply can't find the magical touch that locates the data you seek. What a letdown, and it sure feels bad. You really wanted your first experience to be a good one, but what's a rookie to do?

Most servers, e-mail or FTP or Web, have a place on them where you can locate answers to the most asked questions on given topics ranging from what does *HTTP* stand for all the way up to a technical explanation of client/server technologies and their implementations. By the way, HTTP stands for HyperText Transport Protocol, which is the native language of the Web. More on that in Chapter 5.

CAUTION

If you're new to the Web, or to a particular part of the Internet, FAQs can ease your way into the fabric of the Net. One of the worst things you can do as a rookie is to ask all the dumb questions asked a thousand times before. Use the FAQs. Excessive dummy-ism will get you flamed!

In most cases, you'll get an excellent response from users or the head of a server if your first question is "Where are the FAQs, ma'am?" (or sir). I said the head of a server, but really meant another term—WebMaster. This person is usually the administrator of a Web server. You'll find this person by e-mail most of the time as `Webmaster@servername.type`; `Webmaster@system2.com` is a possible example (Figure 3-22). These people are professionals in every sense of the word, and they strive to make their server popular and free of problems.

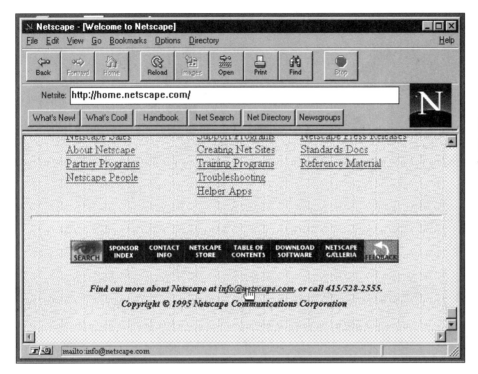

Figure 3-22
Reaching a
WebMaster

Summary

This chapter completes our trek through learning the ins and outs of the
Web and the Internet in general as a primer for the rest of the book.
We've learned a lot about the Internet itself, some more history about it,
and how it can serve our needs. Just like in any society, the Internet has
its own unwritten rules to live by or be told how we should behave. Treat
others with respect, read the FAQs, and have a fun time. Lastly, we've
explored the basics of finding and getting the files that make surfing the
Web such an adventure in online computing. In Chapter 4, we'll dive
right into MSN's Web browser and see what is has to offer us as we
peruse the rest of the Web.

The MSN's Web Browser

As we dive into this chapter about MSN's Web browser, with all of its intricacies, I think it's time to reflect upon the Internet as a whole and what it contains. The Internet is a vast storehouse of data in many shapes, forms, and designs. Each style of data repository is unique in how it is actually stored, retrieved, and otherwise manipulated. How well you prepare yourself for this adventure will largely determine how effectively you'll use the tools named in this chapter.

In this chapter, you'll learn about:

- ◆ Some of the many Web browsers available
- ◆ Related helper applications
- ◆ How to install and configure the Microsoft Web browser
- ◆ How to use the many helper applications associated with the MSN Web browser
- ◆ The basics of the MSN Web browser
- ◆ More advanced uses of the MSN Web browser

For the last of these items, you'll actually make a test run through the Internet.

What's out There

The MSN Web browser (Figure 4-1) is a licensed version of the NCSA Mosaic client under a license from Spyglass, Inc. It offers a wide variety of features and functions to get you through the Web and find the goodies you want to find. It's one of several that are licensed and enhanced versions of the popular NCSA Mosaic client created at the National Supercomputer Center at the University of Illinois at Champaign-Urbana. NCSA Mosaic is available free from a good many locations, but directly from the source at `ftp.ncsa.uiuc.edu`. If the client is free, why buy a commercial version of the same thing?

Well, one thing that commercial vendors do is to spiffy up the product and clean up the rough edges, perhaps adding a few extras or beefing up what's there. This is exactly what many vendors have done with this venerable tool. If you download the NCSA Mosaic client—and I'll show you how later on in this chapter—you'll notice that the filename is MOS20B4.EXE. You'll find similar naming schemes everywhere, but this name says it's a beta copy of Mosaic. What's a beta version?

Figure 4-1
MSN's Web browser

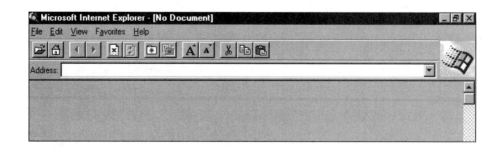

Beta software is that for which the software developers have started a project, written quite a bit of the code, and tested it for functionality. This code is pretty stable and has most of the bugs worked out of it, but the program is still not quite ready for prime-time commercial usage. NCSA's Mosaic, shown in Figure 4-2, is still in the beta stage of development, and it has been for over a year. Quite a long beta, you may quip, but this software is under development by several programmers at the university. Mosaic comes in two flavors—16-bit for the Windows 3.1 users, and also in a 32-bit form that is also intended for Windows 3.1 but that requires the Win32S add-in library set, which allows you to run 32-bit Windows applications inside the normal 16-bit Windows 3.1 environment. This file is called W32S125.EXE and is available at the same site as Mosaic.

Since it's in the beta stage, you can expect to see some problems with the NCSA Mosaic client. Nothing earth-shattering, but some users of the product have reported it's crashing their systems for no apparent reason. On most systems, it runs just fine and serves the purpose well. It is at

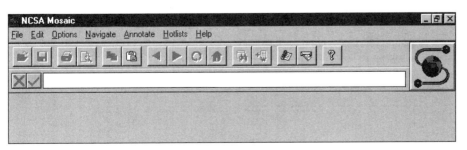

Figure 4-2
NCSA Mosaic's
Main window

this stage that the commercial vendors take over from Mosaic in developing it more fully, or other vendors create their own competing products such as Netscape. With this in mind, let's take a look at some of the other Web browsers out there and a little of what they can do for you.

The first browser we'll look at is Netscape from Netscape Communications Corporation, shown in Figure 4-3. At the time of this writing, it was in version 1.1 and was available in both 16-bit form for Windows 3.1 and 32-bit form for Windows 95. The product is completely different than Mosaic in style, but performs much the same functions. Netscape can be obtained for a test run at the site

```
ftp.mcom.com/netscape/windows.
```

Cello, shown in Figure 4-4, is another tool developed much like NCSA Mosaic in that it was written at a major college, in this case, the College of Law at Cornell. Cello is a breeze to use and configure. You can get a copy at

```
ftp.law.cornell.edu/pub/LII/Cello.
```

Cello uses a slightly different style of hypertext links than does Mosaic or Netscape, but the result is still the same. You can go from site to site at the blink of an eye, or the click of the mouse as it were.

WinWeb (Figure 4-5) is yet another neat Web browser; it is from

Figure 4-3
Netscape
Navigator
version 1.1

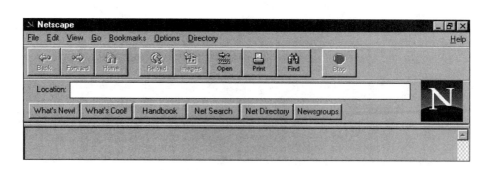

EINet, the makers of the Enterprise Integration Network. They are a major Internet provider whose WinWeb browser is free for noncommercial use. WinWeb is available from

```
ftp.einet.net/einet/pc/winweb.
```

When you download and extract the ZIP file, start it after adding it to the program list or just double-clicking on it with Explorer. The startup default option takes you to the EINet home page of

```
galaxy.einet.net/galaxy.html.
```

You can change this to any other site you wish, or none if desired. You'll notice that WinWeb has many of the features of Mosaic or

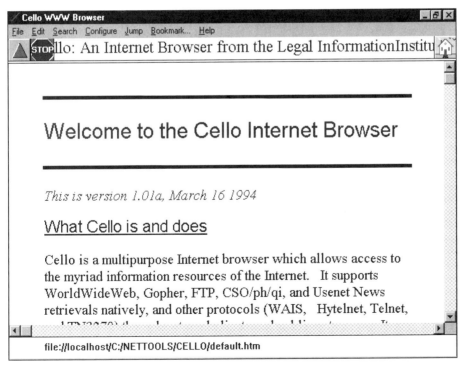

Figure 4-4
Cello from
Cornell
University

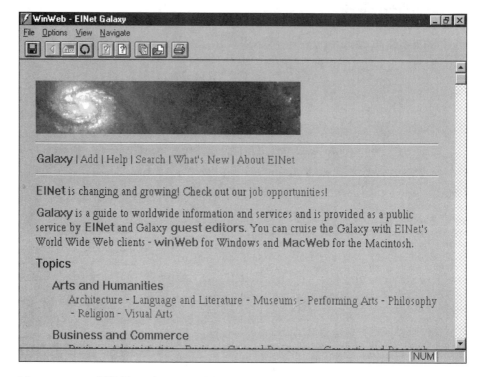

***Figure 4-5*
Winweb
browser from
ElNet**

Netscape—a FILE option, an ability to navigate forwards and backwards, means to create hotlinks, and more.

Terms and Functions

As we've progressed with this book, we've learned a good many new terms and acronyms. This section will present several more that will give you the basis for following discussions on the Web. As with many of these terms, the first is formed as an abbreviation of an actual protocol used to enable a specific Internet function. *HTTP* stands for HyperText Transfer Protocol, which is the means by which Web data are accessed. When you use the Web, you use sites that employ the HTTP methodology of Internet connectivity. One example of such a connection is to the home page of my Internet provider:

```
http://www.interoz.com.
```

You're already familiar with *FTP*, which is the File Transfer Protocol and is how Internet site move files around. *URL* stands for Uniform Resource Locator, which is how the Internet establishes standard addresses and Web connectivity. Such an address helps the client know how to connect to the Web site. These browsers are dependent upon your entering the location of the destination site, and they use URLs to perform this task. The URL represents the link to the site, such as:

```
www.interoz.com
```

shown in Figure 4-6. Breaking this address down, it means a Web site (the "www") located at site interoz, which is a commercial server. The address `ftp.law.cornell.edu`, on the other hand, refers to an FTP site on the server law at site Cornell, but this Internet node belongs to an educational institution. The site name is more appropriately called a *domain*, which is just that—in this case, a domain that Cornell

Figure 4-6
The home page of InterOz

University controls and that is registered with the InterNIC. No one else can have the name Cornell after they've registered it.

Home page is the term used to denote the opening listing of a Web site. This is the most important part of any Web site, as it serves as the first impression that any visitor receives of the site. It should grab your attention quickly and say concisely what the site is all about. A gopher is a site that serves as a central server to data and repositories of information. The word "gopher" is taken in several contexts, but the one that interests us is that a gopher "runs errands and takes care of getting information from specified locations." What this means is that when you log on with a gopher client and ask for something, the Gopher searches the Web using other gopher servers that house these immense databases to fulfill your request. You've seen an example of a gopher in Chapter 3, but it bears repeating here as we'll soon be using the Gopher quite a bit more. (See Figure 4-7.)

Figure 4-7
A run with the Gopher at the University of Minnesota

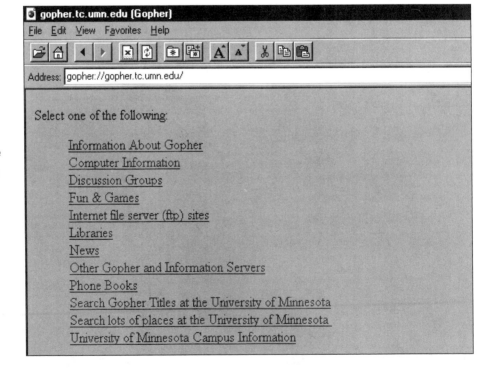

With Archie, Gopher, Jughead, and the many other search tools available, there's still room to get lost on the Internet and the Web. When you just can't find anything at all, try using a *Worm*! Yes, just like the little wiggle worms in the yard, the Web Worm makes its way through the little nooks and crannies of the Web looking into all aspects of it to find the data you seek (Figure 4-8). Normal Worm searches can take minutes, hours, or a day to find the data once you launch the search.

One more interesting aspect of the Web is the *HTML* document that presents the data in the form shown in these figures. HyperText Markup Language is the procedural language used to add the enhancements to a normal text document that form the fonts, draw the lines, and place objects within the HTML file. It allows for buttons, check boxes, data entry fields, and a host of other functions.

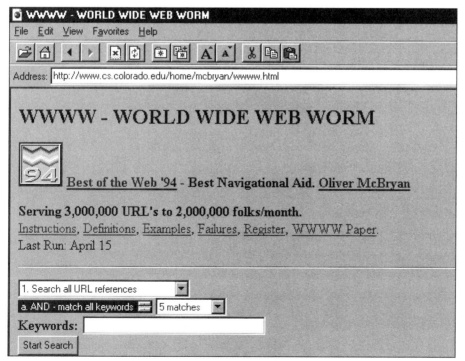

Figure 4-8
A WWW Worm
search

Below is a short sample of HTML code:

```
<HEAD>
<TITLE>Chameleon Getting Started</TITLE>
</HEAD>
<BODY>
<a href=http://www.netmanage.com><img
src="masthead.gif"></a>
<h1>NetManage</h1><h2>Introduction and Getting
Started</h2>
<p>
<img src="bullet.gif"><i><b>Welcome!</i></b>
<p>
Your NetManage software is a Windows software
package that connects you to the Internet.
The suite of easy-to-use applications will help
connect you to the world's largest network and
guide you through its online information.
</BODY>
```

Figure 4-9 shows the resulting picture generated by the HTML code itself.

Figure 4-9
A Web page
generated by
the sample
code

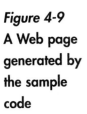

Related Helper Applications

Now that you've got a good feel for the many browsers available, let's examine a few of the helper applications I mentioned in the last chapter. All across the Web, you'll see and do a good many things at sites and get more interested in more activities. Some of these sites actively use sound, pictures, and movie clips to present their information. The majority of Web clients do not have built-in viewers and functions to handle this type of data. What you'll need are one of several *helper applications* that receive the data as the client gets it and then process it as required. Some of these applications are:

- ◆ **MPEG32H.ZIP**—MPEGPLAY, which displays MPEG animated movies or image files.
- ◆ **GS261EXE.ZIP**—A GhostScript viewer, which displays PostScript documents in Windows.
- ◆ **QTW11.ZIP**—A QuickTime movie player using the Windows Media Player.
- ◆ **LVIEWP1A.ZIP**—LView Pro is an image file editor for Microsoft Windows 3.1, Win32S, and Windows NT. It loads and saves image files in: JPEG, JFIF, GIF 87a/89a, TIFF, Truevision Targa, Windows and OS/2 BMP, ZSoft's PCX, and PBMPLUS's PBM, PGM, and PPM formats.
- ◆ **WHAM.ZIP**—Wham allows you to play and record WAV sound files.

While this list is not all-inclusive, it is representative of what you'll encounter as you travel the Web. One utility that you should get right away is the GhostScript interpreter. In most cases, when you find these utilities on the Web, they'll have associated document files in text, Winword, and other formats; but, more often than not, these document files will be in PostScript format. This one viewer can save the day for you when the only format is PostScript.

> **TIP**
> While it may take time away from surfing the Web, one of the best things you can do is to acquire the helper applications first and configure them. You'll enjoy the Web more as you surf it then.

If you don't have these helper applications running, don't despair, because it won't cause harm to your Web client. You'll just not get the full enjoyment of the Web with sound and movie clips.

Where to Get These Helper Applications

There are two sites that most commonly have these applications:

```
ftp.law.cornell.edu/pub/LII/Cello
```

which is the Cornell Law School, and

```
ftp.ncsa.uiuc.edu/Web/Mosaic/Windows/Viewers
```

which is the NCSA home for Mosaic itself. Another place that serves as a mirror site to NCSA is

```
ftp.sunsite.edu,
```

which has many of the same files as NCSA, but not all of them. NCSA and SunSite are very busy at all times of the day. If your Internet provider doesn't have good, fast links, you may never get onto any of these sites. I recently switched providers for this reason. Remember back in Chapter 2 where we talked about TCP and routing and some of the reasons one may never be connected?

Installation of the MSN Browser

In this section, we'll install the MSN Internet Plus Pak tools. As we do so, there will be some changes to the way MSN looks and connects, but not many. In Chapter 3, we installed MSN and went for a test spin, so here we'll give it the add-in tools to use the Web via MSN.

CAUTION

At the time of this writing, MSN's Internet connectivity was largely a long-distance call unless you lived within local calling distance to a major city.

I'm not trying to run you off MSN before you get started, but all links that I found to the MSN Internet were 9600 to 28.8K baud connections. Due to the different kind of link, MSN Internet cannot use the same dialup link as regular MSN does. While my local MSN link gets me a 14.4K baud link, the Internet dialup I use to Atlanta, Georgia, is 28.8K and is long distance for me.

Basic MSN before the Web

We talked about MSN and some of its tools before, but the main difference in MSN before and after the Internet tools are added in is the dialup link itself. (See Figure 4-10.)

What Will Change?

I used a different Internet provider than MSN before MSN came along, and I had Windows 95's dialup networking configured to connect to my provider. When you access the Control Panel, there's a setting for Networks, and one for Dialup Networking.

**Figure 4-10
The MSN
Connection
window**

> ⚠️ **CAUTION**
>
> If you have special dialup functions configured, you'd do well to write down your settings for these two options, as MSN Internet setup will change them slightly as it makes MSN Internet the default dialup.

What else will you lose from the installation? Not a lot except perhaps 10 or 11 megabytes of disk space for the immediate installation. I highly advise that you get a handle on directory names, as you'll find yourself downloading files and such as soon as you really get to the Web's internals. There's lots to see and do on the Web, and invariably it requires some other programs to make it happen. I'd conservatively plan on allocating 20MB of disk space (above and beyond the Plus Pak) to downloading, decompressing, and installing a lot of these programs.

Archives, Archives, Everywhere

Speaking of which, let's take a minute to discuss these archives. As you cruise the Internet, you are certain to have to deal with archives, perhaps sooner than you realize. The many files that reside on your computer range from executables (EXE and COM), to data (text, databases, and spreadsheets), to pictures (PCX and bitmaps), to audio and video files. Many of these file types are made up of bits and bytes of information that form the file using repeated characters. Text files like the one used to create this chapter are an example of highly compressible data. The rate of compression varies from a ratio of 1:1 for binary types such as executables to 20:1 for some pictures and audio files. What would you rather download? A 500KB file, or a 75KB file?—naturally, the 75KB file because it takes less time and less money as you are connected to your favorite FTP site.

Archives come to the rescue! These files contain the data files just mentioned in a compressed form. The three most common archive format extensions you'll see are ZIP, LZH, and EXE. The ZIP file is primarily based upon PKWare's compression technique. The LZH format is based upon the compression program called Lharc, by Yoshi. The EXE archive is a ZIP that has been turned into a self-extracting archive. Other formats exist for different operating systems, but these are the ones you're most likely to run across. The archive is one in which one or more files have been crunched down in size and then stored together into a "container" file. The archive format looks for repeatable characters in a file. These repeatable characters are quite necessary for normal use, but they are extraneous in an archive. Because they are repeated, the compression engine removes them and replaces them with tokens, or symbols, of these same characters.

Consider the sentence below:

Tom and Tommy went to Thomas's house to play.

It's easy to see the patterns in this example. "To" is one, "om" is another, "to" is a third, and the spaces between the words are yet another. Instead of taking 36 characters to hold this sentence, an archive may only need 20 characters to do the job. The space savings are obvious and constitute a prime reason why you'll see that almost all files on an FTP site are in some kind of archive.

Performing the Installation

Now that we've gotten passed all of the basics and how-tos of the Web and such, let's get down to the brass tacks of actually installing the MSN Internet Plus Pak. I'll install it from my CD-ROM that has the Plus Pak on it, but using the floppy disk version isn't much different, except that you must supply the correct disk when asked. When I say to insert the CD-ROM to install, I mean also to insert the required disk as prompted, if you are using a floppy drive.

To start things rolling, start Explorer and navigate to the CD-ROM drive where you've inserted the disc. Before proceeding, it's wise to have a good backup of your Windows 95 directory. I've never had any problems with the installation process, but a word to the wise is sufficient. Change to the directory containing the SETUP.EXE program, and double-click on it. You'll get a welcome message and a warning that Plus Pak can't install correctly if other apps are open and are using files that Plus Pak has to use or change during the install process. Heed this warning as it could save possible corruption of data files! Click on Continue, and you'll get a screen in which to enter your name and organization if you want to. This is not required but a good idea. After pressing onward, you'll get a screen with your product identification number.

TIP

Write your product identification number down! You will need to supply it if you ever need to call Microsoft for support of Plus Pak.

After you click Okay, SETUP will do a search for installed files to see what it does and does not need to install. Next, you'll be asked where you want to place the Plus! files. Notice setup defaults to the drive and directory where Windows 95 is installed. If you install very many applications, your drive where Windows 95 is installed will quickly fill up. This screen allows you to specify an alternate location for Plus!, as shown in Figure 4-11.

Setup will perform a cross-check of installed files and then offer you two options—typical or custom installation. Typical is just that—the files required to perform the job for the user who only wants to get to the Web and back. Custom installation, shown in Figure 4-12, allows you to install as little or as much as you desire—or the entire kitchen sink! A full install of Plus! takes up about 11MB of disk space.

If you select typical installation, Plus! presses onward with the installation, placing the typically needed files on your computer. If you

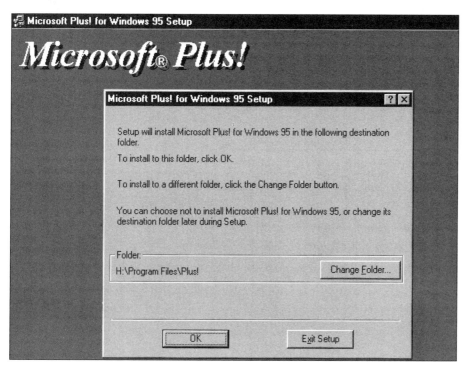

Figure 4-11
Changing the default location for Plus!

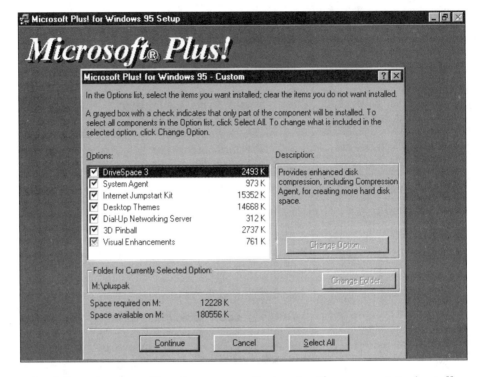

Figure 4-12
Options for custom installation

selected custom, you'll get a screen that asks if you want to install a really nifty program called System Agent, which performs many tasks for you in the background, such as disk defragmenting, Scandisk, and such. Give it a try, and I'm sure you'll like it! Installation proceeds to install the required files.

Once the files have been installed, you'll get a nice welcome to the Internet and an offer to help you decide how to connect to the Internet (Figure 4-13).

If you choose Help, you'll get the Internet Help Wizard, which will tell you all about connecting via MSN, a local area network, or a separate Internet provider. Take a minute to peruse this information, as it may well come in handy someday. It's one of the more informative help topics. Click on Next to press onward. Setup now asks you how do you want to connect, by MSN or by your own provider. We'll select MSN, since this is what the book is about. The next screen simply says that

Figure 4-13
**Welcome to
Internet Setup**

more files will be copied to complete the setup. Click Next to press on.

A very key question comes up next. "Are you already a member of MSN?" it will ask. Back in Chapter 2, we installed MSN and joined up, so your account should be active. Make sure you have Yes selected, and click Next to continue. Some disk activity will occur, and then you'll see a screen that acknowledges you're connecting to the Internet via MSN (Figure 4-14).

Click Okay and then enter the area code and prefix that you'll be calling from. MSN Internet will now call to log on and find the closest number for you to connect as well as update your installation with required data. You also have the ability via the Settings button to change how you connect to MSN Internet by changing the modem or any modem settings. At any rate, click on Connect to press on. Confirm your current MSN account ID and password at this point, and click on Connect again.

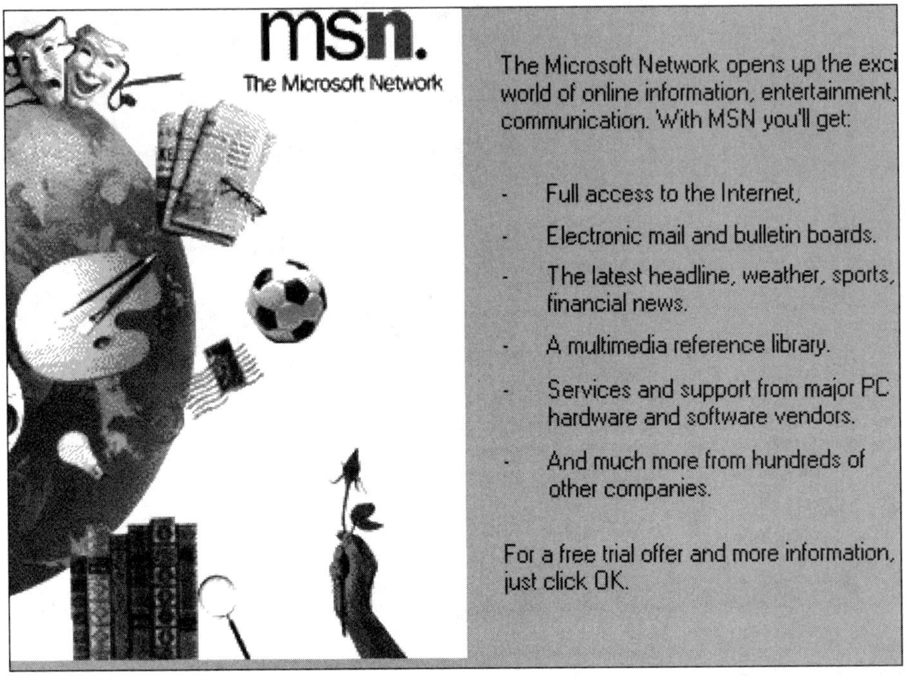

Figure 4-14
**Welcome to
MSN Internet!**

msn.
The Microsoft Network

The Microsoft Network opens up the exci
world of online information, entertainment,
communication. With MSN you'll get:

- Full access to the Internet,

- Electronic mail and bulletin boards.

- The latest headline, weather, sports,
financial news.

- A multimedia reference library.

- Services and support from major PC
hardware and software vendors.

- And much more from hundreds of
other companies.

For a free trial offer and more information,
just click OK.

After signing on and transferring data and files, MSN Internet
returns to give you a screen to finish configuring the software. The first
thing you'll have to do is select the dial-in location if a local one is not
available (Figure 4-15).

Notice that both entries are blank to start with; the figure shows
the numbers after I have filled them in with my primary connection
and backup point of contact. Click Okay to continue the installation.
Follow the prompt to choose a Desktop Theme for your desktop (Figure
4-16). A Desktop Theme is nothing more than a predefined desktop
based upon several customized settings for colors, screen blankers,
mouse pointers, sounds for actions that occur, and such. You can also
just keep your current desktop settings. Take a minute to explore these
settings, and you may just find one that suits you! This is a welcome
personal touch Microsoft has added to the software to put newer users
at ease with the system.

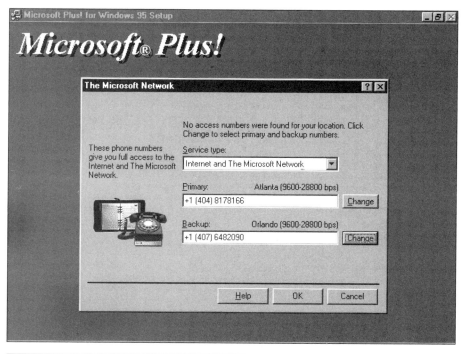

Figure 4-15
Selecting dial-in location

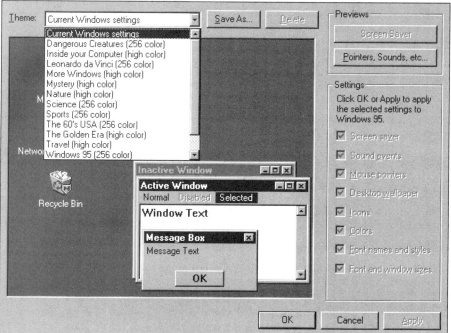

Figure 4-16
Desktop Themes new to Windows 95

With these settings out of the way, you're almost ready to connect to the Web by way of MSN! Last, you need to let the computer reboot for the changes to take effect and the new software to come into play. Make sure all applications are closed and data files saved, and then click on Restart Windows.

When Windows 95 restarts, nothing looks as if it's changed until you start MSN for the first time.

Overall, what's changed now after the installation? When you start MSN, you'll have one more choice to make as to where you connect to MSN. Start MSN and then click on Settings to select Access Numbers, where you'll now see that MSN is accompanied by Internet and The Microsoft Network. (See Figure 4-17.)

To see the next visible clue that your system has changed, start the Control Panel, where you'll see an addition for Desktop Themes and one for Internet. Desktop themes is self-explanatory, but if you double-click on Internet, notice the option to choose the dialup networking

Figure 4-17
Choose how to connect.

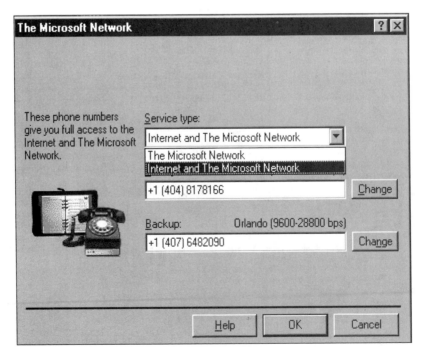

location (Figure 4-18). If you click on that option, the Microsoft Network now appears where it didn't before. You'll see the two Internet dialup connections as well. It is here that you can change where you make your other Internet connection, if you've defined one before installing MSN.

TCP/IP and the MSN Browser

Last, if you have a DNS (a Domain Name System, as discussed in Chapter 2) configured as I did, it will be changed to support the MSN Internet connection. This wasn't a big deal for me because my Internet provider supplies the IP address each time I connect. This is called *Dynamic IP Addressing* as opposed to the fixed IP addresses that some Internet providers use. In order to use the MSN Web browser, you have to connect via the MSN connectivity point. So, we've done all that can be done, and now it's time for the moment of truth! Let's start the MSN Web browser and get to work.

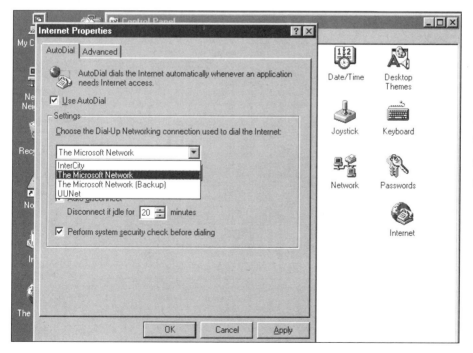

Figure 4-18
**Control Panel
dialup Internet
choices**

Configuring the Browser

Now that we're this far along, this section will show us how to configure the Web browser, where to connect, how to change some of the settings for optimum connections for the modem, and how to create lists for our favorite sites. Then we'll go get some of those helper applications that we have mentioned.

Where to Connect

Connection to the MSN Internet POP is controlled through the standard MSN Settings dialog box. After starting MSN, click Settings and then Access Numbers. We've done this before, but now let's look at the alternate locations. You'll see two sets of access numbers just as we set them up, as Figure 4-19 shows.

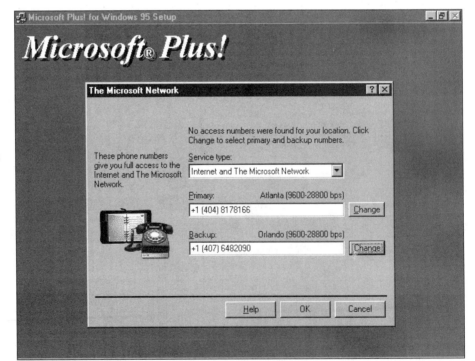

Figure 4-19
Selecting access numbers

Only now, let's make a change. I usually dial into Atlanta, Georgia, and then Orlando, Florida, as the alternate. If I wanted to restrict dialing into the system to one node, then I would set both entries to the same location. Click the Change button, select a Country, and then select a State/Region. The country defaults to the U.S., and selections should be the same as when we set them up earlier. Next, choose the phone number to dial. You may notice the list is kind of slim at the moment, but Microsoft is working hard to provide more and faster connection points as time rolls on.

Why would I want to set my normal and backup dial-in points to the same number, you may ask? One reason is the cost. In several situations, you may find that the initial primary number is a local call, whereas the backup is long distance, so setting them to the same number prevents long-distance calls. So what, you can set the primary to the number and leave the backup blank, right? Sure you can, but if the primary is busy, MSN redials up to 5 times before calling it quits. With both primary and backup set to the same number, MSN now dials 10 times before quitting! If MSN doesn't answer within 10 tries, something else is wrong and you needed the afternoon off anyhow. Experience has shown that even if a node is very busy, 10 redials should get you in unless it's totally hopeless.

TROUBLESHOOTING

Q. *I try to start MSN, but all I get is weird noises and a No Carrier error message. What's wrong?*

A. Your local phone lines could be so noisy that a clean connection is not possible. You can check this by connecting with different online services, if you have them, using the same modem. You may also need the C1D2 setting for your modem. Change these settings by clicking on Settings, Modem Settings, Connection, and then Advanced. In the Extra Settings field, type in **C1D2**, which is case insensitive. Click on OK three times, and then try it again.

Favorite Places

Tell MSN to connect, and let's go! You do that by double-clicking on the Internet icon that was placed on your desktop during the installation (Figure 4-20).

After starting, the Microsoft Internet Explorer (the MSN Web browser) automatically goes to its home page of

```
http://www.microsoft.com/IExplorerHome
```

which is at Microsoft Corporation in Washington state. This is a really cool home page, just what a home page should be—concise and to the point as to what users will see when they log on to this server (Figure 4-21).

Figure 4-20
The Internet Icon on the Desktop

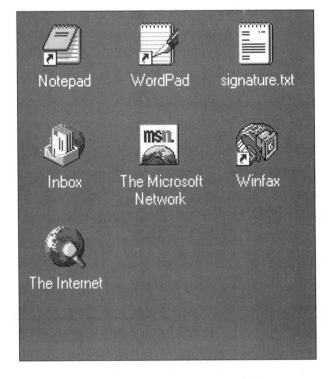

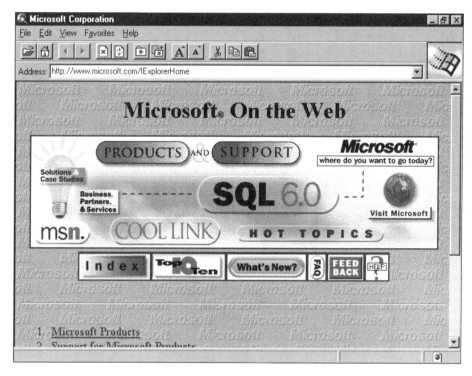

Figure 4-21
**The home page
for MIE**

Taking a little side trip, let's look at one of the best time-saving features browsers have in common, and that's "favorite places." Look at the top of the browser, and click on Favorites to get the drop-down menu showing your favorites. Mine has one place defined, and it's the home page of my Internet provider. Clicking on that takes me directly there (Figure 4-22).

Once there, you can use the vertical scroll bar to see the rest of the home page, which extends downward some distance, and you'll see all the hotlinks in blue. Clicking on one of these takes you to another area of this site, or it might take you to Hong Kong for that matter. This is the very essence of the Web and its fabric. Scrolling down the page, I come to one of my favorite links, the Bikinis Are Wee page. Clicking there takes me to a very interesting page, so we'll add it to the favorite sites list. Sitting on this page, click on Favorites at the top of the page, and then on Add to Favorites to save it for later use! You'll get a box that

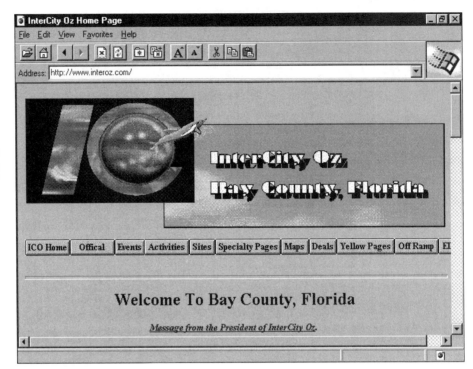

Figure 4-22
The home page for InterCity OZ

shows current favorites and prompts you for a name for this new addition (Figure 4-23). You can accept the given name or choose your own. Finally, click on Add to complete the transaction. That's it!

Helper Applications

The next part of our journey is getting one of these helper applications I've mentioned. Recall from an earlier discussion that the site name was `ftp.law.cornell.edu`. So, in the address field of the browser, type this in:

```
ftp://ftp.law.cornell.edu
```

and then press [Enter]. You'll see the welcome screen to Cornell University, so click on the blue underlined "pub," then "LII," and then "Cello." You're there! (See Figure 4-24.) Notice that while you were

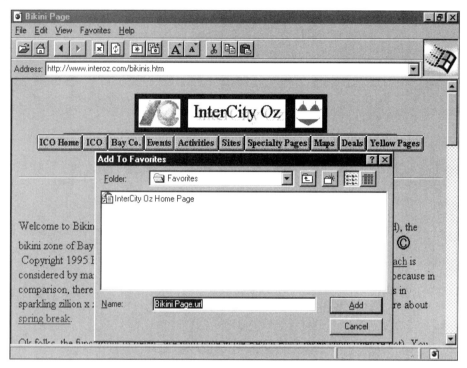

Figure 4-23
**The Add
Favorite Site
menu**

navigating the directory tree, the mouse pointer changed from an arrow to the hand symbol whenever you crossed a hotlink. Neat, eh? This way you always know where the link is on the page.

Line up the hand cursor on the file called WINGIF14.ZIP and click once. I should note here that the heavy blue underlined words are directories, whereas the thin underlined words are files. When the download actually begins, you may see a message that says it doesn't know how to handle the file and prompts you for what to do. Just tell it to save it as the name of the file and pick a folder to store it. The transfer completes, and you've just downloaded your first file from the Internet via the MSN Web browser! Not too hard, was it? Now, save the site by adding it to your list of Favorites as you did earlier. Now the next time you need a file from Cornell, just open the Favorites menu and select the Cello entry.

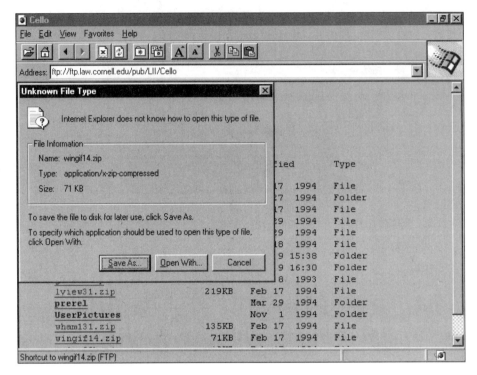

Figure 4-24
The FTP site at Cornell by way of the MSN Web browser

Setting Up History Lists

As the saying goes, history repeats itself, and that is true for the MSN Web browser. MIE has a setting so that it can remember as many sites as you'd care for in a history log. Click on FILE in the upper-left corner, and you'll see a list of the last sites you visited. If the list exceeds 10, then a bottom entry is called More History, which you can click on to see all sites up to the limit set in the View➤Options➤Advanced menu (Figure 4-25, I have 300 set for the moment). Take a minute to peruse the Options menu, in which you can change the default home page used upon logon, the colors, and the amount of disk cache to use while online. This disk cache keeps a listing of the most recently visited sites and makes return to those sites faster.

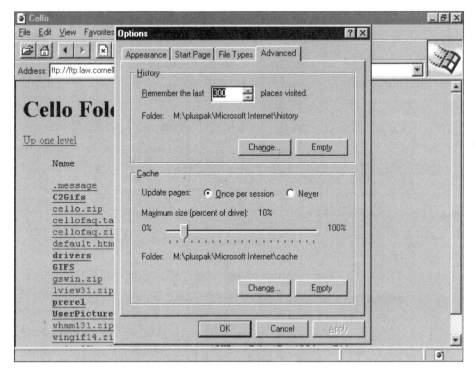

Figure 4-25
**The View➢
Options➢
Advanced menu**

We've done a lot up to now, and we're ready for a little more playing on the Web. The next section will show you how to make your way around the Web with some basics, because Chapter 5 will be a full in-depth run across the Web using the Microsoft Web browser.

Some Basics of Using MSN's Web Browser

Okay, we've whet our appetite on the Web, so let's take a bit closer look at it—but now we'll make a round trip to an FTP site, visit the Gopher at the University of Minnesota, play around EINet, and then keep track of all these fun places as we spin our own Web.

Getting around URLs

URL stands for Uniform Resource Locator, as we've said before; a URL is uniform because all sites can have their names broken down into these fundamental parts: the type of Web connection, the server name, and the type of site. The first place we'll go see is the Microsoft home page as usual before we change that to something else, like my Internet provider's bikini page! Connecting up to the Web, we go there automatically. If you're still running MIE, then enter the URL `http://www.microsoft.com/1ExplorerHome`. Let's pick apart the home page and see if there's really anything interesting for us to make us want to come back:

◆   The entire bottom line of options is the most critical to any site—an index, the top 10 items, what's new, FAQs, feedback form, and help!

◆   The hot topics of the site.

◆   For vendors of products, a support and services hotlink is crucial to member support.

From this list, you can see there are several items that every good site should employ to give it a compelling reason why the user should come back. Web sites make their money by being good and offering a solid base of user support and useful content. Many sites earn their living by referrals for product sales because a user found the product on the Web site and either called by phone to place an order or did it over the Web site itself! Yes, you can even order merchandise over the Web using a credit card if you're not skittish about this. Many sites utilize secure transactional methods for these and other sensitive matters. Make sure the prospective site does so before you post your credit card number.

Now that you've seen some basics of a home page, let's click on the list number 4 to go to MSN and then click on item 1, to get one of the coolest Web pages I've seen in a long time! This is what Web pages are all about (Figure 4-26).

Frequently Visited Places

Still at Microsoft Internet Central, add this page to your Favorites as we did earlier. There is one thing about the favorites: When you add one, the name of the site is added as well. As we'll see in later chapters, sometimes the URL is added to the list instead of the name. MIE adds a text name you can remember such as `Microsoft Internet Central` instead of something like `http://www.mic.microsoft.com` that would make you wonder what MIC really is. Favorite places are stored in a folder called History under the directory where Plus Pak was initially installed, so from this you can see the link between Favorite places and historical sites.

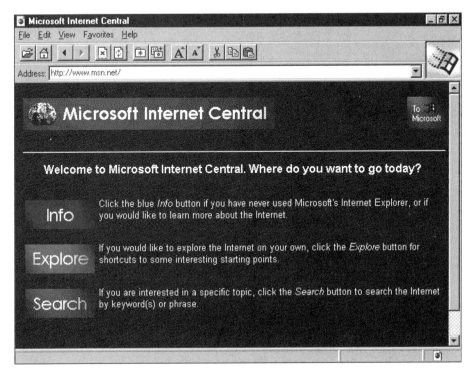

Figure 4-26
Microsoft
Internet Central

More on History

Historical sites are those which you've visited and then passed on your journey to other sites. Favorite places are those that, while passing through history, you've added to some permanent storage on your PC for reference later. But, doesn't the history do the same thing? Yes, but when you end your online session, the history-cached locations go away! Favorite places stay listed for each subsequent online session.

GopherSpace

One of the fun things I mentioned earlier is Gopher, the little rodent from the University of Minnesota (Figure 4-27). You can find his home at

```
gopher://gopher.tc.umn.edu
```

and you can get there by typing in the address above in its entirety in the Address field. Unlike an HTTP site, the Gopher presents a purely text screen. Seldom will you ever see a gopher site with graphics. There

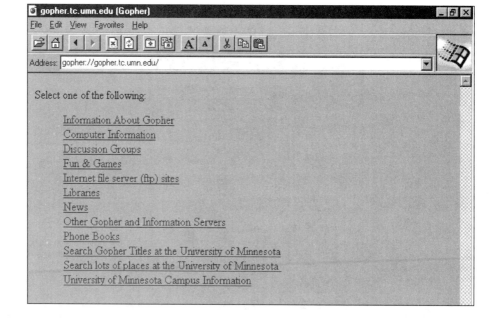

Figure 4-27
The gopher server at the University of Minnesota

are gopher servers all over the Web, and this is just one of them.

Notice the changed colors of two options, Other Gopher and Information Servers and Search Gopher Titles at the University of Minnesota. These two are different colored because I have followed those options and returned. The color coding serves to let you know where you've already been. Gopher servers can be used to find almost anything on the Web. Click on the Search Gopher Titles option, and it'll take you to the appropriate screen. A sample gopher search might use any keyword for a topic. Let's say you wanted to find any subject matter on the Oklahoma bombing. In the title search area, enter any text appropriate to the subject and press Enter. The search returns any hits on the topic, a "no results found" message, or an error message saying that the server was too busy to process the request. All too often, you'll get a busy line, as gophers across the Web are heavily used. Just as easily as you added Web sites to your Favorites list, you can add gopher searches as well.

Summary

This has been a very exciting chapter about Web browsers in general and the Microsoft Web browser called Microsoft Internet Explorer, MIE, in particular. Microsoft has made a credible step into the Internet providers' arena with a self-contained product offered as an add-in to the Windows 95 operating system. We've seen how well MIE integrates with Windows 95 and how easy it is to set up and operate. We've seen how we have the ability to use our own Internet provider if we want to or to adopt MSN as a complete online services system. In this chapter, we've seen how to get around the Web a little bit with FTP, Gopher, and the WWW sites themselves. In the next chapter, we'll take a jaunt around the Web in a more detailed manner with all of these tools, and we'll tune MIE for our own preferences. See you in Chapter 5!

 Let's Go for a Spin!

Up to now, we've completed all of the prerequisites to get onto the Web with the Microsoft Web browser. We've installed both MSN and the Microsoft Internet Explorer. In Chapter 4, we explored a few of the prerequisites to becoming familiar with the Web—we got our feet wet as the saying goes.

In Chapter 5, not only will our ankles get wet, but we'll plunge in as we learn all about:

◆ Getting around the Web with the many Web resources
◆ Shopping on the Web
◆ Handling the many files on the Web
◆ Gaining a more detailed view of the Gopher

Getting around the World Wide Web

The Web is a vast repository of data and services scattered around the globe. So, how is a poor soul supposed to find these data? In this section, we'll explore the Web using several tools designed to help us find all sorts of data. We're going to keep this overview of these tools kind of short since we don't want to spoil the fun in Chapter 6, where we'll put these tools to fuller use and explain them in more detail while using the Microsoft Internet Explorer.

A Word about Files

Before we get started with this chapter, we must prepare to deal with files and other data types on our journey across the Web. With that in mind, we need somewhere to store the data on our hard drive. Pick the drive where you want to keep this information, and then create these directories:

- **Download**—to store the files we'll retrieve from the Web and across the Internet
- **Locations**—to provide one common location to store the URLs that we'll save for our favorite places so as not clutter up the Windows 95 directory area
- **Working**—to process the files we download and test them for virus content
- **Holding**—to provide a temporary holding area for files and such until we decide what to do with them

These are recommended directory names, but feel free to name them anything that suits your tastes or desires. As time goes on and you acquire more software for the Web, you'll begin to use a lot of disk space. To keep things together, some people may be tempted to put all of these utilities into one directory. *Resist this temptation!* Putting all of these files into one location can be a recipe for disaster.

Here's why. There's a critical program called *WINSOCK.DLL* that is the core to your access to the Internet as a whole. This program provides the communications link between your client helper application, albeit your connection itself, and the operating system such as Windows 95. Windows 95 comes with its own *WINSOCK* file and thus doesn't need any other program of the same type or design. In fact, other Winsocks directly conflict with Windows 95's Winsock. Because of this, you need to take special precautions to ensure that the Winsock that may come with one of these helper applications does not overwrite the Winsock in the Windows 95 home directory. You also need to check that the PATH statement in your AUTOEXEC.BAT file doesn't include two paths that both point to a Winsock file, and that the Windows 95 Winsock isn't missing. This is a guaranteed recipe for disaster.

CAUTION

Avoid having multiple *WINSOCK.DLL* files in the PATH or in the Windows 95 home directory, as this situation will cause a loss of functionality for the Microsoft Internet Explorer and other Web utilities.

Use the Windows 95 Explorer to make sure this isn't happening to you: Start it, select *Tools*, then select *Find*, and then click on *Files or Folders*. At this point, tell it to look for the *WINSOCK.DLL* file and tell it to look in *My Computer*. FIND will search your entire hard disk for all occurrences of the desired file. You can do this for most any cases in which you want to check for multiple instances of the same file. It's a great tool for cleanup as well as preventive medicine.

Archie

Archie has long been a favorite personality on the Web because of his unique ability to locate files scattered across cyberspace. Archie operates by way of another database, one that is located across numerous servers. Archie scans the Web servers approximately weekly and builds a database of files and the FTP servers they reside on. This database can be found at key Internet sites across the world. This search across the servers is done for you automatically by the Gopher client. To perform such a search, do the following:

1. Connect to MSN and the Internet, if you've not already done so, and start the Microsoft Internet Explorer.
2. At the address field of MIE, type
    `gopher://gopher.tc.umn.edu/` and press [Enter].

3. Select "Internet File Server (ftp) sites."

4. Select "Search FTP sites with Archie (gopher+ version)," which will get you a bit better search across the Web. In reality, it doesn't matter if you use the "gopher+" version or not. Both return equally useful data.

5. Click on "Search of archive sites on the Internet."

6. Type in a filename (I used WSARCHIE for my example) and press [Enter].

The search will start and be conducted from Archie server to Archie server looking for your file (Figure 5-1). When it completes, hopefully it will include what you're wanting. In the case of the search above, it returns a few hits.

When the search is done and the file(s) are listed, you can retrieve them by simply clicking on the hyperlink.

Figure 5-1
Archie searches for a file.

Veronica

If you recall from earlier discussions, Archie is used to find files using a global search mechanism. This search is rudimentary in type and design, but it works quite well most of the time. The main thing is that Archie uses one of about a dozen Archie servers to find the files. If it's not on one server, then you'll have to pick another server and retry the search. An Archie server will have previously compiled a database from a large list of FTP sites, and it is this database that is searched.

Veronica does much the same thing, but with gopher servers around the world. "Veronica" stands for **V**ery **E**asy **R**odent **O**riented **N**et-wide **I**ndex to **C**omputerized **A**rchives. Veronica is "rodent oriented" because of its all mouse-driven, computerized archives. Veronica rebuilds its databases approximately every two weeks by scanning the menu structures of the sites it monitors and building its own indexes into the databases. Part of the information stored by Veronica is the home site and location where a data item is stored.

Let's perform a simple search to demonstrate Veronica, and then we'll press onward to the next topic. Log on to MSN Internet if you've not already done so, or connect to your own Internet provider. Start the Microsoft Internet Explorer from your desktop, and enter

```
gopher://gopher.tc.umn.edu
```

into the address field. When you come to the opening screen, perform the following steps to look for "sharks" (Figure 5-2):

1. Click on "Other Gopher and Information Servers."
2. Click on "Search Titles in GopherSpace using Veronica."
3. Halfway down the screen, click on "Search GopherSpace by Title word(s) via PSINet."
4. Enter the keyword to use in the search.

In the third step, take some care in stating where you want to search. You should try to use a server close to you to speed up the search and retrieval functions, but it's not at all mandatory. I used PSINet because it's always worked for me! If you get a message that says there are too many connections, you'll have to try another server or try again later.

Jughead

Veronica is a global searching tool for gopherspace. It excels at wide searches, but what about data at one particular site that you know are there but just can't find? This is where Jughead comes into play. "Jughead" stands for Jonzy's Universal Gopher Hierarchy Excavation and Display. What this really means is that Rhett "Jonzy" Jones, the author of the program, is providing us with a tool to dig deep into the inner workings of one particular site to find what we're seeking.

Figure 5-2
Veronica searches for sharks.

Jughead starts up much as Veronica does in that you specify a server to start at and perform the search. Let's go to the author's home server of

```
gopher://gopher.utah.edu
```

just as you'd do for a gopher server. Enter this address, and you'll get a screen like Figure 5-3:

WAIS

"WAIS" stands for the Wide Area Information Service, which is an excellent tool for searching the Web when neither Veronica nor Jughead finds your requested item. Why? Because whereas Veronica is a global gopher search tool looking at *titles* of documents and Jughead looks at the individual server itself for the data, WAIS searches the documents themselves in a full-text search methodology. WAIS takes a

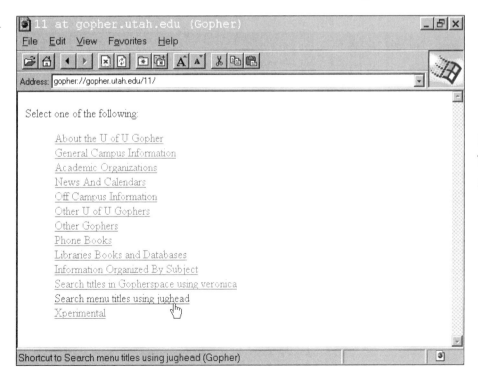

Figure 5-3
The Jughead search engine

little bit longer, but it's searching a considerably larger pool of data much more intensively.

To search with WAIS, you'll need a WAIS client, since this function has not been included as a client in the Microsoft Internet Explorer. The U.S. Geological Survey usually has the program in an archived form called *WWAIS24.EXE*, which is a self-extracting archive. You can get the file at

```
ridgisd.er.usgs.gov/software/wais.
```

Once you have it downloaded, copy the file to some directory and run it. This will extract the program files into a usable form. From Windows, run the program, and you'll get a screen such as Figure 5-4 below:

A typical search of a WAIS server might be for documents on specific items, such as the Japan gas attacks. To see what might be found on this topic, execute a WAIS search by starting WinWAIS and following the steps.

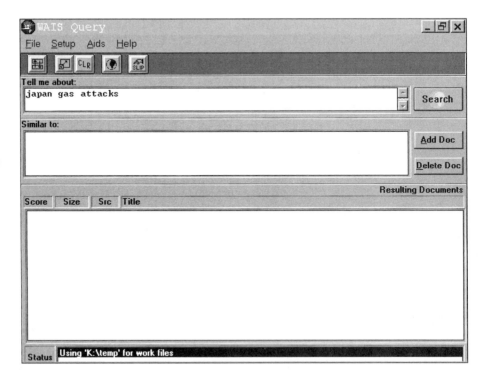

Figure 5-4
A WAIS search tool called WinWAIS

1. Pick a WAIS server by clicking on File, and then Select Sources. Use the ALLSRC option under the Source Group field. This shows you all of the WAIS servers.

2. For this search, I picked the ANU—Pacific Relations server since I was looking for something in that region. Click on the Done button to proceed.

3. In the Similar To field, you can enter text that causes a search for which the response will be close in sound to the search pattern.

4. In the Tell Me About field, type in **japan gas attacks** and click on the Search button in the upper-right corner of the screen. WAIS heads off to the specified server as noted at the Status field at the bottom.

When the search completes and returns the relevant data, you'll get a screen similar to Figure 5-5 below. From this, you can double-click on one of the documents that appear to get the full text of the article.

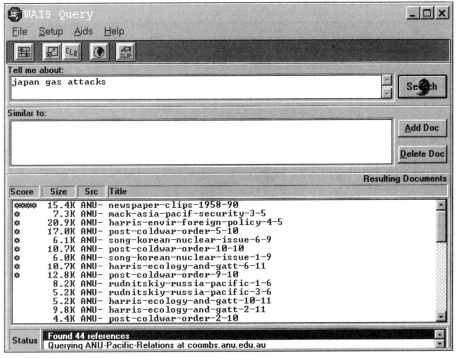

Figure 5-5
WAIS search results

The Web Worm

The Web Worm, a nifty service, is used to find virtually any resource by title or URL across the Web. It does it by having as many as five *knowbots* running at one time. A *knowbot* is a Web search tool that knows all about one particular aspect of the Web and what to search for in conjunction with your search parameters. This Worm can be found at

```
http://www.cs.colorado.edu/home/mcbryan/WWWW.html
```

as shown in Figure 5-6.

Just as its name implies, the Web Worm worms its way around Web servers into every little nook and cranny, dutifully looking for your document. To do a search, enter the scope of the search in the Select field and then give it a set of keywords to use in the search. You can use Boolean search parameters like OR and AND to limit the search. You

Figure 5-6
The WWW Worm search tool

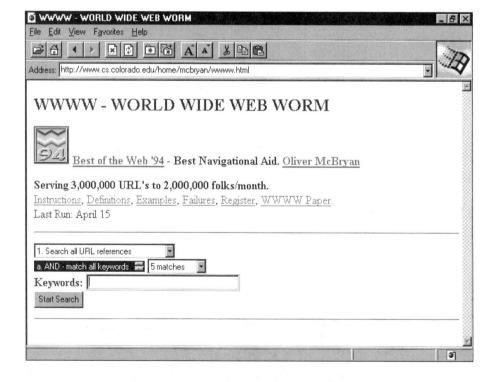

should note that the search may take some time to complete, so don't get key-happy in the meantime.

World Wide Web Search Engines

Many of the available Web search tools are collected at one home page (Figure 5-7). You may choose to launch most of your searches from here. This is definitely a key home page to remember. It's here that you'll find Veronica, Archie-like search engines, Jughead, WAIS, and more. When you get to this site, page down through all of the information, and you'll be amazed at what's here! You can find this collection of Web searchers at

```
http://cuiwww.unige.ch/meta-index.html.
```

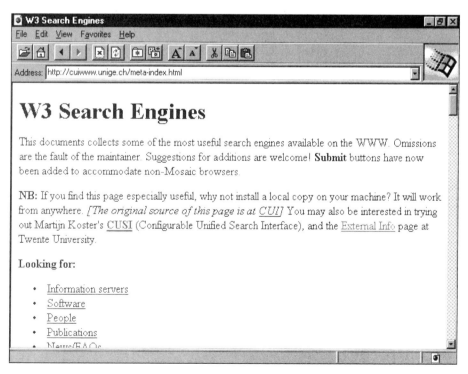

Figure 5-7
Web search engines

This is an awesome search and retrieval tool set for the novice user. It's the one place on the Web I know of that you can find 99 percent of all of your search needs at one site.

Newsgroups

Newsgroups are messaging centers that carry conversations about topics of all kinds. Imagine that you're carrying on a conversation with a friend, and two other friends are not around but you wish they could be there to hear what's going on. Well, take a copy of your question to your friend and that person's answer, and post these on the electronic version of a message cork board, and you have a newsgroup! You put your message on the board and then leave. One friend comes by after you've left, reads your message, and writes a reply on the lower half of your note. Now, yet another friend comes around and sees your message and the first friend's reply and writes down his or her own reply to either your original message or the reply to your message. A reply to the reply to the first reply, and you now have a *thread* going on. Just as a thread weaves its way through a garment to form the fabric, so does a message form a discussion. In most situations, you need a news reader client to do this, but you can also get news using the Gopher by going to

```
gopher://gopher.msu.edu:3441/1threaded
```

as shown in Figure 5-8.

Note how newsgroups are organized here. To get to the page shown in the figure, you would see entries such as "alt" and "comp" and "biz." These are the categories that exist on the Usenet. Usenet is the Internet structure that links the news servers from location to location so that all of the news is posted to all servers. Table 5-1 lists most of these groups by name and subject matter:

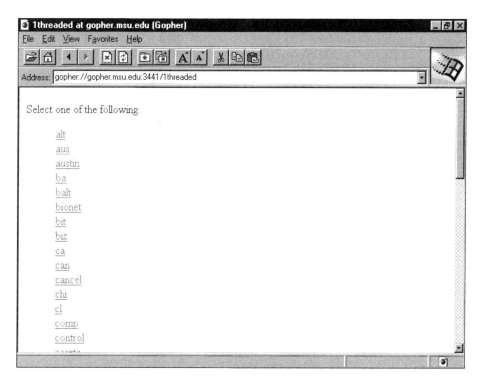

Figure 5-8
Getting newsgroups via Gopher

Table 5-1 Usenet Categories

Group Name	Purpose
alt	Alternative subject matter
biz	Business-related interests
comp	Computers and related topics
med	Medical and hospital topics
misc	Miscellaneous interests
rec	Recreational fun groups
sci	Science and technology
soc	Social issues

These groups are but a sample of the hundreds of newsgroups that you'll find on the Web. I've given you one newsgroup server to start, and you can explore the Web to find more. It's important to note that you have to have rights and permissions for a news server to use it. These are usually accomplished by your Internet provider. MSN has newsgroups now and should have full access available by release time of Windows 95.

Not only can you get newsgroups, but, as Figure 5-9 shows, you can get news from around the world and the Web by going to

```
gopher://gopher.tc.umn.edu/11/News.
```

This Web page lets you see the news from Chicago, the University of Minnesota, and elsewhere.

Telnet

Telecommunications networking is a means to communicate with servers of all types for the purpose of extracting information when your

Figure 5-9
Getting news from across the Web via Gopher

client and the server are not of the same type. Since this is most of the time, Telnet can sometimes be the only way you can access a particular server. Telnet is a basic style of communications in which your dialup connection serves as a smart terminal to the server. Virtually all of today's communications programs have the capability to access a server by basic means much as you might dial into a bulletin board in your local home town. On the Web, you can connect to a number of servers via MIE or by way of a Telnet client (Figure 5-10).

I have a program that gets me into CompuServe in a more automated way, but what if I'm at the house of a friend who has an Internet connection, and I need to check e-mail on CompuServe? I just Telnet into the CIS server and follow the prompts. Nothing could be easier, right? Well, not exactly. Telnet gives you the capability to communicate with a variety of servers around the world, but it won't allow you to download files! You can check information like weather at

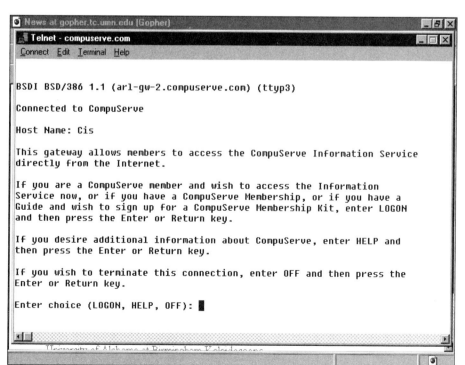

Figure 5-10
Telnetting into CompuServe

```
telnet://downwind.sprl.umich.edu:3000
```

by way of Telnet just as you can using the Microsoft Internet Explorer. By now, you may have heard of Telnet clients that work as a client in other systems, but the Microsoft Internet Explorer's Telnet comes with the installation. There's nothing extra to install such as with Netscape, in which you must download a Telnet client and then tell Netscape where the Telnet client is located on your PC. The Microsoft Internet Explorer comes with the Telnet client built in.

Shopping on the Web

This section is a shopper's dream and the bill payer's nightmare! We'll discuss the various ways you can shop on the Web, places to go, and things to look for as you surf the Web. Just think of it—no lines to wait in, no lines to check out through, no overcrowded parking lots. What more could you ask for except a higher credit line?

Plenty, and the Web has it. As you browse the stores, you'll run across those that use video and sounds clips as well as graphics to advertise what you'll be getting. In foreign countries, many have kiosks that assist you in finding the right size to fit. Remember that we have a propensity to think in terms of standard sizes and fits, whereas our friends across the water use the metric system and different shoe sizes than our own, so we need to learn to be versatile and flexible. Many of these foreign vendors will help you with this task.

Need a Book?

This is a fantastic subject that deserves some attention. As you cruise the Web, you'll undoubtedly need to brush up on some of this new information you're absorbing, so why not find a book on the subject to take with you on your next plane or car ride? Let's head off to the Computer Bookstore at

```
http://www.nstn.ns.ca/cybermall/roswell/roswell.html
```

and look at a fine selection of books (Figure 5-11).

You'll have a variety of options and things to do here, but I want you
to click on the last hyperlink to search the store for a book that'll tell you
more about TCP/IP. The previous chapters just gave you a tremendous
appetite to know more about how your connection works, so let's get more
information! To search their bookstore, perform the following steps:

1. Click on the "Search the bookstore" hyperlink located at the
    bottom of the home page.
2. In the field provided, enter the term **TCP/IP**.
3. Click the Search... button, or press ⌷Enter⌷.

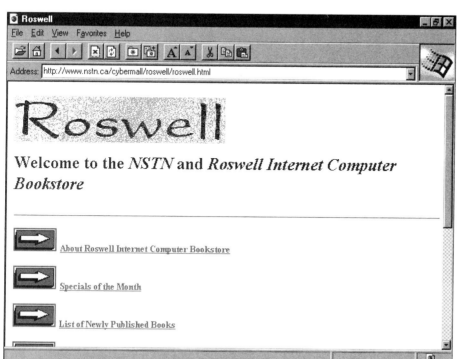

Figure 5-11
Roswell Internet
Computer
Bookstore

Notice that the returned information appears to be all jumbled up, and it's hard to read until you look closer. What you'll see are hypertext jumps to each book at the store. Clicking on one of them takes you to a screen that tells you all about the selected title (Figure 5-12).

There's a store on the Web where you find maps and related items. This store has maps of all shapes, styles, and designs for all occasions. There are street maps, country maps, topographical maps showing elevations, and much more. If you're interested in maps of all types, visit

```
http://www.delorme.com
```

and take a look at what they offer (Figure 5-13).

Computers don't always rule the Web. There's a fun store run by Scholastic, Inc., located at

```
http://scholastic.com.
```

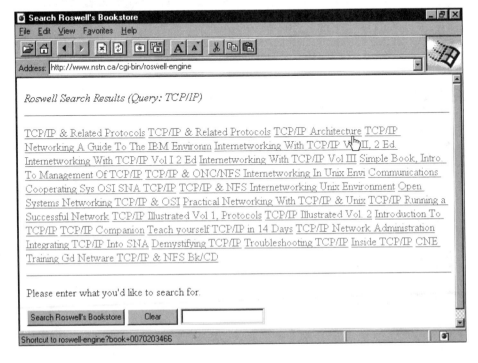

Figure 5-12
Getting more information about the selected book

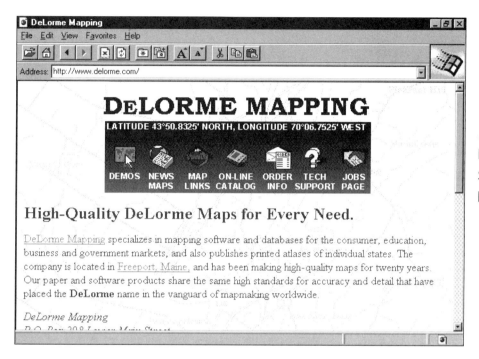

Figure 5-13
Delorme's Map
Store at
Freeport, Maine

When you get to this site, you'll actually be getting to the WAIS, Inc., site in which Scholastic maintains a hyperlink to its location. At the WAIS home page, scroll down to nearly the bottom of the page and click on "Scholastic" to get you there (Figure 5-14). Note the link to CMP Publications at nearly the same spot on the home page. (CMP is the parent firm of more than a dozen of the most popular computer industry trade journals.)

Before long, and perhaps by the time this goes to print, Scholastic should have their own Web site at

```
http://www.scholastic.com.
```

Services and Sales

As businesses become more modernized and fully integrated with communications services, you'll see more and more businesses that are establishing an online presence on the Web. Companies that are

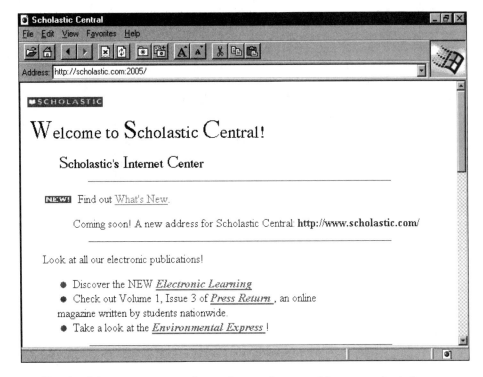

Figure 5-14
Scholastic
Central

really looking to expand and reach a wider marketplace are discovering the Web as a diversified business opportunity. And what an opportunity it is! Let's say that you make device ABC and sell thousands of these widgets each month. To build each widget, you need five component parts plus your assembly plant. Each of these five parts is built by five different companies, but these five companies make only their respective parts and sell them only to your company. That's quite a limited scenario for these five businesses, but this happens all the time in the real world. What could they do to enhance their opportunities?

Well, your company can have a Web site that advertises your product, but each of these five businesses could have a hyperlink on your home page to it's own product descriptions and sales. It's a way for them to diversify into wider areas, as well as being a way for you to make more money because you're effectively selling space on your Web page. Because each of these businesses may have something of interest to you, you could add these to your favorite places in the Microsoft Internet Explorer. This is what Scholastic has done at the site mentioned earlier. The site is owned by someone else, but Scholastic has a link on that page to it's own business interests.

As you continue surfing the Web, you'll find companies such as Dell Computer Corporation online with their own Web presence at

`http://www.us.dell.com` (Figure 5-15).

Here, you'll find product information, spec sheets, software, desktop systems, and much more. For instance, you can learn how you can get various levels of support for your Dell products.

While we are on the subject of computers and software, check out the site at

`http://www.awa.com/microstar/`

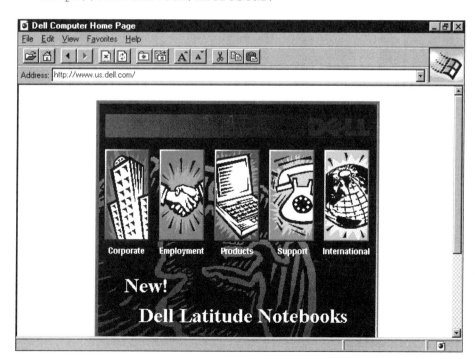

Figure 5-15
Dell Computer Corporation

for shareware (Figure 5-16). They've been dealing in kids' software, shareware, and games since 1987. They include an e-mail form you can fill out if you want to see how to get your shareware listed with them.

If you're a music buff and want to see what's been out on the market lately, check out the Compact Disc Connection at the site

`telnet://cdconnection.com` (Figure 5-17).

These folks carry about 110,000 CDs of all types of music guaranteed to suit the most discriminating tastes.

When you get there, you'll learn that they have a European section including German folk music. If you would rather access their system via a BBS, call them at 408-985-0162 using eight data bits, no parity, and one stop bit at the 14.4K baud rate. This site demonstrates a clear use for Telnet: Searching a database of over 200,000 total titles through a Web server would be quite slow.

Figure 5-16
Microstar
Software Club

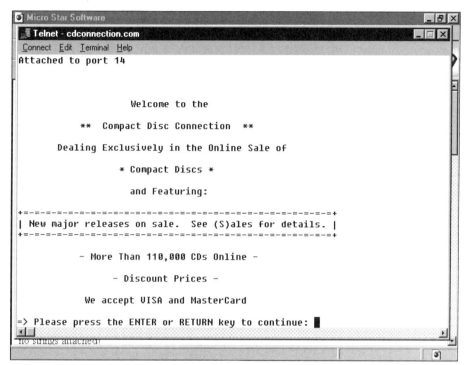

Figure 5-17
Compact Disc Connection

 **TIP**

Telnet sites are faster to access when there are more data to search and retrieve, but the presentation isn't as pretty as on Web sites. If you just want a quick look at a site and don't need to download anything, Telnet is a better choice.

If you are disabled or have disabled employees, check out Americans with Disabilities, located at

```
http://www.human.com/mkt/access/index.html
```

where you can get information on the requirements for businesses spelled out in the Americans with Disabilities Act of 1990. You can also learn how to incorporate your business by going to the Company

Corporation located at

```
http://Incorporate.com/tcc/home.html
```

where you can find all the advice you need. Sole proprietors that are growing and seek the benefits of small corporation status will like this site. I've added this one to my own list of favorite places for later reference.

Just as there are sites for music and computers, so are there sites for earrings, cars, sports buffs, and much more. One of the things that's abundant across our globe is malls and crowds. In the next section, we'll head to the mall but leave the crowd behind!

Mall Shopping with a Mouse

This is perhaps one of the section that diehard mall shoppers would most love to see and use if they had computers. You can see just as many services here as you can when you're actually in the mall nearest you, but you'll have to go get your ice cream from your freezer instead. Just don't drip it on the keyboard.

CAUTION

All of the services mentioned here use online credit card services to place and fulfill product orders. Most vendors have taken steps to assure the protection of your credit card number, but no system is yet 100 percent foolproof. Know whom you're dealing with if someone calls by phone for verification of your credit information.

The first place we'll visit and add to our favorite places is the CommerceNet located at

```
http://www.commerce.net
```
(Figure 5-18).

**Figure 5-18
CommerceNet's
information
page**

This organization is working to encourage more use of the Web as a delivery system for businesses and a medium for businesses across the globe to carry on commerce.

One really neat location that you'll love to add to your favorite places is the Index of Services located at

```
http://www.shore.net
```

which provides about 145 links to products and services of all types and designs. You can learn to be hypnotized, or find memory for your computer, or find out about acupuncture, or investigate a host of other products and services.

You can learn about our Canadian friends by tuning into their CyberMall at

```
http://www.visions.com/netpages/.
```

Figure 5-19
The Canadian Mall connection at CanadaNet

This site provides quite a learning environment for the non-Canadian surfer to discover what our northern friends have to offer (Figure 5-19). There are sections on real estate, tourism, career opportunities, the arts and humanities, and much more.

The mall at the Stanford Shopping Center provides a unique look at mall shopping, as this location provides the distinctive look of a real mall. You can find them at

```
http://netmedia.com/ims/ssc/ssc.html.
```

This mall is billed as the one of the few open-air shopping malls in the U.S. Located just outside Stanford University, it's a gorgeously landscaped mall! As opposed to the locations we've talked about earlier, this mall Web site lists the stores and how to contact them as well as a map location for the store (Figure 5-20).

Figure 5-20
**The Stanford
Shopping
Center**

The Internet Shopping Network

One of the most fun places is the Internet Shopping Network. Located at

```
http://shop.internet.net,
```

this place is a veritable gold mine of shopping pleasures (Figure 5-21).
As soon as you go to this URL, you'll be asked for your membership
number. If you're not a member, then you can browse through the stores
and window fronts! Membership is free, but you have to create your
membership by providing your credit card information for billing
purposes when you order products and services.

You can find out about food, electronics of all types, computers and
related devices, food at the mall, products for your home, and more. It's
quite a shopping extravaganza, and all done with the mouse and a bit of
patience—and a credit card!

Figure 5-21
The Internet
Shopping
Network

Need a Few Files?——The FTP Connection

No one entity has as much to offer the computing enthusiast as does the Internet. E-mail, chat, research databases, and FAQS (Frequently Asked Questions) are among the many facets of the Internet. But the most prolific source of information is the archived file. This section will delve into many aspects of the archive file, the many formats, and just exactly what to do with these mysterious forms of data. After getting through this section, you may consider upgrading your hard drive!

What Do You Do When You Get a File That Is Compressed

As you read in Chapter 4, file archives are an omnipresent fact of life on the Internet. We described some of the principles and benefits of archives there; here we will take a closer look at the kinds of file archives commonly found online.

NOTE

Although this section discusses four specific products, these are by no means the only ones capable of handling the job we're talking about. These utilities are perhaps among the more popular, but the reader is urged to seek out more sources before purchasing any one utility for an expressed purpose.

ZIP File Formats

The ZIP format was made famous and widespread by PKWare, a company excelling in data compression techniques. There are a few other companies marketing ZIP compressor engines, but this discussion will center around PKWare because it is the de facto standard for ZIP archives. It is a shareware product and can be purchased on many computer store shelves. You can also contact the manufacturer directly:

PKWare, Inc.
9025 N. Deerwood Drive
Brown Deer, WI 53223
ph: 414-354-8699
BBS: 414-354-8670
fax: 414-354-8559

Nearly all ZIP files that you'll see are based upon PKWare's compression engine. Those few that are not are most assuredly in a fully compatible ZIP format. All of PKWare's tools are DOS-based and command line–executed. PKZIP is used to create the archive, PKUNZIP to decompress it, and ZIP2EXE to create self-extracting archives from the .ZIP form.

There are two common formats—version 1.10 and version 2.04g—that are widely used at this time. Version 1.10 has been around for a very long time and served well in its lifetime. Due in part to larger data files, slow transmission lines, and the like, PKWare recognized the need to improve upon it's already successful version 1.10 product.

Version 2.0 came out with a much improved compression engine, but it introduced several bugs that negated many of the gains and resulted in unstable archives. Several patches and changes later, version 2.04g was a more stabilized and far better product than earlier version 2.x archivers. While this discussion seems to center around the PKWare product rather than the archives it produces, it's vitally important that you understand this difference in ZIP versions to ensure that you get the best archive you can.

CAUTION

ZIP archives between version 2.0 and version 2.04 may be unstable and could easily corrupt your files.

So, how do you know if you've got a version 1.10 or a version 2.*xx* archive? You don't, really, until you attempt to use the archive. Version 2.04g is backward compatible with version 1.10 and previous versions of version 2.*xx* and handles them with an ease which will be transparent to you. Using the "-v" viewing option with PKUNZIP does not reveal what version was used to create the archive. What is required is to use the "-vtm" option, which displays technical information about the archive and pauses the display between screenfuls.

Entering the command with this option PKUNZIP -vtm TEXT on one of my own archives yielded the output shown in Figure 5-22.

To get detailed help instructions, type in **PKUNZIP /?**. Be sure that your PATH is set to the PKUNZIP.EXE file, or that you're current directory is where the PKUNZIP.EXE file resides.

```
Searching ZIP: TEXT.ZIP

            Filename: AGENTS.TXT
           File type: text
          Attributes: --w-
       Date and Time: Feb 14,1995   02:15:00
  Compression Method: DeflatN
     Compressed Size:    11754
   Uncompressed Size:    31176
   32 bit CRC value: 627e5fdf
          Created by:    PKZIP: 2.0 under MS-DOS
   Needed to extract: PKUNZIP: 2.0

            Filename: COMPUSER.TXT
           File type: text
          Attributes: --w-
       Date and Time: Feb 14,1995   02:15:00
  Compression Method: DeflatN
     Compressed Size:     2481
   Uncompressed Size:     6252
   32 bit CRC value: f80ef299
          Created by:    PKZIP: 2.0 under MS-DOS
   Needed to extract: PKUNZIP: 2.0
More - Space for next screen, Enter for next line_
```

Figure 5-22
Displaying the contents of a ZIP archive

Create new archives with the command:

```
PKZIP -a TEXT *.TXT
```

which will add all of the text files in the current directory to the archive TEXT.ZIP, as Figure 5-23 shows.

```
C:\TEMP>pkzip -a text *.txt

PKZIP (R)   FAST!   Create/Update Utility   Version 2.04g   02-01-93
Copr. 1989-1993 PKWARE Inc.  All Rights Reserved.  Shareware Version
PKZIP Reg. U.S. Pat. and Tm. Off.   Patent No. 5,051,745

 ▌ 80486 CPU detected.
 ▌ EMS version 4.00 detected.
 ▌ XMS version 2.00 detected.
 ▌ Using Normal Compression.

Creating ZIP: TEXT.ZIP
   Adding: AGENTS.TXT    Deflating (63%), done.
   Adding: COMPUSER.TXT  Deflating (61%), done.
   Adding: DISKHELP.TXT  Deflating (60%), done.
   Adding: FILENAME.TXT  Deflating (62%), done.
   Adding: LICENSE.TXT   Deflating (75%), done.
   Adding: REGISTER.TXT  Deflating (61%), done.

C:\TEMP>_
```

Figure 5-23
Creating a ZIP archive

Decompressing the same archive is accomplished by using the PKUNZIP program, like this:

```
PKUNZIP TEXT
```

which extracts all of the files from the TEXT.ZIP archive, as shown in Figure 5-24.

PKWare isn't the only company that markets a ZIP processing program. If you own PCTools for Windows from Central Point Software, you already have a powerful ZIP compressor/decompressor that you can activate via the File Manager functions. This program is the exact opposite of PKWare in terms of usage. It is purely Windows based point-and-shoot functionality. You don't have to remember any commands, any syntax, or where to place the files (Figure 5-25).

An excellent shareware product that provides a nifty Windows shell around many archiver programs is WinZip (Figure 5-26). Currently at version 5.6, it has a simple and effective interface to the archiver programs. WinZip splits the difference between PCTools and the command line–driven PKWare products by presenting you with a clean Windows interface like PCTools and the same functionality of PKWare.

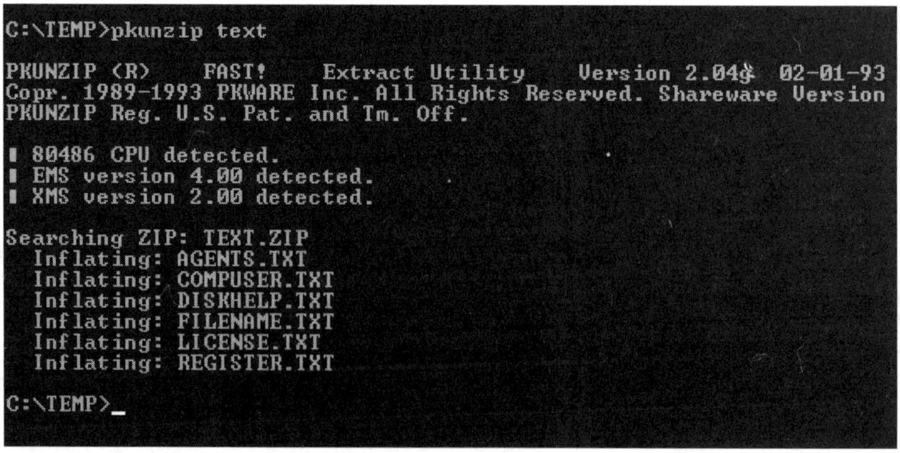

Figure 5-24
Decompressing the contents of a ZIP archive

```
C:\TEMP>pkunzip text

PKUNZIP (R)    FAST!    Extract Utility    Version 2.04g  02-01-93
Copr. 1989-1993 PKWARE Inc. All Rights Reserved. Shareware Version
PKUNZIP Reg. U.S. Pat. and Tm. Off.

■ 80486 CPU detected.
■ EMS version 4.00 detected.
■ XMS version 2.00 detected.

Searching ZIP: TEXT.ZIP
   Inflating: AGENTS.TXT
   Inflating: COMPUSER.TXT
   Inflating: DISKHELP.TXT
   Inflating: FILENAME.TXT
   Inflating: LICENSE.TXT
   Inflating: REGISTER.TXT

C:\TEMP>_
```

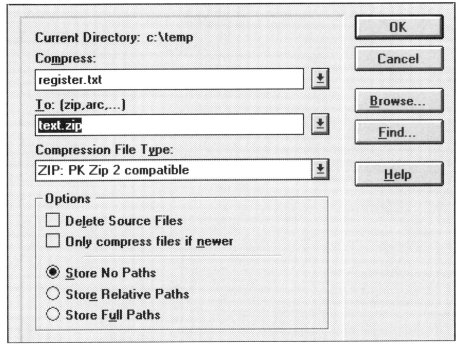

Figure 5-25
PCTools for
Windows'
archive handler

Name	Date	Time	Size	Ratio	Packed	Path
agents.txt	02/14/95	02:15	31,176	63%	11,754	
compuser.txt	02/14/95	02:15	6,252	61%	2,481	
diskhelp.txt	04/13/92	01:13	6,571	60%	2,631	
filename.txt	02/14/95	02:15	1,950	62%	744	
license.txt	02/14/95	02:15	22,941	75%	5,873	
register.txt	02/14/95	02:15	9,857	61%	3,859	

Figure 5-26
The WinZip
archiver
program

Selected 0 files, 0 bytes   Total 6 files, 77KB

The result is a powerful yet easy-to-use tool with which you can manage all of those Internet archives with ease. Note, however, that WinZip requires the archive programs as separate packages, whereas PCTools does not. WinZip can be ordered from the author at:

Nico Mak Computing
P.O. Box 919
Bristol, CT 06011

LZH File Formats

We'll now explore another type of archive, one called LZH, which is based upon the compressor known as Lharc, by Yoshi (Figure 5-27). It uses the LZW (Lempel-Ziv-Welch) compression technique to achieve results close to those of PKWare's product. The best part of this is it's free for noncommercial use, and free for government agencies.

Lharc does its magic similarly to PKWare in that it too looks for repeated characters and strings of data, which are replaced by tokens to represent the data. PCTools for Windows handles LZH files by itself, but WinZip requires the LHA.EXE program to be present.

Lharc is quite easy to use (Figure 5-28). The document file that comes with it explains all the options used by the program. The two

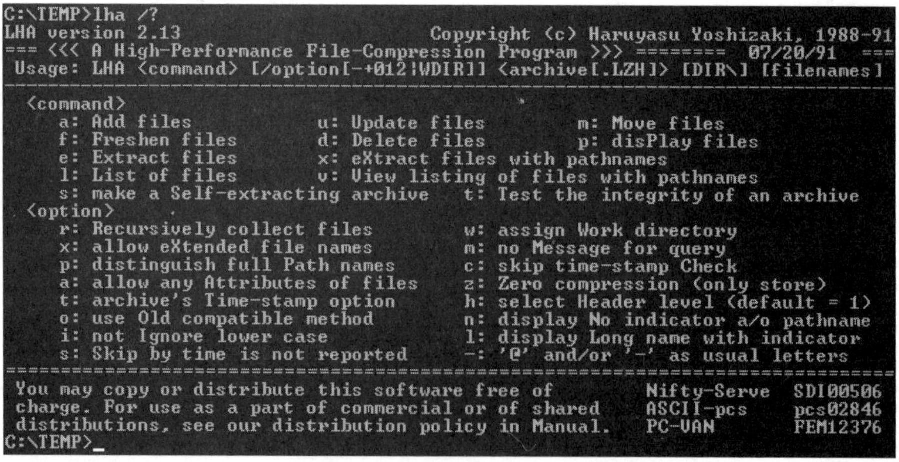

Figure 5-27
The Lharc program's options

```
C:\TEMP>lha /?
LHA version 2.13                    Copyright (c) Haruyasu Yoshizaki, 1988-91
=== <<< A High-Performance File-Compression Program >>> ========  07/20/91  ===
 Usage: LHA <command> [/option[-+012|WDIR]] <archive[.LZH]> [DIR\] [filenames]

  <command>
    a: Add files            u: Update files         m: Move files
    f: Freshen files        d: Delete files         p: disPlay files
    e: Extract files        x: eXtract files with pathnames
    l: List of files        v: View listing of files with pathnames
    s: make a Self-extracting archive   t: Test the integrity of an archive
  <option>    .
    r: Recursively collect files        w: assign Work directory
    x: allow eXtended file names        m: no Message for query
    p: distinguish full Path names      c: skip time-stamp Check
    a: allow any Attributes of files    z: Zero compression (only store)
    t: archive's Time-stamp option      h: select Header level (default = 1)
    o: use Old compatible method        n: display No indicator a/o pathname
    i: not Ignore lower case            l: display Long name with indicator
    s: Skip by time is not reported     -: '@' and/or '-' as usual letters
=============================================================================
 You may copy or distribute this software free of     Nifty-Serve   SDI00506
 charge. For use as a part of commercial or of shared ASCII-pcs     pcs02846
 distributions, see our distribution policy in Manual. PC-VAN       FEM12376
C:\TEMP>_
```

```
C:\TEMP>lha a text *.txt

Creating archive : text.LZH

==>   39%  AGENTS.TXT    oooo
==>   40%  COMPUSER.TXT  o
==>   40%  DISKHELP.TXT  o
==>   38%  FILENAME.TXT  o
==>   26%  LICENSE.TXT   ooo
==>   39%  REGISTER.TXT oo
Copying TMP to ARC ... done.

C:\TEMP>_
```

Figure 5-28
Compressing files with Lharc

programs differ more in their file formats than anything else.

Figure 5-29 shows an example of decompressing an LZH archive.

Lharc can be found at FTP sites

`ftp.oar.net/pub/dialup/pc/compress`

and

`ftp.cyberspace.com/pub/dos/utils.`

Alternatively, you can do an Archie search using the keyword
LHA213.EXE and specifying the Archie site.

```
C:\TEMP>lha e text

Extracting from archive : TEXT.LZH

Melted    AGENTS.TXT    oooo
Melted    COMPUSER.TXT  o
Melted    DISKHELP.TXT  o
Melted    FILENAME.TXT  o
Melted    LICENSE.TXT   ooo
Melted    REGISTER.TXT  oo

C:\TEMP>_
```

Figure 5-29
Decompressing files with Lharc

EXE File Formats

This section delves into EXE or self-extracting archives. You now know about ZIP and LZH archives, but what are EXE archives? You're already familiar with the EXE file type, used for the executable, or program, files on your computer. These are the ones that launch an application of some sort and do something. EXE archives are similar in that they can be invoked and executed as programs.

Basically, an EXE is a ZIP or LZH with a wrapper around it to perform the extraction process for you. ZIPs require PKUNZIP or a compatible decompressor, and LZHs require Lharc or a like decompressor like PCTools for Windows or WinZip. To do the same job, these self-extracting files contain a miniature version of each of these programs within the archive! You can't see it, but it's there (Figure 5-30).

You use the command line option "-s" to do this, as shown in the example.

ZIP2EXE requires no options as the program already knows what you want to do and does it (Figure 5-31). Neat!

TIP

If you plan to send files to someone and you don't know if they have the required decompressors, use a self-extracting archive.

Figure 5-30
Creating a self-extracting archive with Lharc

```
C:\TEMP>lha s text

Making SFX of archive : TEXT.LZH

Extract    AGENTS.TXT
Extract    COMPUSER.TXT
Extract    DISKHELP.TXT
Extract    FILENAME.TXT
Extract    LICENSE.TXT
Extract    REGISTER.TXT
Copying TMP to ARC ... done.

C:\TEMP>_
```

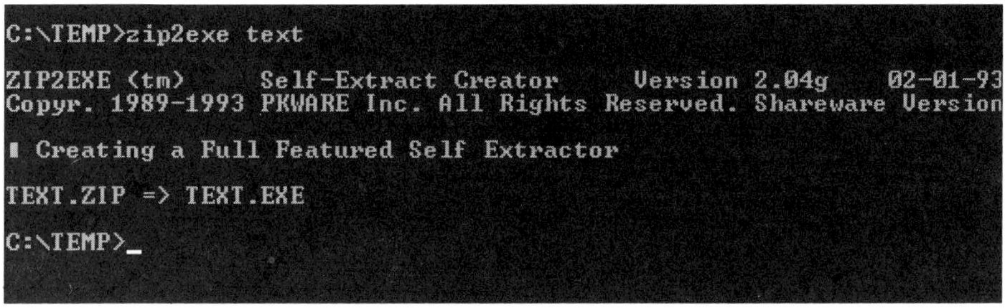

```
C:\TEMP>zip2exe text

ZIP2EXE (tm)     Self-Extract Creator     Version 2.04g     02-01-93
Copyr. 1989-1993 PKWARE Inc. All Rights Reserved. Shareware Version

∎ Creating a Full Featured Self Extractor

TEXT.ZIP => TEXT.EXE

C:\TEMP>_
```

Figure 5-31
Creating a self-extracting archive with ZIP2EXE

The beauty behind EXEs is that they are transportable between PCs and users. So what, you say? What if the person receiving the file has zero knowledge of archives, or computers, or life in general? They have to have some way to handle the files, and to do so in the simplest manner. Not knocking the new user, far from it, but do you remember when you were first learning computers? Tough, wasn't it? Well, self-extracting EXEs can ease the worries and problems relating to archives.

WinZip has the ability to create EXE files by sending the required options to the respective program. PCTools for Windows, however, does not.

Other Internet Archives and Files

In your travels of the Internet, you will see files with extensions like TAR and Z. These two represent UNIX-based file compression methods that PC users seldom have utilities to work with. Another format is ARC, but it is rarely used. It is more common on other online services like CompuServe and Prodigy. Two more types are the PAK and ZOO archives, but I have never seen them on the Internet, and they are seldom seen in general. Another common file format, but one that is foreign to PCs, is the PS or PostScript file. This file has special formatting that enables superb documents for desktop publishing systems, but many applications produce PostScript files in other formats and with other extensions.

Files by Way of the Web

While we're on the subject of PostScript, let's go get the *GhostScript* program I mentioned in Chapter 4 and use it as an example of how to process an archive file. Since this book is about Web browsing, let's first get the file by way of an FTP:// style of connection. To try an alternate approach, we'll go get a second file archive called WS_FTP32.ZIP, which is a standalone FTP program—standalone because it needs nothing more than a connection to the Internet to do its work. I'm going to show you this alternate method because, if you recall, I mentioned that MSN is used to create the connection to the Internet, and you use the Microsoft Internet Explorer to do your Web surfing. Should something happen to the Microsoft Internet Explorer, at least using WS_FTP you could do some things in life. If you have an FTP tool handy, you can always download an e-mail program so you can carry on with mail, or download another browser if necessary.

Fire up your Internet connection via MSN, and then start the Microsoft Internet Explorer. We'll get the GhostScript program first. With MIE running, enter

```
ftp://sunsite.unc.edu/pub/micro/pc-stuff/
ms-windows/winsock/apps
```

into the address field and press [Enter]. When you get there, single-click on the file WS_FTP32.ZIP. (See Figure 5-32.) When the Windows 95 Explorer opens and asks what do you want to do with this file, tell it to save the file to a directory of your choosing. If you've not already done so, this would be a good time to create a working directory to download your files to and check them out for viruses.

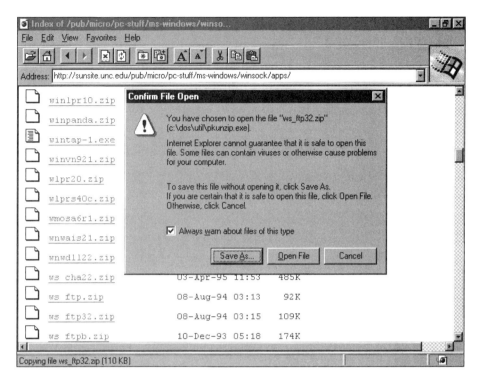

Figure 5-32
FTPing by way of the Microsoft Internet Explorer

WARNING

Even if sites have been said to be checked for virus content, it *is always* your responsibility to ensure the file is clean before processing it on your PC. Neither the site nor the uploader assumes any responsibility for virus content.

You've gotten the FTP file, and while you're there get whatever programs you want or can think of for later use. One possible file is WSARCHIE.EXE, which is one of the self-extracting types we talked about, and another is EUDORA14.EXE, a mail reader. Go ahead and download EUDORA14.EXE as our self-extracting example.

Processing Those Files

Now that you've gotten the files and placed them into the temporary directory, let's process them by expanding them into their component parts. On my system, I created a temporary directory called K:\TEMP where all of my applications temporary files are placed. When I shut down for the day, this directory gets deleted as part of my system's cleanup. I've also created a working directory called New Files where I move these newly downloaded files for processing. Keep in mind that as you extract these archives, they recreate the files within them and write them to the disk just as they existed when someone compressed them. As this decompression occurs, other files in the same directory with the same name risk getting overwritten. To prevent this, each of the decompression engines has internal settings that check for this condition, and notify you if a file with a given name already exists.

In one less-than-exciting situation, a person had created an archive in which the name of the executable program was the same as that of the archive itself! As the archive was extracting, the executable file was overwriting itself and preventing extraction of the other files. True story! So, move the Eudora file to the working directory, use Windows 95 Explorer, and double-click on the name of the file. Eudora will extract itself into its component parts, which are only three files to start with.

Extracting the ZIP files is a little bit more work than that, but not much. Navigate to the Start button and run a DOS session. Change over to the directory where you moved the WS_FTP32.ZIP program, type this command line

```
drv:\path\pkunzip ws_ftp32
```

and press Enter. *Drv* is the drive letter name, and *path* is the fully qualified directory for where your PKUNZIP.EXE program (or

equivalent) resides. If you have this location in your DOS PATH=
setting, then just type

```
pkunzip ws_ftp32
```

and press [Enter]. The component parts of WS_FTP32 will extract and
provide you with the program.

> **TROUBLESHOOTING**
>
> **Q.** *I tried to extract the files, but I got the error message
> that said the disk was write protected, and the extraction
> was aborted.*
>
> **A.** It's possible that the drive you're trying to extract the
> files to is in fact full! Other possibilities include disk
> corruption preventing the files from being written to disk.
> Yet another possible fault is that the disk is indeed write
> protected. Some disk compression utilities will purposely
> write-protect a disk if they detect some unknown problem
> with the disk itself. This is done as a safety measure.

Set up your FTP program just as you would any Windows 95
program, and now you've got your own FTP client WS_FTP32 is useful
in that way because if you use WSARCHIE instead of the Microsoft
Internet Explorer, then Archie searches require an FTP client to
retrieve the located files. On the other hand, you can use Gopher in the
Microsoft Internet Explorer to find, browse, and download files all in one
program! Neat, yes? I think so. It's a major step in making the user's life
on the Web easier and more enjoyable. The next section on Gopher will
demonstrate this unique search-and-retrieval method.

Gopher—Another Friend on the Web

Haven't we come a long way in this chapter? We sure have, and now, this close to the end of the chapter, is the time to explore Gopher more intensively. It will be interesting to look back on some of the things we've done and consider how we could do them with Gopher. FTP? Sure can. Find files on the Web? Yes, the Gopher gives us the same kind of FTP access we just obtained using the Microsoft Internet Explorer. Adding these to our favorite places menu tree has allowed us to build a nice permanent history of these spots of interest. So, let's complete this chapter by doing some more things with Gopher.

What Really Is Gopher?

After all of this talk, what is this furry rodent all about? Gopher, besides being the mascot of the University of Minnesota, is perhaps the one tool that comes closest to solving all of your needs. With the Microsoft Internet Explorer, you've got full usage of the FTP, Telnet, Web browsing, and News functions, but using the Gopher function and taking it off to the Home of Gopher at UMN, you can perform almost anything on the Web besides active mail that an aspiring Web surfer could need in an average day's playtime.

Gopher is the all-knowing and all-understanding trooper of the Web. Just like the good gophers (or "gophers") of the world awaiting their next task in life, Gopher waits for our command. To refresh your memory, the definition of a gopher is someone that runs errands and performs tasks for someone. The good gopher remembers where he or she went in the past and the most efficient way of getting from here to there. Our gopher remembers by the way of the favorites menu, where we keep a list of the permanent locations, and by way of the history log, where we can keep the last *xxx* number of places visited.

Gopher is Archie. Gopher is FTP. Gopher is Telnet. Gopher is Veronica. Gopher is the Web. Remember that when we jump into Chapter 6.

Where Is the Rodent?

The little varmint's home is the University of Minnesota, as we've said before, but in reality the dude is sitting at the ready just under the cover of your PC. And you wondered what that noise was in the last section where we dealt with files. Gopher had some pretty large files to drag back to you, and accidentally bumped into the side of the modem coming back! Oooops!

But really, Gopher is just under your fingertips awaiting your next command. When you get more accustomed to the idea, Gopher is a set of keystrokes away from performing your next errand. The section coming up next is designed to set your thoughts into motion for what we're going to be doing in Chapter 6, which will be making an extremely in-depth use of the tools we've discussed thus far. With that said, let's preview Chapter 6's wild cruise through the Web.

Cruising with Gopher

We've made a very long trip across the Web, so let's make a recap of all of the tools at our disposal for working the Web to its fullest potential. Before starting the trip, we discussed handling the critical file called *WINSOCK.DLL* and how to prevent disasters in communicating with the Internet. We started out plundering the Web with our first friend called Archie. Archie is a file search-and-retrieval utility that is accessible by way of Gopher, or by using a standalone utility such as WSARCHIE that we retrieved. Archie lets us search all across the Web knowing only a few letters of the name of the file, and Archie does the grunt work for us.

Our next friend of the Web is Veronica, who looks for documents that match a specific keyword pattern. Veronica performs these searches across multiple servers, allowing you to use keywords found in the *title* of the document. Veronica is a more global tool with a lot of flexibility. The next part of the tour was with Jughead. Similar to Veronica, Jughead differs in that it looks at a specific server rather than the Web in general. It really gets down deep on that one server and does a very thorough job of search and retrieval. When all else fails, WAIS allows us to search the breadth of these documents in a complete text search into the internals of the document rather than just the *title* or keywords of the document. It takes longer than Jughead or Veronica, but for obscure searches or documents, WAIS is the way to go.

When finding this information gets particularly difficult, try the Web Worm or other Web search engines. These tools of the Web look into the very depth and the heart of the Web for the site or related data, and they could easily be your one-stop shopping tour for Web searchers. When you can't find the data this way, it's time to ask around of others that may have been there. You can do this by way of the newsgroups, which are an electronic version of the meeting room where you can ask questions and see what other people think about something.

After you've found what you want, or if you need an alternative to the Web to get somewhere, Telnet could be the way to go. Telnet is a basic and simple form of terminal communications where you connect the Microsoft Internet Explorer to a server and interactively type in your commands, unlike the Web tools we've been using where you mouse-click to your destination. Telnet is one of the least used tools, but it could possibly be one of the simplest to operate.

You worked hard at getting around the Web, so now we went shopping at some sites we found while gophering around looking for other things. We found a few books on TCP/IP to enhance our newfound knowledge, and then we got our spouse some flowers for putting up with us! Yes, there's a host of things that can be found for sale on the Web, and we went to a few of these online shopping malls to see what was there. Amazing, wasn't it? You can still spend to your heart's content and not have to put up with a single rude customer cutting in line. What a concept!

Summary

Quite a jaunt around the Web, to be sure. By now, you should have the basics of the Web with the Microsoft Internet Explorer down pat, and be ready for Chapter 6, where we'll explore the depths of the Web even more and find out some interesting things about the electronic highways and byways that the rest of the world is calling the Information Superhighway. In reality, this term has just sprung up, but the Internet and the Web have existed for years. Is the Info Highway a new thing? Hardly, but the resources on it may be new to you. I'll see you next in Chapter 6, where we'll do our best to plunder these resources.

Finding the Needle in the Haystack with the Microsoft Internet Explorer

Everything we've done so far has been geared toward getting you settled into using the Microsoft Internet Explorer and some of the things you can do with it.

This chapter will present you with:

◆ More detailed information on functions of the Microsoft Internet Explorer
◆ How to search the Web from several different perspectives
◆ How to use a variety of tools to do the search
◆ What to do with the results of the search

With these points in mind, let's begin our journey into cyberspace with the Microsoft Internet Explorer. In Chapter 7, we'll make much the same journey across the Web, but with Netscape Navigator.

Microsoft Internet Explorer—a More Detailed View

This section will help you get the most out of the Microsoft Internet Explorer; for instance, you'll learn to tweak it internally and to use some related tools. Just to repeat something I said earlier, if you already have an Internet provider that's a local phone call for you, you can still use that option and start the Microsoft Internet Explorer on that connection. When MSN gets more Internet connections, and most of them are at the 28.8K baud rate, you might consider switching to them. One big benefit of using the MSN Internet connection is that you can switch from the Internet to MSN's native service with the click of the mouse!

Menus and Options

The Microsoft Internet Explorer has several menu functions that bear a deeper look at, so start your Internet connection if you've not done so already. MIE will balk at some of these choices if you're not online. Let's take a look at some of the menu options that you'll use more as we get farther along.

The File Menu

The first function is the File menu. Choose it now and select Open. This menu option allows you to reuse any one of the URLs from a previously visited site, or you can type in a new one if you wish (Figure 6-1). When you open the menu, notice how the Address field is empty. You can now click on the down arrow at the right side, and a list of the last 25 sites that you've been to will appear. There's a check box at the lower left of this screen that says Open in new window. This means that when this URL is accessed, the main Microsoft Internet Explorer window stays in place (its contents stay intact), and this new URL is started in a brand-new window. You may want to use this option if the new destination site is something you just want to peek into, and then come right back to where you began.

At this same screen, you can select *Open File* or use the hotkey Ctrl+O, which means that a previously saved location can be reopened by using the html code of the site's Web page. Back in Chapter 4, we looked at some sample HTML code in which the attributes of the Web page were saved to your local hard drive. The code includes, among other things, the URL of the site in a hypertext link. Also, remember that we call these links *hotspots*. If you saved the Web page as HTML code pages, and not text, then you can simply open the file from disk and have that site's Web page at your disposal. See the next section on Save As to tie this together.

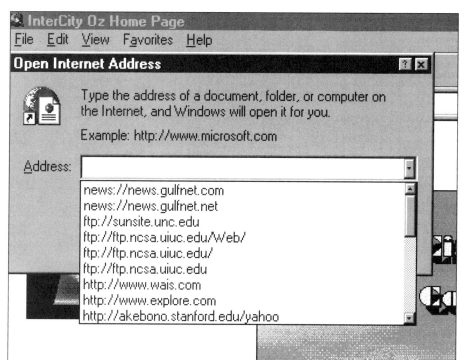

Figure 6-1
Opening a previously accessed site by File➢Open

The next File menu option is the Open Start Page; clicking on this will take you back to the home page that you defined in the View➤Options Start Page tab. We'll dwell more on this in a later segment of this section, but it's important that you at least be aware of it.

This next File option is called Save As, in which you can save the contents of a Web page to your local hard disk for quick return to that site later. Well, in the history, you could save the URL to favorites, right? That's true, but you saved the URL address itself and not the Web page in its entirety, which is what *Save As* does. Let's go to the site `http://www.microsoft.com` and test this function. Since I use this site so much through the course of the day, I can put it in my favorites or save it as an HTML file locally as opposed to via the Favorites menu. Do this by selecting File, Save As (or use the Ctrl+S hotkey) and then pointing the Windows 95 Explorer to your desired location. Pick the file type, either pure text or HTML code. By the way, when you do disk-oriented things like this and you get this screen to locate something on your computer, you're actually running the Windows 95 Explorer utility. It was started when the Microsoft Internet Explorer requested the file-saving function be activated.

Why would I want to save the entire Web page as opposed to just the URL as Favorites does? Both do the same thing, right? Yes, they do, but saving the HTML code allows you to see what the authors of the Web page were doing and how they created their page. As time goes on and you learn more about the Web, you may get interested in learning how to create your own Web pages or even go into business doing this. I'm not saying to plagiarize the code, far from it, but looking at how others have done it is a great way to diversify your own talents. Think of it as part of the learning about the Web, and the sharing of knowledge that exists for everyone's benefit. Another benefit is the ease of reading about a site.

Look at example of how a Web page is saved, first in HTML code (Listing 6-1), and then in pure ASCII text format (Listing 6-2):

```
<HTML>
<HEAD>
<TITLE>InterCity Oz Home Page</TITLE>
<HEAD>
<BODY>
<center>
<img src ="icozdph.gif" width=600 height=180><br>
<center><a href="iconbar.map"><img border=0
src="iconbar.gif" ismap></a></center>
<hr size=5>
<p>
<h2>Welcome To Bay County, Florida</h2>
</center>
<p>
<center><font size = "-1">
<b><i><a href = "messages.htm">Message from the
President of InterCity Oz</a>.</i></b></font>
<p><b><blink>
```

Listing 6-1
**A Web page in
HTML format**

And now look at the same output in pure ASCII text format:

```
<Picture>
<Picture>
_____
Welcome To Bay County, Florida
Message from the President of InterCity Oz.
```

Listing 6-2
**The same Web
page in ASCII
format**

The difference is as clear as night and day. While you're still learning your way around the Web, it's best to stick with the ASCII text until you're ready to tackle HTML code, but it's nice to know there's an option to get to the bottom of it if you'd like.

Page Setup and Print are standard Windows functions, and I'll not bore you with them other than to say that if you want to alter the page settings here, it's the same as if you did it by way of the Control Panel. The Create Shortcut option will add the current Web page to your desktop as a shortcut in Windows 95. At present, the only option for this is on the desktop, but you can use the Windows 95 Explorer to make a copy of the shortcut and place it into any folder of your choosing. You can then delete the shortcut on the desktop. This is the roundabout way of doing things, but it's the only way we can do this for now. I'd use this setting if I had places I go to most often and didn't need to, or want to, go through all of those steps to get online just to go to one place. Just double-click on the desktop icon, and the Microsoft Internet Explorer takes care of the rest! Really neat stuff.

The last item on the File menu is the More History option, which you can follow to see the many places you've been to in the past. Once again, this menu has all of the common attributes of the Windows 95 Explorer in that you can edit, copy, cut, or otherwise edit the heck out of the selected item!

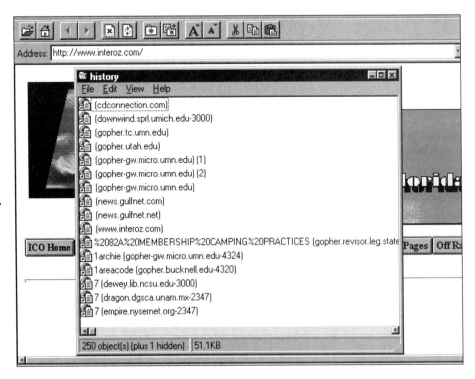

Figure 6-2
Opening a previously accessed site by File➤More History

The Edit Menu

The Edit menu provides standard editing options such as Cut, Copy, and Paste (Figure 6-3). One word of caution, though, is that the Find option in this menu *is not* the FIND function located in the Windows 95 Explorer! This Find is to locate text within the current document.

The View Menu

The View menu has quite a few options that need to be talked about while we're online (Figure 6-4). The top three, Back, Forward, and Backspace, all refer to navigating the Web from where you are right now. If you start from site A, then go to site B, and then on to site C, you can get back to B simply by hitting the [Backspace] key! Hit [Backspace] a second time, and you return to site A. Unfortunately, there's no *forward* key at this time, but there is a forward button on the toolbar. See the next section for that item.

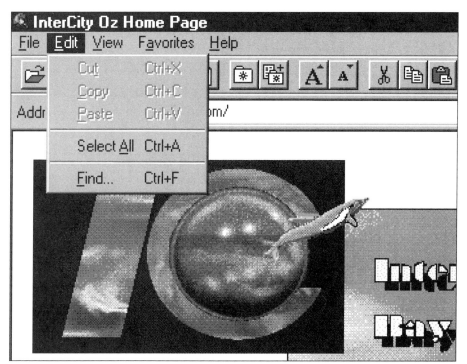

Figure 6-3
The Edit menu

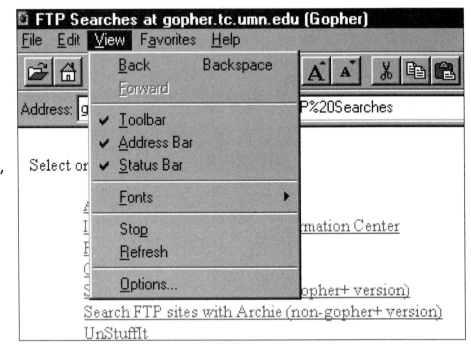

Figure 6-4
The View menu, first three options

The next three options, also grouped together, activate the various toolbars and status lines that you can get from the program. You'll see the standard toolbar, in which you can change various parts of the way the Microsoft Internet Explorer looks or acts on screen, at the top of the screen. The Address bar is where you type in the URL of the site. The Status bar is located at the bottom of the screen; it tells you what's happening with the program at any one time, or else it simply tells you where you've got the mouse placed on screen.

The next option controls the fonts, allowing you to adjust the size of the text displayed from the Web page (Figure 6-5). This is a setting you can change anytime you decide your eyes need some relief. You don't have to reboot or restart the Microsoft Internet Explorer to do this. It's interesting to note that if you change the size of the font, then the Web page automatically resizes the text on screen so that it fits between the sides of the display.

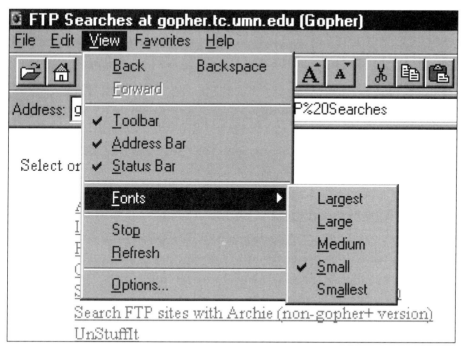

Figure 6-5
**Changing the
font sizes**

The next two items, Stop and Refresh, do just what their names imply: stop the current action, whatever it may be, and refresh the screen display. These actions are useful at times when you may go from page to page on the Web and the host server doesn't send all of the data. The last menu option is called Options, and it deserves some attention as well. There are four tabs to this menu option: Appearance, Start Page, File Types, and Advanced. Let's look at these in turn to see what they offer us on the Web.

Appearance has three sections to itself. They are Page, Shortcuts, and Addresses. Page defines how our screen colors will look for the text and the background. If you don't alter anything after installation, it defaults to blue text on a white background. Shortcuts defines how the hypertext links look on screen. Mine is set to the defaults of a maroon type of color for sites already viewed and a deep pink for pages not yet viewed. In the Addresses section, you get to choose how the Web sites are stored in your favorites section. For instance, one of my frequently visited places is http://ftp.ncsa.uiuc.edu, which is the NCSA

FTP site. What would you rather remember: "NCSA FTP site," or the URL in bold above? The English version, of course! Showing simplified addresses does just that—it stores the English version of the URL.

Click on the Start tab, and you'll see one more set of options that allows you to specify your home page. The home page is where you go by default if you want or need a standard place to go. Figure 6-6 shows a callout for the little house at the far left of the toolbar. Clicking on the house takes you to your home page. The Start tab lets you define your home page or use the default of Microsoft. The File Types tab lets you create or destroy associations with files. For instance, if the file ends with the ZIP extension, in File Types you can say that if you double-click on any ZIP file, then application XYZ is started to process that file. In my case, and in Chapter 5 where we handled files, I set the ZIP extension to point to a shortcut to my C:\DOS\UTILS\PKUNZIP.EXE program, which then unzips these archives. It's a really neat way to automate part of your system.

Figure 6-6
Changing the history and cache settings

"the little house at the far left of the toolbar"

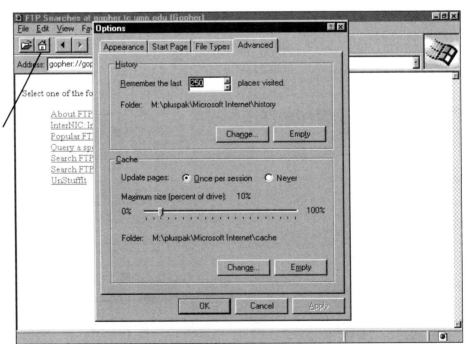

As the last of the View options, we'll look at the Advanced tab. It's here that you can adjust the number of sites kept in your history, and you can also define the percentage of disk space (and the location) of the history *cache*. The *cache* is a temporary location where frequently accessed data is stored, usually because it's faster to access the cache than it is to access the original source location itself. This is true for the Web. Even if you're on a 28.8K baud link, your local hard disk is still infinitely faster!

Favorites

When you're at a really good site that you'd like to remember, add it to your Favorites list (Figure 6-7). You already know how to accomplish this, but what does it really mean? What does it do for you, or *to* you? Let's take a few minutes and explore this. The Microsoft Internet Explorer has the capacity to hold as many sites in its history or cache as you do disk space, but the downside is that it'll make your system run a bit slower. Not really noticeable at first, but it'll creep up on you for sure.

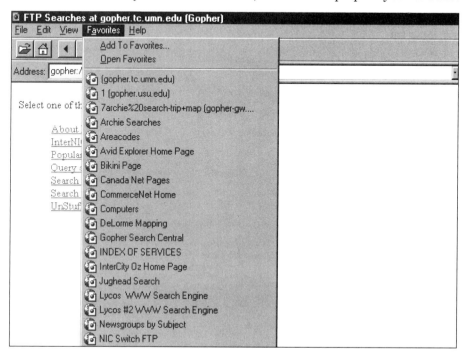

Figure 6-7
My Favorites menu opened up to show my places

Click on Favorites, and you'll see two options. One is to Add to Favorites, and one to Open Favorites, plus you'll see the current list in the favorites tree. The number in Figure 6-8 take up 23KB of disk space and include 21 shortcuts. Notice the tree structure of Windows 95 Explorer showing where my favorites are stored.

The really interesting aspect of this is that this isn't a file, but rather a shortcut to the Web site! Edit the shortcut, and you'll see that the real URL is stored within the shortcut, not the text name of the site. So, when you add the site to Favorites, you're really just creating a Windows 95 shortcut to that site. Fascinating stuff!

CAUTION

If you're not careful, your Windows 95 home drive will become full of all sorts of files! You should always double-check where your programs are storing files when you install the program.

Figure 6-8
A Windows 95 Explorer view of favorite places

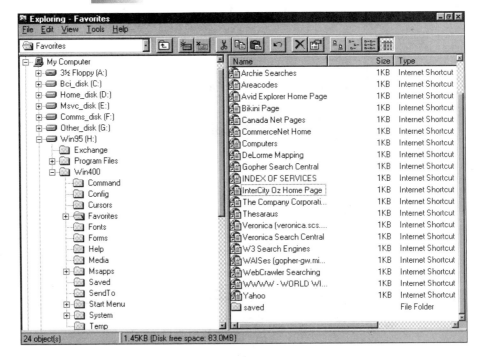

Clicking on Add to Favorites brings up a menu prompting you for information about the new location such as which drive and directory to place it on, and the name for the location. If you want to go to a site recently added to Favorites, click on Favorites and then click on Open Favorites, where you'll be presented with a window of all your current favorite sites (Figure 6-9). Double-clicking on the icon takes you there right away.

You can also get there by single-clicking on a site and then choosing File➤Open while viewing the Favorites list. All of the rest of the Favorites windows menu options are standard Windows 95 functions, so I'll not go into those at this time.

Firewalls and Proxy Servers

This last section before we jump into Web searching involves two seldom-discussed options of TCP/IP, *firewalls* and *proxy servers*. A firewall is a security measure the server itself has implemented to

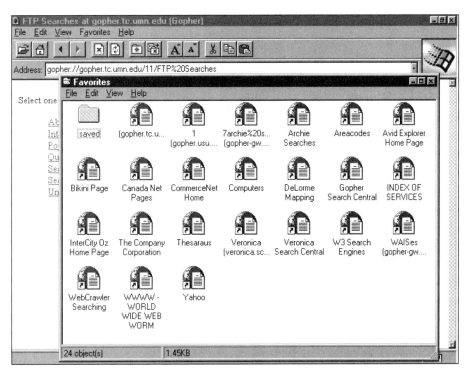

Figure 6-9
Going to a favorite place

control access based upon different criteria such as who belongs to a users' group or is included in a predefined set of IP addresses. This type of security is meant to stop unauthorized surfers from crashing the gates anytime they want. Firewalls prevent breeches in attempted entry where such is not allowed. Think of the firewall inside a home. It stops the flames from spreading through the walls, or at least it slows them down. The computer-based firewall does the same task.

When two or more physical networks are connected together but only one of them is publicly viewable and usable, that one is a proxy server. The other may be an in-house experimental network that the public has no need to see or use, but that the MIS folks in-house need to test. One of the systems in the hidden network could in fact be a Web server in development, available to users on the same IP segment but not the public at large. On MSN and the Internet, we do not use proxy servers. If you're on a network and will be running the Microsoft Internet Explorer, ask your network administrator if you're running proxy or not.

Searching the Web

Now, it's time to cross the line from study to learning while having fun and doing! We're going to do more of what we did in Chapter 5, searching the Web and finding documents, getting files we may need on our trips, and generally seeing as much of the Web as possible. While we're cruising the Web, we'll gather these things and place them into an organized set of folders. From the folder where you installed the Plus Pak, create a set of subfolders and name them:

- ◆ **Files**—Where we'll keep all of the files we may get
- ◆ **Documents**—Obviously, for documents
- ◆ **References**—URLs we save as the favorites
- ◆ **Sites**—Lists of your favorite places
- ◆ **Other**—For the odds and ends of Web life

With these things mind, we're going to set out to accomplish a few tasks. We'd like to plan a vacation trip from the Gulf Coast to the northern tier of states westward to Washington State, down the Pacific Coast to Northern California, and then southeast to Arizona and back to the Gulf Coast. All the while we're planning this trip, let's keep an eye out for any documents that may inform us about the areas we'll pass through, scenic routes, camping areas (as we'll be in our camper), and groups or agencies that could help us in times of emergency. If we run across any software that will help us on this effort, we'll download it and process it for later usage.

Each Document Has a Title

Almost all documents on the Web are categorized by what are known as *keywords*. A keyword is one of perhaps several words that briefly describe the document and make finding the document a lot easier. This book is titled *Web Browsing with The Microsoft Network*. When it goes to bookstores, the store may know it by the title as a matter of course. However, some stores may have hundreds of very closely related books. In this sense, it'd be awfully hard to find the book just searching on the name. There could be a dozen MSN books by different publishers and authors. In that case, the publishers would all be different, as would be the authors, but the titles would still contain "MSN." The publisher's name would be a keyword, as would be the author's name. Every book has an ISBN number that is unique to it, and thus the ISBN would be a keyword.

Keywords make our lives easier on the Web by providing us with a mechanism for easier searches.

TIP

Think of what the document is supposed to be about, or be doing, when you specify the keyword search. Keep it as closely related to the subject as possible.

> **CAUTION**
>
> If you specify too many keywords, that's about as bad as using a bad keyword. It almost always causes the search to fail, or find irrelevant documents.

So far we've been talking about keywords, but the section head spoke of titles for documents. Quite a few document search-and-retrieval systems are organized by indexing the documents and creating keywords out of their titles (Figure 6-10). When this happens, the search is carried out by ranking the found documents by an index of hits and is weighted by a score.

From this set of results, you'll see that a search for "shark" doesn't always return the desired results! Close, but not always! Look at the rest of the found items, and you'll see the ranking I mentioned. Results

Figure 6-10
Searching the EINet Web Searcher for "shark"

like these clearly show how keywords work for, or against, you in your quest for information.

Broader Searches—by Category

When you're looking for a specific document, you're likely to have a hard time searching for just that one. In all likelihood, you may benefit from a wider search across more servers than looking in just one location. It's during these times that performing your searches in a more diffused manner will help you the best. Consider using tools like WAIS for this, or the Lycos search engine (Figure 6-11) at

```
http://lycos.cs.cmu.edu
```

or at their alternate site of

```
http://query6.lycos.cs.cmu.edu.
```

These sites allow searches at just about any level. If your browser supports the use of forms—and the Microsoft Internet Explorer does—then try the forms-based searches in which you can narrow down the search patterns and generally set the scope of the search.

When you get to the Lycos site, you most assuredly should add it to your favorites. Add it to your list of Sites that you created earlier, since you're likely to use it a lot.

Multiple Search Options

There are numerous ways to search the Web for information, and the next main section will go over more, and more in-depth, ways to do this. The data are endlessly scattered all across cyberspace, it seems, and the only organization beyond the search engines at each site is provided by utilities such as those we'll use soon. The first way of two in which you can do more with the Microsoft Internet Explorer is to open a new URL

Carnegie Mellon

Lycos ™

The Catalog of the Internet

A 1995 GNN Best of the Net Nominee. Over 23 million queries answered.

You're looking at the number one ranked content provider on the Internet according to the experts at Point Survey.

- Search the big Lycos catalog (5.07 million web pages), or if you have forms, use the Lycos search form to set the number of hits, and other options. You can also try the Windows NT-based big Lycos catalog.
- Search the small Lycos catalog (434k web pages), or if you have forms, use the Lycos search form to set...

Figure 6-11
The Lycos WWW search engine

and create a new window when you get to the site. This is accomplished by clicking on File and then Open, then either type in the URL or pick one from the History scroll box. For this to work, you must check the box marked Open in new window. Alternately, if what you want to do is access a site by way of its home page that you've saved to disk, then instead of typing in a URL or picking from the History box, perform an Open File action. This presents you with a Windows 95 style of list box to pick the .HTM file to open.

If you have two modems, a second, but more expensive, way to help find data faster is to create a second data link to the Microsoft Network. Windows 95 is quite capable of handling a pair of 28.8K baud links, and I did it daily while writing this book. I use the Microsoft Internet Explorer on the native MSN Internet dialup link, and the other modem is dialed into my local Internet provider running those tools (Figure 6-12).

On one modem, I have the Microsoft Internet Explorer using the W3 Search Engines, and the other modem is performing an Archie search

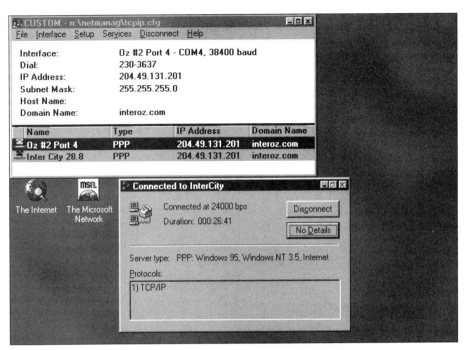

Figure 6-12
**Running MIE
and my own
Internet
provider
simultaneously**

for files. While this seems to be an expensive proposition, diehard Windows fans finally have an operating system that fulfills our needs for handling high-speed data communications flawlessly. You bought Windows 95 for its look and feel, the improved handling, but some of the real gains have been in the printing and communications sections of the operating system. If you've got the money to spare on an extra modem and an Internet provider, then two data links will get you through the Web even faster. You've basically got to ask yourself how much your time is worth when you go online. With the price of 28.8K baud fax/modems down at about $250 on the street for external units, it's getting easier to justify such an investment. Microsoft has done a superb job of making sure that there are as many connection points as possible around the country, and the world for that matter, so that you're sure to find a local calling point for MSN. For the time being, most of the MSN Internet connections will be long distance for the majority of us.

A Little More about MIE

One of the last things I want to go over is that from all of this, you can see that although the Microsoft Internet Explorer isn't the most fully capable Web browser on the market today, it certainly does its job quite well and offers a goodly amount of value for the average Web surfer. Best of all, it's provided with the Plus Pak as part of the deal. Many of the Web tool vendors on the market today already have suites of tools including FTP, Telnet, Gopher, Archie, Finger, Whois, and more. These tool sets are very good, and most have matured in the marketplace quite well, but they don't come free.

Microsoft had, at one time, announced plans to enhance the Plus Pak later this fall with its own flavor of many of these tools. That'd make Plus Pak a very neat and tidy collection of the most useful, and most used, Web tools that you'll ever need. In an earlier part of this chapter, I showed you how the Microsoft Internet Explorer can be used to access most of these Web functions. So, why would you want to get the enhanced Plus Pak if and when it comes out? Well, because most of these tools are customizable for their own individual functions. The Microsoft Internet Explorer is customizable for itself, and not for Gopher or Telnet. When I say "customizable," I mean that you can save the new configurations for these tools for your most frequent actions.

In the meantime, you can go to any one of the many FTP sites across the Internet and get your own tools, as we've shown before. Most of them are freeware, no extra money required, but some are shareware and have registration fees associated with them. I've not found any really bad Internet tools out there, but some are better than others. You can get these if you want, or wait for Microsoft to release the Plus Pak enhancements this fall (not a guaranteed date, but it's a good bet that Microsoft is interested in getting its own tools out there to compete with the other vendors). In this next section, while we're looking out for our vacation trip planning, we'll look at how some of these existing Web tools can complement the Microsoft Internet Explorer, and where you can get them.

What Would You Use?

As we run the gamut of tools and technology for Web browsing, let's apply several of these helper applications while we're in the Microsoft Internet Explorer and work on our vacation trip for the fall. We've got to plan the route, think about rest areas, identify sites to see along the way, and more. We may not find everything we're searching for, but let's give it a try anyhow.

Archie

What in the world is Archie good for on a vacation? Let's go find out. Using one of the favorites I saved from a few sections back, I selected

```
gopher://gopher.tc.umn.edu/11/FTP%20Searches
```

to get a screen like the one in Figure 6-13.

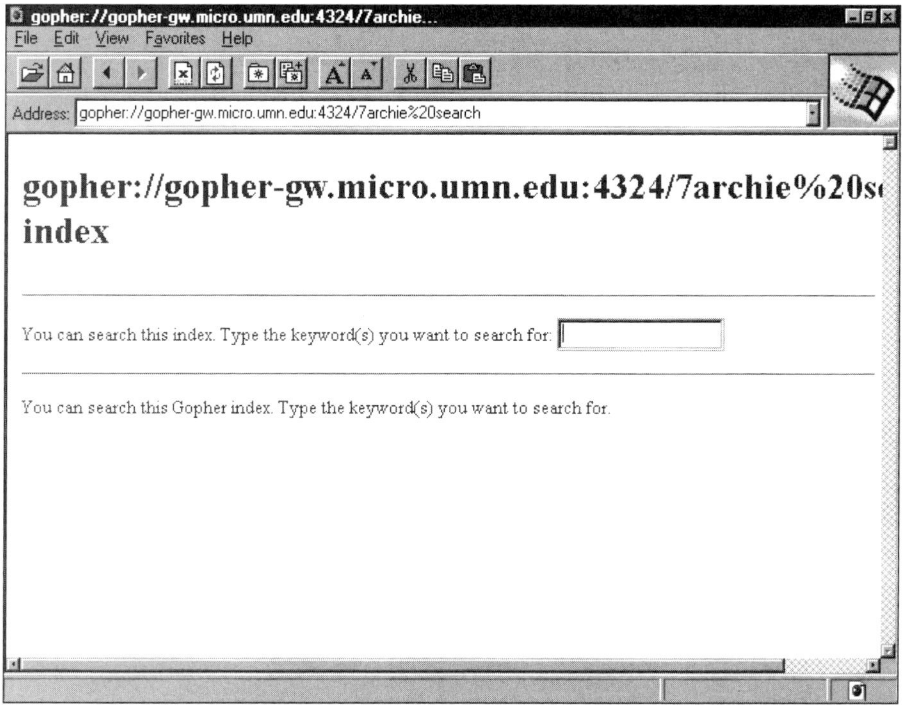

Figure 6-13
Archie Searches taken from favorites

See? I didn't have to remember anything but to click first on Favorites and then on the Archie Searches that I saved. What? You didn't save it? Shame!, But just type in the URL above, and off you go! Now you can save it to Favorites just as I did. Okay, perform the search on your first topic, which is going to be the maps we may use. If you remember, there's a Web site that works with maps, but let's see what Archie has to say.

Using the keyword of "maps," I got about 40 hits, or matches, of various things that make up maps or parts of maps. Some were GIFs of various overhead shots of the U.S., and some included weather reports across the U.S. You can subscribe to this list server by sending a message to `LISTSERV@VMD.CSO.UIUC.EDU`; make the body of the message

```
sub wx-talk your_name_here
```

replacing *your_name_here* with your real name. This location is a list server that automates numerous requests including subscription to and from, getting more lists, and getting help.

The maps we found really weren't exactly what I had in mind for us, so let's widen the search parameters a bit and use the keywords "trip map" together.

This time, I got a new set of results for files on FTP sites relating to trips (Figure 6-14).

Veronica

We've been through Veronica a few times, so let's try it again from the angle that we're planning our trip and see what can evolve from this set of queries. First of all, let's see what kind of scenic sites we can find along our path. I've got a few searches going at the moment, so let's think about what to do relating to our travels. We need to think about places to park our camper, so let's look for a guide of places to stay.

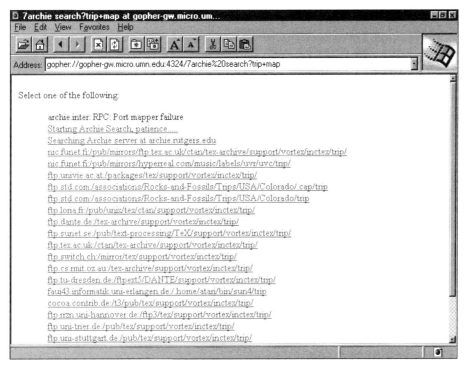

Figure 6-14
Archie Results from multiple keywords

There's a lot of camping across the states, and we need a guide to these locations. Some are for a minimal fee, some are for members of camping and travel clubs only. We also need to know where along the planned route to stay.

So, let's find a Veronica site that'll do these things for us. Open your Favorites and head off to the site we saved a long time ago:

```
gopher://veronica.sunet.se:2347/7.
```

Let's do a search using "camping" and "guide" as keywords. As shown in Figure 6-15, it should return dozens of hits for camping sites, guides, and also information for disabled campers.

So, with that done, I wanted to look for maps that could get us from here to there and back. First, I tried a keyword of "maps." That was so general that I got over 1300 hits. Second, I tried a search using the

Figure 6-15
Veronica search return for camping

keywords "tour maps," which caused the server to time out while performing my search. These time-outs occur frequently as one works during the evening hours, such as 5 P.M. to midnight Eastern Standard Time, because this is the period of heaviest use. I did a Veronica search using the keyword "roadmaps" and got two hits. One of these was a document that lists the tourism councils or other locations where you can get state road maps across our nation! The URL is

```
gopher://ftp.cac.psu.edu/00/genealogy/
roots-l/GENEALOG.ROADMAPS.
```

It lists all of the pertinent information. How's that for a useful search? Sometimes it may take a few tries using different keywords, but you can usually find what you want if you're patient.

Jughead

Jughead was next in turn to try for this excursion. So, back at the W3 Search Engines, I found the Jughead search option and then went to

```
//liberty.uc.wlu.edu:3002/7
```

used the keyword of "camp," and was greeted by a slew of hits ranging from Internet camps to learn about the Web and such, all the way to summer camps for kids. I didn't find anything really relating to our purpose, so let's try "campground" and see what happens. That didn't work too well, either. I tried several sites, and none were very successful. We wanted to find maps for our trip as well, so I used the keyword of "maps" and got two hits of sites that have maps. Unfortunately, I got the ever-present error message about the site being too busy to respond to my request to download the documents.

We have to keep in perspective what Jughead is for—detailed searches at one server. If the server is geared toward software development, then the chances of finding references to campsites will be next to nil. I kept searching about eight servers that held possibilities, but none worked. For our purpose of vacation planning, Jughead didn't do us much good at all.

WAIS

In a previous chapter, you saw how WAIS allows you to search across a wider spectrum of sites when you don't know exactly what you want, but you do know parts of it. We've seen how Archie has found a file or two for us and Veronica has been useful in finding road maps. Let's use WAIS for the same topics and get into another useful source of information.

Back at the W3 Search Engines, choose the WAIS Directory of Servers Index (gateway access) and search with the keywords "travel guide." This brings up a number of hits on traveling and a few guides to the Internet.

As you can see, several services do not lend themselves to successful searches of the Web by some subjects, and others are quite good. Veronica found many things for us. The only other WAIS type of search that had any relevance to this subject was through

```
http://galaxy.einet.net/www/www.html
```

using the keyword of "campground," and this was more of a general Web search than a WAIS-specific search (Figure 6-16). This example shows how the lines between Web resources can sometimes get blurred very quickly.

The Web Worm

Among the most useful tools to search the Web are the Web crawlers, or worms as they're sometimes called. Let's head off to the magical world

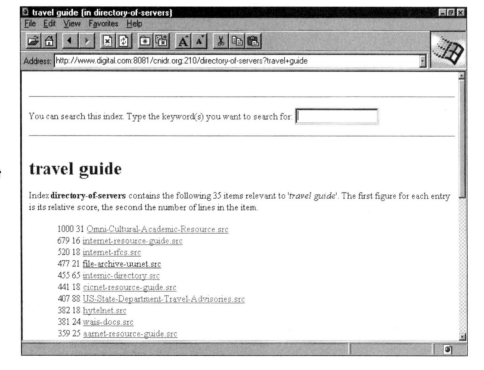

Figure 6-16
A WAIS-like search at EINet for travel guides

of the Web Worm at site `http://webcrawler.com/`, which you saved into your Favorites list. Actually, you should have saved the Web Search Engines listing, but this URL just mentioned is in the hypertext link on the W3 page. At this site, you can tailor your search to use multiple keywords uniquely or in combination, such as "road **or** maps" or "road **and** maps." For this search, I've used the keyword "campsites" to see if we can find a place to stay. The search resulted in 59 hits (Figure 6-17). Only 25 of the hits were displayed because I told the crawler to return only the first 25 hits. If I adjust the search to return 100 hits, we'll get all of the found documents shown in the scrolled window.

After adjusting the return specifications, we now get back 56 of the 59 hits. Paging down a bit we see the Arizona Park Service listing for it's state's parks. This is exactly what we want to see; unfortunately, not all states have their parks listed, but this is a start! You can conduct similar searches at this Web Crawler to see what can be found

Figure 6-17
Web Crawler results returned for campsites

for maps. I used the keyword "roadmaps" and got 288 hits! Scrolling downward through this listing revealed quite a few maps, but most were Internet road maps. We want state maps or the like. Use this methodology to continue your search, and your vacation plans will soon smooth out!

CAUTION

Some maps and related data on the Web may not be updated to reflect current road conditions. It's always wise to consult with a state's tourism council or highways department to be sure. Use the list we got earlier for the road maps.

Let's next use the keyword "campground" to find a guide or information that'll help us stay overnight when we get to an area along the route.

This search turned up 121 hits; it displayed the top 100 hits since we still have the return specs set to 100 from a previous search. As an aside, the return set is defined at 25, 100, and 500 hits. I set mine to 100 since I don't like looking at more than that many. If the search returns over a thousand, or even 500, you need to narrow it down anyhow unless you are prepared to see that many.

Finally, we'll have the Web Worm search by the keywords "travel software," turning up 1400 documents on the subject! Scrolling down through the list shows us, among other things, online registries for hotels and other services! Another item we were looking for. Not exactly a campsite, but nonetheless it'll do if there's a need. Many of these organizations will register you right online using your credit card. Again, the usual caution is urged if you do this, because many services are not yet secured for financial transactions. With this done, let's turn our attention to other Web search engines that may help us with our plans.

Web Search Engines

Head off to the collective Web Search Engines page that you saved, or type in

```
http://cuiwww.unige.ch/meta-index.html
```

if you didn't save it from an earlier search. When you get to this site, choose the CUI World Wide Web catalog by clicking on the link to the right of it. This takes you directly to the CUI searcher, or you can remain at the collective set of searchers, your choice. At the searcher, enter the keyword of "camping," and you'll get a whole bunch of hits involving quite a few aspects of camping, traveling, and the like! This is clearly one of the things we were looking for, and this search is well worth saving or even printing the results. For you mobile travelers carrying a modem, keeping them electronic will save you a lot of paper and space as well. It's easy to see where frequent Web surfing adds up in the resources department and begins to load down the old hard drive. It's here that you see how it pays to organize functions *before* you start a planning effort like this.

On the Web Search Engines page, go all the way down to the Documentation part and look for an entry called NCSA Docfinder. In its entry field, type the word "campground" and submit the request. If the servers work for you the way they did for me, this search will return five hits on the search keyword, all of them listed as HTML pages (Figure 6-18, over the page). Remember those? The Web pages you're looking at are composed of HTML code. The five hits that were returned are posted as HTML links, so to speak. If you wanted, you could just type

```
http://docfinder.ncsa.uiuc.edu:7999/
bin/finder?campground
```

into the address field for the Microsoft Internet Explorer, and the same results would come back.

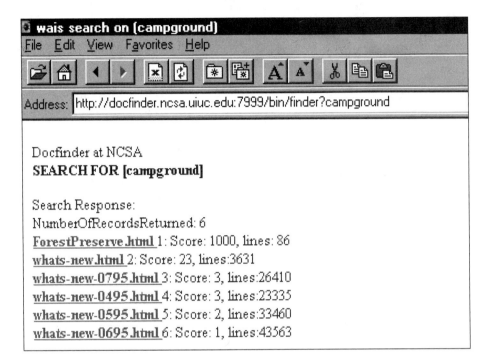

Figure 6-18
Docfinder at NCSA for campgrounds

In making one pass through a set of sites, I ran across a reference to an Explorer site where I found The Avid Explorer at

```
http://www.explore.com.
```

Here you can plan a trip, check ski conditions at popular western resorts, and such (Figure 6-19). They've got a weather page where you can get updated reports on conditions on the slopes or the roads. There are links to travel guides of all sorts both domestic and international at this same page, but about half way down. I should mention that this is the same weather site as at the University of Michigan, but Web-ized into something more palatable than a Telnet site.

Telnet

As we said in the last chapter, Telnet is a methodology in which we use our PC as a smart terminal and connect to a remote server somewhere.

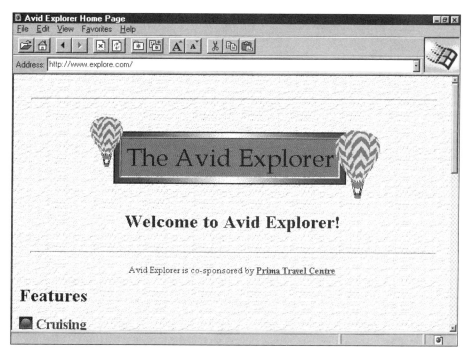

Figure 6-19
The Avid Explorer home page

This lets us appear just as if we were another one of those *dumb terminals* usually associated with minicomputers or mainframe Big Iron systems. As we connect to these systems, it's important that we remember that sometimes a time limit is placed upon us for the connection. For instance, if we start a search and it doesn't return anything within 60 seconds, the search fails either because too much data are being returned or because indeed nothing was there. However, if the search takes 90 seconds, then the entire Telnet connection could be broken due to the server believing that the connection was terminated on our end when it really wasn't. So, when you're Telnetting to a system, remember this little issue.

Speaking of which, let's take off to the one Telnet connection that I know will help us in our quest for a nice vacation, and that's the same weather site you just saw on the Web at the University of Michigan at the address of

```
telnet://downwind.sprl.umich.edu:3000.
```

When you get there, you will see that the menu system is very clear as to its purpose and content. You can look for thunderstorm warnings and watches, tornado watches, and other critical pieces of information. Sites like this one, if you're a traveler with mobile communications, can be really useful as a distant eye in the sky for you. But, then again, if I were out in a big camper like this, I'd have my satellite-dish TV set tuned into a local channel and not just watch the races!

Another neat place to visit if you have an account is CompuServe's Weather connection (Figure 6-20). You can Telnet into there by typing in `telnet://compuserve.com` and following your normal logon procedures.

When you get online, enter the CIS command `go cis:weather` and follow the instructions for the type of terminal you have, and then choose the part of the world you want to see. I've chosen the U.S. and then entered **2** for the short-term reports. From there, you can make your selection about the type of report. This information is usually

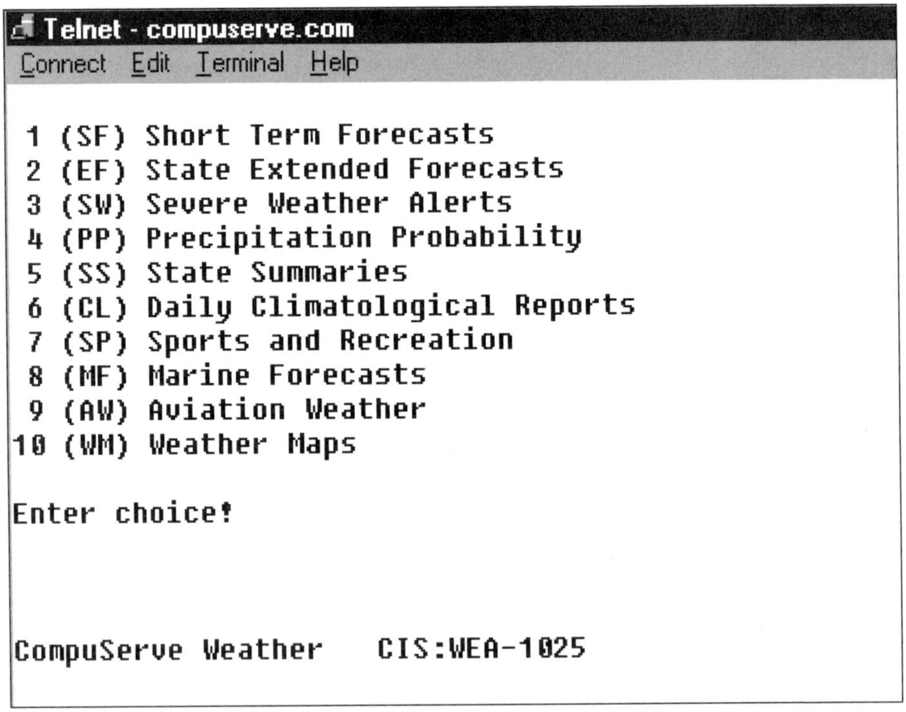

Figure 6-20
CompuServe's Weather On-line

```
 Telnet - compuserve.com
Connect  Edit  Terminal  Help

 1 (SF) Short Term Forecasts
 2 (EF) State Extended Forecasts
 3 (SW) Severe Weather Alerts
 4 (PP) Precipitation Probability
 5 (SS) State Summaries
 6 (CL) Daily Climatological Reports
 7 (SP) Sports and Recreation
 8 (MF) Marine Forecasts
 9 (AW) Aviation Weather
10 (WM) Weather Maps

Enter choice!



CompuServe Weather    CIS:WEA-1025
```

accurate, but with all things in an online service, updates may be a bit late or just scheduled for a few hours in between each one.

Yahoo

If there's one site that interests me above others, it's the site called Yahoo located at

```
http://akebono.stanford.edu/yahoo
```

which is another excellent source of information. It's presented in menu style, and not much in a particularly searchable order. It's got a listing of some of the most intriguing subjects. Once there, take the option called Environment and Nature, then go to Parks, next onward to National Parks, Forests, and Monuments, where you'll get a list of some of our nation's best parks and recreational areas (Figure 6-21).

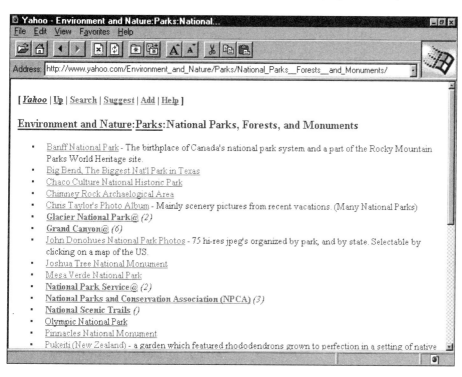

Figure 6-21
Yahoo Site with National Parks listing

We can take this process one step further and check for places to go and things to see while we're roving about the Western United States. Navigate back to the top level of Yahoo, take the track to the following URL resource, and look what we found!

```
http://www.yahoo.com/Business/Corporations/Travel/
Tour_Operators/
```

It's a listing of tour operators across the world, but we can see specific ones for the Pacific Northwest, canoe trips, rafting, and much more! It's everything we were looking for in a camping or travel setting for sites and recreation. Checking for a hotel one level back listed tons of hotels and reservation chains, but most (if not all) of them were for ritzy and upscale hotels. Judging from that listing, I don't think there's a rustic inn in the Olympic Mountain Range.

Lycos Search Engine

Performing a search at

```
http://lycos.cs.cmu.edu
```

with the search words "camping guide" yielded 16 hits of documents. The Lycos search engine is one of my favorites because I can tailor the search to include documents that have a *hit ratio* of 0.*xx* to 1.00 where *xx* is any number (Figure 6-22).

Repeating the Lycos search using the keywords of "travel maps" yielded some interesting results in that we got maps for countries in Europe and some for the U.S. as well. Looking at the listing a bit further, I found an interesting set of maps at

```
http://nearnet.gnn.com/gnn/bus/Travel.html
```

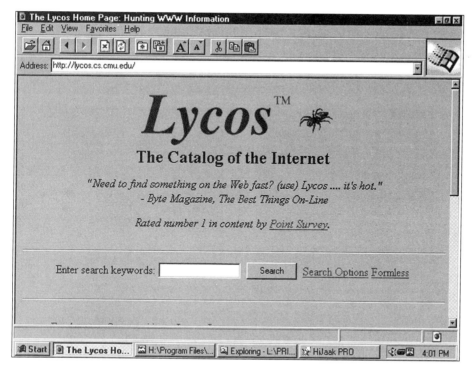

Figure 6-22
A Lycos search

in which I could get time-sensitive maps planned out for my trip at Fodor's Worldview maps (Figure 6-23, over the page), and where Mountain Travel*Sobek will help you plan out an active outdoor vacation trip.

I repeated the search, but this time I went for "reservations" to see what, if any, help we can get with accommodations. Remember that we're driving a self-contained camper, so we really don't need a hotel but a campground to park in. In this search, we could get reservations for the rest of the world, but nothing for campers and camping in places we'd like. Once again, the camper gets nixed in our searches. Wouldn't it be nice if we could find an agency that caters to camping and outdoors travel of this type? Sure would!

Now, for the $64,000 question: Have you been saving all of these searches to favorites? Or are they in your history log? In a few sections, we'll be taking a look at the many sites we've visited, how they've affected our system, and what we can do with all of the data we've accumulated over the span of this chapter.

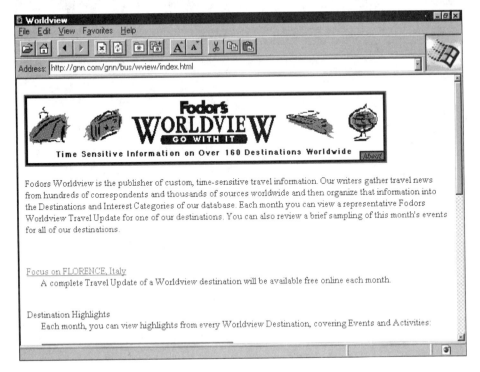

Figure 6-23
Fodor's
Worldview

Newsgroups

Newsgroups afford us the opportunity to interact in a different manner than we've grown accustomed to, by posting messages to people asking what or how they did something. It's especially nice to be able to ask someone how they did it, or where they went on trips, before completing your own plans. What we'll do is to keep in mind our topics of maps, camping spots, hotels, and files that we may be able to use. Before getting into this, a refresher on newsgroups is in order. News is broken down into component categories of alternate subjects, computer groups, social groups, and many others including the recreation group. To access these, we need to get onto our news server. This is usually the one assigned by your Internet provider, but it will be any of the newsgroups found on MSN in our case.

First, I'll take this from the stance that you've got your own Internet provider as I do, and we'll plunder the newsgroups that we've got by virtue of these accounts. Second, we'll turn to MSN itself to get around the forums and the many newsgroups there. To start the show, make the connection with your provider, and start your favorite news reader. Since I use the Netmanage Chameleon product, I'll show how it works and then compare it with WinVN, which we downloaded a few chapters back. If you didn't get it and forgot the FTP site where it was, go to `ftp://micros.hensa.ac.uk` and look in the `/mirrors/cica/win3/winsock` directory for the file named `winvn926.zip`. Unzip the file and follow the instructions in its accompanying documentation to set it up. Once that's done, we'll be ready to work with it. But, for now, just sit back and relax while I show you how my news reader works. When we get done with these two, we'll then do the same thing with the Microsoft Internet Explorer.

After I start it up, NEWTNews, as it's called, presents me with the opening screen (Figure 6-24). I have to log on my news server, or tell it which news server to use if I've not yet done that. Since I did that a long time ago, NEWTNews automatically checks for new groups and gets new articles. This is how I've customized it for my own needs.

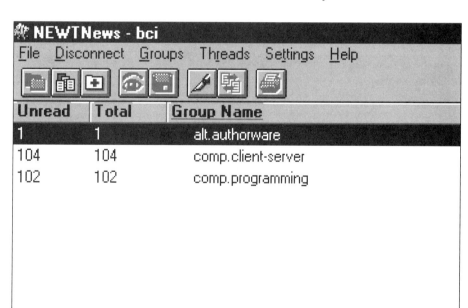

Figure 6-24
The NEWTNews news reader from Netmanage, Inc.

With this done, let's check to see if we can find a newsgroup that closely corresponds to our interest in camping and is relevant to planning our trip. In this case, we're likely to find something in the rec group. So, I look for it by selecting the rec group as the first choice, and then I type in "camp" to filter it down even further. Nothing! I can't believe that at all! So, I use a filter search that says Text to match as I tell it to search all of the newsgroups by name. This time, I find a camping topic, but under the `fsu.freenet.camping` newsgroup. Now that's a twist and a half, but we've found something at last (Figure 6-25).

Adding this newsgroup to my subscribed selection automatically updates my subscribed-to list of groups and looks for new messages posted to that group. At the time of this writing, there were none, but we'll post one using NEWTNews and check it out with WinVN next. Posting a message to a newsgroup is almost identical to creating an e-mail message, except instead of sending it to someone, you're posting

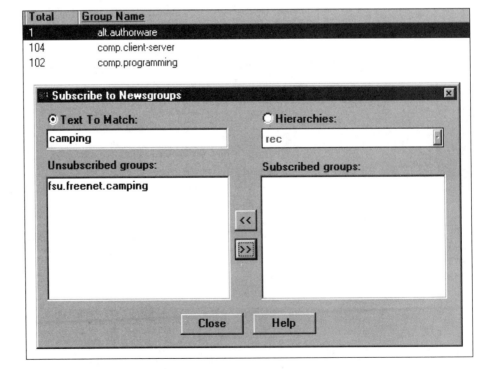

Figure 6-25
Newsgroup
selection
completed

it to a bulletin board. Remember our discussion from Chapter 4? Okay, so we've subscribed to the only camping newsgroup we've located, we've posted a question to it, and we're waiting for a reply.

> **TIP**
>
> A newsgroup message could take up to an hour to be posted, or more, depending on the server and how busy it is at that time.

Let's start WinVN and check to see if the message was posted. You need to remember that our newsgroup is called `fsu.freenet.camping`, since we'll need that for our subscription list. We've allowed about five minutes for the message to be posted. Many news readers have settings where you can adjust the time frame in which you automatically check for new messages. My NEWTNews is set to every three hours, although I seldom am online for three hours at one time. A more reasonable time hack would be 15 minutes if you were really working the news heavily. When we start WinVN now, the `fsu.freenet.camping` group isn't in my subscribed-to list of news. I put it there by selecting Group, then selecting Find, and then typing in the full name of the newsgroup. Alternatively, you could just scroll down nearly 12,000 newsgroups until you found the one you wanted. WinVN doesn't segregate the groups like NEWTNews does. When the group is added, it is updated with new messages, and there's ours! (See Figure 6-26.) Double-clicking on the group brings the list of messages on screen, and then we can read any message by double-clicking on it.

The last thing we'll be doing with newsgroups is to go into MSN itself and see what's there in the way of newsgroups for the same topic. Stop WinVN if you've not done that yet, and save any parameters if you want. Since you're already logged onto MSN and the Internet, you don't have to do anything special except to start MSN by double-clicking on the MSN icon on your desktop. Go to Categories, then to the Interests,

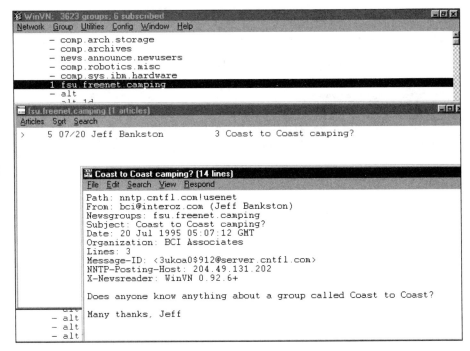

Figure 6-26
WinVN reading
newsgroups

Leisure, and Hobbies subcategory, then to the Travel forum, and finally inside that forum double-click on Travel Internet Newsgroups. This forum has two newsgroups, `alt.airline` and `alt.travel` (Figure 6-27). As more and more of MSN matures and comes online, expect to see more newsgroups added into the structures where you can get news as part of your daily roaming through MSN.

Mailing Lists

The last thing we've got to discuss in this section is mailing lists. A mailing list is much like the dreaded stuff you get in the regular mail, but it's generated by a server on the Internet. The best part of this is that you can subscribe to it, get it for a few days or weeks if that's your pleasure, and then turn it off! Water faucet on, water faucet off! Don't you wish you could do this with your daily rash of junk mail? We're not so lucky. The flipside to this coin is that if you change Internet addresses, the mail server knows not the difference, and you miss the boat.

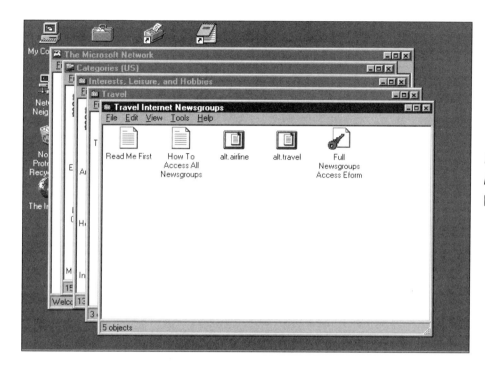

Figure 6-27
MSN
Newsgroups

CAUTION

You *must* subscribe and unsubscribe from mailing lists using the exact same e-mail name each time! Failure to do so will cause your requests to be ignored, and frustrate you as the mail keeps coming in!

Subscription is done by e-mail. The general format for subscriptions is

```
subscribe list-name your name.
```

If I wanted to subscribe to the World Wide Web new announcements list server, the actual form would be

```
subscribe www-announce Jeff Bankston
```

which I would mail to the CERN server (Figure 6-28) so that CERN would now send me all of the new announcements each time a new Web site came online, an FTP site went active, or similar Internet events were announced. I should note here that on my e-mail client, my name maps to my Internet address of BCI@INTEROZ.COM, which is what the mailing list server looks at when communicating back to you, not my real personal name. The current address of this server is www-announce@mail.w3.org. This is a great way to stay on top of new systems as they become available.

Handling the Results

Boy oh boy, have we gone around the block with Chapter 6 getting things together. We've seen how we can traverse the Web to our benefit, but what did we do with all of that information as it accumulated?

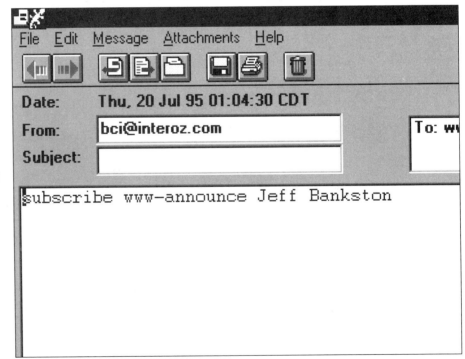

Figure 6-28
Subscribing to a mailing list

Where did it go, or where did we want it to go? Is all of this newfound Information Highway dribble worth the effort we went through to get it? Well, let's analyze some of the results of these many searches to make that determination.

Saving Searches

The primary way we've saved searches is by way of the Favorites menu tree structure. If you followed along with me as I added sites to my Favorites, you saw that it didn't take that very long to fill up the visual tree. As we did so, the on-screen limit of 23 objects was filled up, and I have 34 total in my Favorites. You can see this by clicking on Favorites and then Open Favorites and looking at the scroll box that comes up. At this screen, select View, then select Arrange Icons, and then choose how you want these objects to be arranged in this screen. A couple of points of interest are worth mentioning here. The first is that you can arrange by the date that sites were added so that you can see a historical perspective of where you were and what you did or where you visited. Why is that interesting? Set the View option to Details and look at the Favorites list now! You get a really quick view of how often and when you were at a site, and when it was added to the list (Figure 6-29).

One more perspective is to look at hard disk space being used by storing Favorites. Mine are located on `H:\WIN400\FAVORITES`, where I see 34 objects each using 1KB of disk space. No big deal, they're not using much space, right? Wrong! Depending on how you have your hard disk partitioned, you could be losing a whole bunch of disk space. Mine is set so that the cluster size, or the storage unit on this partition, is 4KB in size. What this means is that when data objects are stored on my disk, they occupy the disk in 4KB increments. If I have a 8KB file, then it uses two allocation units exactly. Well, that's in a perfect world, not in ours. From the last time you ran Windows 95's Explorer and looked at the Internet shortcuts, they occupied only 1KB apiece. This means that each favorite saved uses a 4KB allocation unit to store a 1KB data file.

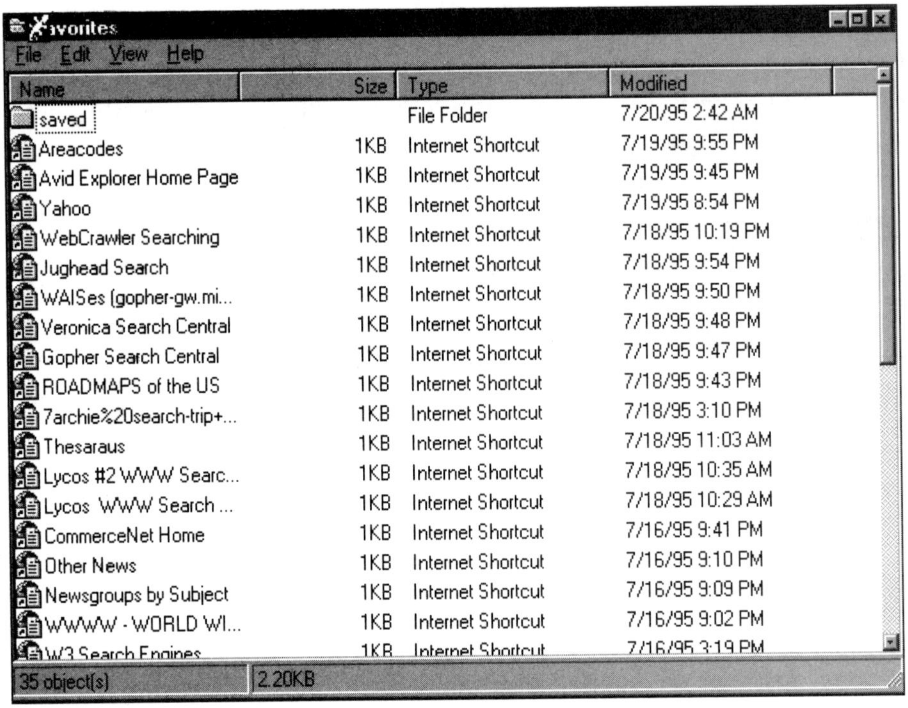

Figure 6-29
Favorites with
View set to
Date and
Details listing

Name	Size	Type	Modified
saved		File Folder	7/20/95 2:42 AM
Areacodes	1KB	Internet Shortcut	7/19/95 9:55 PM
Avid Explorer Home Page	1KB	Internet Shortcut	7/19/95 9:45 PM
Yahoo	1KB	Internet Shortcut	7/19/95 8:54 PM
WebCrawler Searching	1KB	Internet Shortcut	7/18/95 10:19 PM
Jughead Search	1KB	Internet Shortcut	7/18/95 9:54 PM
WAISes (gopher-gw.mi...	1KB	Internet Shortcut	7/18/95 9:50 PM
Veronica Search Central	1KB	Internet Shortcut	7/18/95 9:48 PM
Gopher Search Central	1KB	Internet Shortcut	7/18/95 9:47 PM
ROADMAPS of the US	1KB	Internet Shortcut	7/18/95 9:43 PM
7archie%20search-trip+...	1KB	Internet Shortcut	7/18/95 3:10 PM
Thesaraus	1KB	Internet Shortcut	7/18/95 11:03 AM
Lycos #2 WWW Searc...	1KB	Internet Shortcut	7/18/95 10:35 AM
Lycos WWW Search ...	1KB	Internet Shortcut	7/18/95 10:29 AM
CommerceNet Home	1KB	Internet Shortcut	7/16/95 9:41 PM
Other News	1KB	Internet Shortcut	7/16/95 9:10 PM
Newsgroups by Subject	1KB	Internet Shortcut	7/16/95 9:09 PM
WWWW - WORLD WI...	1KB	Internet Shortcut	7/16/95 9:02 PM
W3 Search Engines	1KB	Internet Shortcut	7/16/95 3:19 PM

35 object(s) | 2.20KB

It wastes 3KB. If you have your disk partitions set for 8KB clusters, meaning that you have partitions from 256MB to 511MB in size, you are losing 7KB with each Favorite saved. If you had 200 Favorites saved and were wasting 7KB on each partition, then you'd be wasting 1.4MB of disk space storing 200KB of data files!

Why am I telling you this? Because as you surf the Web more and more, your disk usage will certainly go up. Some things like Favorites could be stored to floppies if you wanted to save disk space. The same point holds rue for seldom-used utilities. Just a little point of interest I thought I'd throw out to our new surfers.

Caches and the Data

There's another matter of interest to talk about relating to disk space and files in connection with MSN and the Microsoft Internet Explorer. A *cache* is a temporary holding area used to speed up certain operations.

Here's basically how it works, and we'll use your CPU and motherboard's cache memory to show the theory. The three critical components of your computer are the CPU chip, the memory plugged into it for storing the data, and the bus structure where you plug in the cards that do things. Along with that bus I'm including the circuit chips that control it. When the CPU has to do something, it has to get its data from the hard drive and then store them in the memory chips. While that is happening, the CPU is basically on hold doing nothing but waiting for the disk drive to send the data. Other things are possible for the CPU to be doing, but for now just accept this. When the CPU gets the required data, it stores some in its *cache* memory, which is inside the CPU chip for the 486s and later processors. It also stores some in the cache memory that's on the motherboard. That particular cache could be from 64KB up to 1MB, usually 256KB these days.

So, the CPU has data to work with right now. That work is completed, and it's ready to do more. Instead of going back to the slower hard drive to get more data, the CPU looks to this cache memory to see if any of the data are there. If they are, then that's where the CPU gets them; otherwise, it goes back to the hard drive. In this manner, the CPU works a lot faster. A cache serves to provide that closer working environment with the CPU.

MSN and the Microsoft Internet Explorer use disk space as a cache to store data that have been downloaded from the Web. It's invariably faster to get the data off of the hard disk than it is to re-download them from the Web. These files that serve as MSN's and the Microsoft Internet Explorer's cache are *not* erased after each online session!

WARNING

If you let the cache directories go uncleaned, then they will eventually cause your PC to slow down and waste large quantities of disk space. They could even conceivably fill up a partition.

To take care of this situation, read on into the last section.

More on Processing Files

Now that we've surfed out hearts out, it's time to clean up and put away the toys for the evening. One part of the process should be a periodic cleaning of the hard drive where these cache files are stored. During the early testing phases of MSN, I found my system with nearly 8,000 files in the cache due to online activity! Quite a pile of files, and it took about three hours to clean them out. Here's how you do that.

CAUTION

While even the best laid plans of mice and men work most of the time, there's no replacement for a good, reliable set of backups. Always safeguard your data before attempting any mass removal of files.

Start up Windows 95's Explorer and navigate to the directory where you installed the Plus Pak.

1. Click on View, click on Options, and then click on the View tab.
2. Click on the View All Files radio button and then click on the Apply tab.
3. After a few seconds, the screen will flicker and come back to normal as Explorer rereads the disk drives.
4. Click on the Okay tab.
5. Now, you can see all files, hidden and otherwise, as well as the cache subdirectory (Figure 6-30).

Delete away to your heart's content, but leave the cache directory itself. Be sure to reverse the process to normal file viewing when you finish.

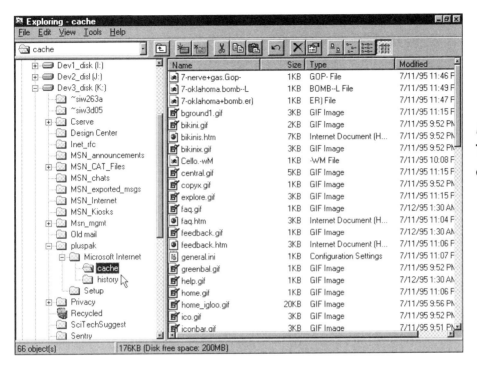

Figure 6-30
The cache sub-directory

Summary

We've made a full circle around the Web visiting a good many resources there and picking up a few new tricks in the process. We learned that the Web can be our friend and enemy at the same time. A tough problem at times, but we made it through while getting some good information about planning a vacation as well. Although the complete trip didn't get planned, we learned that there are quite a few Web resources that can be overlapped to provide us with what we need. No one resource did the job by itself, but collectively, the Web tools came through. We've seen Archie, Veronica, Jughead, and the rest of the gang working together to keep the Web working for us. In Chapter 7, we'll use Netscape to do many of the same things, and we'll see how it compares to the Microsoft Internet Explorer. See you there!

Netscape's Browser and MSN Internet

We've seen how the Web can be our friend, and how it can also be our enemy, hiding all of that good information. The Microsoft Internet Explorer has performed admirably in our initial pass through the Web, and we're ready to press onward to other Web-related matters. More specifically, in this chapter you'll learn all about another Web browser called Netscape Navigator from Netscape Communications Corporation. Currently at release version 1.1 and beta version 1.2, Netscape is one of the most popular Web browsers on the market. There are other browsers out there, but I had room for only one additional browser in this book. Chapter 7 is designed to cover nearly all aspects of Netscape from start to finish. We'll cover preparation, installation, customizations, and general use while we compare it to the Microsoft Internet Explorer.

Introduction

Netscape is a wonderful tool that was clearly designed as a competitor to NCSA Mosaic. If you recall, I said in a previous chapter that Mosaic was still in beta when many other Web browsers had been completed and gone to market. Just before starting this chapter, I learned that Mosaic has gone into final beta, the last step a product normally goes through before being released as a completed product. In the world of software development, no product is ever fully developed; hence, the growing world of browsers is becoming more competitive as time goes on. The following section will offer you a perspective on the browsers we've seen, what we can expect from Netscape, and beta software in general.

Browsers, Browsers, Everywhere!

Did you ever go shopping for something new and see a dozen ads in the paper from a dozen vendors all claiming their product was superior to the others? Sure you did, and it's only natural that this occur for competitive reasons. Software products, including browsers, are no different, but there's still no one consistent standard by which to judge them. In Chapter 4, we talked about many of the browsers available on the market, including freeware offerings such as Cello and Mosaic, as well as commercial products such as Spry and Netscape. All of these browsers have their good points and bad points, a point to keep in mind as we focus on Netscape.

This focus is not meant to imply that Netscape will do the best job for you; after all, everyone's surfing needs are different. Nor is it meant to imply that the Microsoft Internet Explorer, now in its first release, is inadequate, either. All products evolve and mature over time with enhancements, bug fixes, and other related developments, and the Microsoft Internet Explorer is no exception. As version 1.0 of a product, it does an exceptional job. To recap how to obtain some popular browsers, look for them at these URLs:

Product	Location
NCSA Mosaic	`ftp.ncsa.uiuc.edu`
Netscape	`ftp.mcom.com/netscape/windows`
Cello	`ftp.law.cornell.edu/pub/LII/Cello`
WinWeb	`ftp.einet.net/einet/pc/winweb`

Once you've worked with these browsers, you should have a clear idea what you want in a browser. One problem you'll have on the Web is deciding on anything! The Internet is so sprawling, and there's so much to see and get, that you'll download several megabytes of data in an afternoon and spend the next week evaluating each product.

About Netscape and Beta Software

Netscape is available in both 16-bit and 32-bit flavors. The 16-bit form is targeted for the Windows 3.*x* environment, whereas the 32-bit version is native to Windows 95. It was originally developed to work inside of Windows 3.1 with the use of the Win32S subset extensions we talked about in Chapter 4. Win32S allows 32-bit applications to run in the normal 16-bit world of Windows 3.1. In Windows 95, both 16-bit and 32-bit applications will run fine without the use of the Win32S subset files. So, if you've bought or downloaded either version of Netscape, this chapter will apply, although I am using the Windows 95–specific version. The exterior is the same regardless.

Beta software consists in applications that are being developed and are not yet ready for prime time. They exist in forms ranging from early betas that may be unstable and could crash your system to versions very close to release needing only minor refinements. By and large, most beta software is fairly stable, with only minor glitches in its overall performance.

WARNING

If you choose to run beta software on your PC, you are responsible for the overall effects the software may have on your system. Developers make all kinds of efforts to ensure that beta won't cause any harm to your software, but any beta could be fatal to parts of your system, mainly the operating system software. Betas have been known to crash systems and cause monumental damage to the software that resides on the hard disk.

TIP

There's no better safeguard to beta testing that a good set of backups to your data!

The makers of Netscape place the current beta version on their home server, currently

```
ftp://ftp.mcom.com/pub/netscape1.2b5/
```

I will say, despite my reservations about beta software, that Netscape is one of the better betas available to those desiring to play around with development code. Navigator is currently in beta 3 for version 1.2, which could be released by the time this book goes to press.

Installing and Configuring Netscape

This section will cover installing Netscape from both floppy disks as a retail product and from a file archive as you'd download it from the FTP site. Configuration and setup will be the same regardless of how you installed it.

Requirements

Netscape itself is very undemanding of the system hardware. The product comes on two 3.5-inch high-density floppy disks for both 16- and 32-bit versions. It will need approximately 1.3MB of RAM to get started and perhaps another megabyte of RAM to work at peak efficiency. As with many Windows applications, you should plan on having at least 4MB of free memory when you start Netscape.

Netscape is equally undemanding of disk space. The full installation requires about 1.5MB of disk space, and the subdirectories will later use up to another 4MB as you begin using the bookmarks, the favorite places, and the cache system, which we'll get into later.

Installation from Floppy Disk

Start the Control Panel, double-click on Add/Remove Programs, and then insert Disk 1 into your drive and click on Install (Figure 7-1).

The Setup Wizard searches your floppy drives for the presence of an Install or Setup program with which to install your software. This new way to install software is the most desirable method, as Windows 95

Figure 7-1
Adding a new program to Windows 95

uses this system to handle several administrative matters pertaining to the newly installed software. When the installation routine has been located, it will be identified and reported to you as the one that will be installed (Figure 7-2). You are given the opportunity to correct anything here that is out of order or to cancel the installation if you desire.

If the program reported isn't correct, you may browse to find the proper one, step back to make a change, or cancel. Otherwise, click on Finish to press onward. Next, say where you want the program installed. Make your drive and directory selection and continue on. Insert Disk 2 when prompted and click on OK to continue. Netscape creates the program group under Programs, Start Menu; it is called (appropriately enough) Netscape and includes the program executable and the ever-present Read Me file, which is worth reading for the few minutes it takes. Your installation of Netscape is complete.

Figure 7-2
Confirmation to install new software

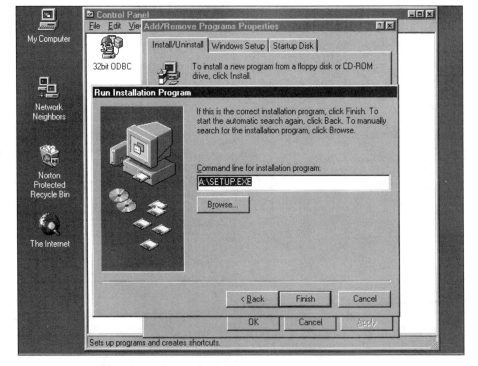

Installation from the File Archive

Installation from the archive is just as quick and painless as installation from floppies. Make a directory for Netscape and copy the self-extracting archive to that directory using the Windows 95 Explorer. Double-click on the archive to expand it into its component parts. Next, double-click on the SETUP.EXE program that now resides in the directory, and everything from that point is just like installation from floppies! Pretty simple, right? I think so too!

Configuration

After installation, start Netscape by navigating through Start and the applications tree to the Netscape program group. (For the sake of togetherness, I moved my Netscape program group so that it's under my Internet group, where all my other Internet tools are located.) When you start Netscape for the first time with the downloaded edition, you have to agree to the licensing agreement shown in Figure 7-3 to go on. *Read*

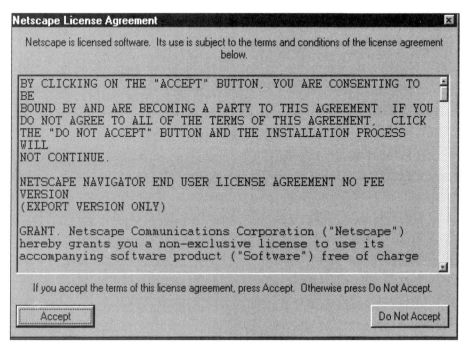

Figure 7-3
Netscape's
license
agreement

the licensing agreement! If you don't agree, then don't go on; otherwise, click on Accept to continue.

Netscape will start up, and if you're not logged on, your Windows 95 TCP/IP Dialup Networking application will automatically start to connect you to your provider. If you're using the Microsoft Internet Explorer and the MSN Internet connection, start that to connect to the Internet. Go online, and Netscape will automatically go to the Netscape home page shown in Figure 7-4. You may prefer to go to some other home page, or none at all. Let's begin customizing Netscape by changing this option. First, however, we must understand the many menus Netscape sports.

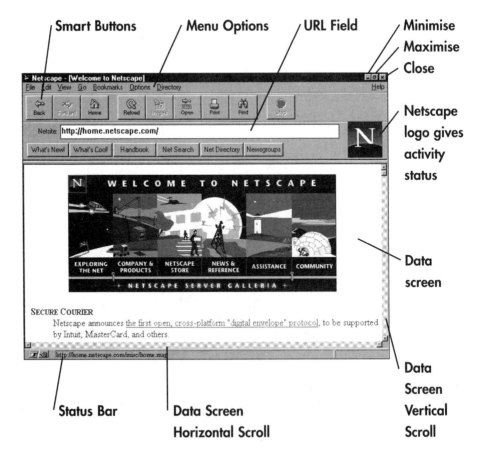

Figure 7-4
Netscape's
home page

When you start Netscape for the first time, it goes to the home page of Netscape Communications Corporation at URL `http://home.netscape.com/`. The Netscape home page banner comes on screen along with any other graphics. All of these graphic images come at a price of slower processing, because they have to be downloaded from the site before you can view them, obviously, but what if you don't care for the graphics? They can be stopped by an option that we'll describe shortly.

NOTE

The Netscape Navigator handbook can be accessed anytime you're online by clicking on the Handbook button (third from the left), which takes you to the Netscape home site.

The Menu Options

At the very top of the screen is the title bar, which tells you the name of the present site. To its far right are the normal Windows 95 icons for Minimize, Maximize, and Close, from left to right. There are seven menu options across the top of the screen: File, Edit, View, Go, Bookmarks, Options, and Directory. Immediately below the menu bar are the smart buttons that execute the options Back, Forward, Home, Reload, Images, Open, Print, Find, and Stop. These are the most common functions that you'll use as you navigate Netscape. Immediately below these smart buttons is the key to it all—the URL field representing where you want to go, or what you want to do, called the Netsite field. We'll be referring to this as the URL field as well. To the right of this field is the Netscape logo; it tells you if you're going somewhere or doing something. It'll blink and change a bit if you're causing something to happen or sit idle otherwise.

Below are buttons labeled What's New, What's Cool, Handbook, Net Search, Net Directory, and Newsgroups. Most of these are self-explanatory, but we'll touch upon them briefly. The next area, and the largest, is the main screen, where the data will be seen and manipulated. The vertical scroll bar is on the far right side of the screen, and the horizontal scroll bar is at the bottom. At the very bottom of the screen is the status bar, which tells you what URL a hotlink on the screen connects with (position the mouse pointer over the hotlink so that it changes to the little hand). This feature tells you beforehand where you're going if you click on a given link. It's also nice to use for charting URLs without actually having to go to them.

The File Menu

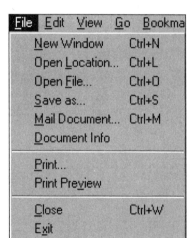

The File menu has the following options:

- New Window (Ctrl+N)— Allows you to go to another URL while leaving the current one on screen. A second window opens for the new site.
- Open Location (Ctrl+L)— Opens a screen in which you can type in the full URL of the desired site. The same thing can be achieved by clearing the Netsite field.
- Open File (Ctrl+O)—Allows you to open a saved .HTM file that you may have saved when you were at a site.
- Save As (Ctrl+S)—Allows you to save the current Web page as either a plain text file or an HTML file. The text style choice allows you to import it into a word processor cleanly, whereas HTML format requires much conversion and cleaning up.

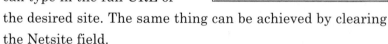

- ◆ Mail Document ([Ctrl]+[M])—Allows you to send the current Web page to someone via e-mail, provided you've made the proper setup, as we'll do later.
- ◆ Document Info—Gives you all kinds of nifty information about the Web page itself: when it was last modified, the type of document, and so on.
- ◆ Print—Self-explanatory
- ◆ Print Preview—Self-explanatory
- ◆ Close—Self-explanatory
- ◆ Exit—Self-explanatory

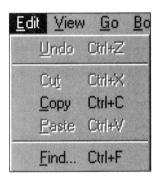

The Edit Menu

The Edit menu contains the following rather standard editing options:

- ◆ Undo ([Ctrl]+[Z])—Undoes whatever you just did, and only that one thing. If you want to undo something, you have to undo it before doing anything else.
- ◆ Cut ([Ctrl]+[X])—Cuts, to the clipboard, the text or objects in the currently marked block.
- ◆ Copy ([Ctrl]+[C])—Copies, to the clipboard, the text or objects in the currently marked block.
- ◆ Paste ([Ctrl]+[V])—Copies the text or objects from the clipboard to the current location of the cursor.
- ◆ Find ([Ctrl]+[F])—Locates the desired text in the current document.

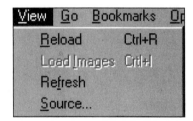

The View Menu

The View menu has the following options:

◆ Reload (Ctrl+R)—Downloads the entire current Web page to your PC. When you first went to the site, you got that Web page, but if your local copy of the page becomes corrupted for some reason, you can always refresh it using Reload.

◆ Load Images (Ctrl+I)—If you have Options➤Auto Load Images (described later in this section) turned off, graphics won't load when you access Web sites. The off setting greatly speeds up your Web surfing. When it is in effect, the View Load Images option lets you load the images for the current page; it does not remain in effect for later.

◆ Refresh—Refreshes the current Web page text by redrawing it on screen.

◆ Source—Allows you to look at the HTML source for the current Web page. If you're ever interested in how Web pages are made, here's your chance to see how others have done it.

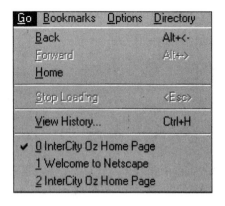

The Go Menu

The Go menu has the following options:

◆ Back (Alt+,)—Moves you back one Web site in a sequence of sites visited. For instance, if you have visited sites A, B, C, and D and then have manually returned to site C, Back will then move you to site B.

◆ Forward (Alt+.)—Moves you forward one Web site in a sequence of sites visited. For instance, if you have visited sites A, B, C, and D and have manually returned to site C, Forward will then move you to site D.

- Home—Takes you to your home page as defined in Options➤Preferences➤Styles and under Start With in the Windows Styles section.

- Stop Loading (Esc)—Does just what its name implies.

- View History (Ctrl+H)—Shows you a textual listing of the latest sites you've visited. You can either go to a given site or just add it as a bookmark to your collection.

The Bookmarks Menu

The Bookmarks menu has the following options:

- Add Bookmarks (Ctrl+A)—Adds the current Web page to your list of bookmarks defined in the Options➤Preferences➤Applications and Directories menu.

- View Bookmarks (Ctrl+B)—Allows you to view the bookmarks previously added from sites. At this menu option, you can edit any bookmark without having to go back to the Web page itself to update it.

The Options Menu

The Options menu has the following options:

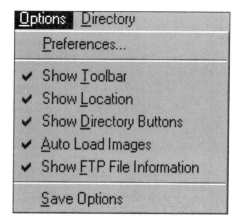

- Preferences—Will be detailed immediately at the end of this block of options. It's so huge that I didn't want to break it up here.

- Show Toolbar—Shows the toolbar.

- Show Location—Shows the URL field box.

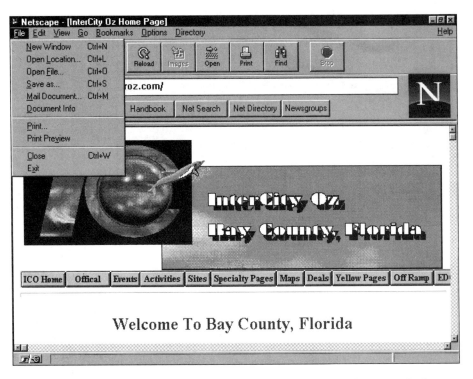

Figure 7-5
Netscape's
Bookmarks List,
where you can
edit an existing
bookmark

- ◆ Show Directory Buttons—Shows the helpful buttons below the URL field entry.
- ◆ Auto Load Images—Enables or disables the loading of graphics files as you access a Web site. Turn this off to speed up access of sites.
- ◆ Show FTP File Information—Gives detailed file FTP descriptions about the FTP server you're visiting.

As mentioned, Preferences leads to a rather complicated menu (Figure 7-6) that offers you the ability to customize Netscape in the following ways via the Set Preferences On box:

1. **Styles**—Controls display of certain features of pages.
   - ◆ Window Styles—Allows you to say how the window styles will be viewed in toolbars: as pictures, text, or both. It's here that you define your starting home page,

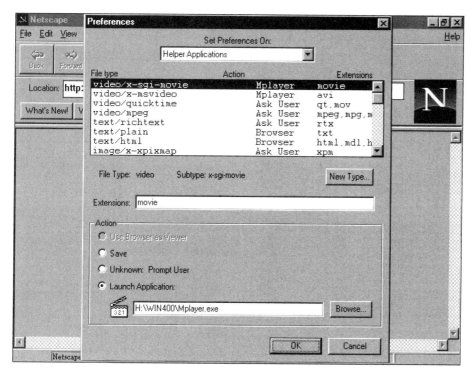

Figure 7-6
The Preferences menu

if you desire one, and specify if that home page is to be
loaded automatically when you start Netscape.

◆ Link Styles—Lets you say how the hotlinks are to be
viewed and includes expiration information. You can
clear all of them out by clicking on the Expire Now
button.

2. **Fonts and Colors**—Allows you to select how Web pages are
viewed on screen for various aspects of the pages themselves.

◆ Fonts/Encodings—It's here that you can define how the
hotlinks look, what the foreground and background
colors are, and what the font is. This is important for
those folks who have sight problems and need the
additional help that a larger font can supply. You can
also specify the Latin or Japanese dialects for the text
itself.

◆ Colors—You can have a lot of fun here customizing how Netscape displays links, fonts, text, and such. It's also easy to get into trouble with font colors.

CAUTION

If you set the foreground and background colors to the same thing, then the text and pages become invisible! Use extra caution when setting colors to avoid this.

◆ Image File—Lets you select an image to use as the backdrop to Netscape.

3. **Mail and News**—Lets you define all kinds of options for your capability to mail from within Netscape and for getting to your favorite newsgroup.

◆ Mail—Lets you define, in order from top to bottom of this section, your mail server, your real-life name, your e-mail account name, such as bci@interoz.com, your company name if any, a signature file that contains an electronic signature of your name and perhaps business name, and if you use 8-bit or MIME mail. Normally, everyone uses 8-bit mail.

◆ News—Lets you define, in order from top to bottom, the IP address or the alias of your news server (such as news.interoz.com), the directory where you want the news to be placed, and how many news articles you'd like to see at one time. This is a great way to limit information overload by keeping the number of messages down.

4. **Cache and Network**—Defines the particulars about the connection itself.

◆ Cache—Defines the size, in kilobytes, of the disk and memory caches and the ability to empty each one of them as it gets cluttered. This cache is where the most recent data from your Web surfing are held. It typically holds images, URL references, and the like. Verify Documents means that a Web document will be verified for validity during an online session.

◆   Network Connections—Lets you specify the network buffers and maximum network connections in this Netscape session. In general, you'll never need to adjust these settings. If you're running multiple screens and a lot of URLs at the same time, you may have to increase them.

5.   **Applications and Directories**—Lets you specify the location of ancillary functions.

◆   Supporting Applications—Lets you say where the Telnet helper application, a 3270 communications application, and an HTML viewer are located.

◆   Directories—Defines the location for temporary files and where your bookmark file is located.

6.   **Images and Security**—Provides information about images and controls the level of security for information exchanged between you and the server.

◆   Images—Allows for color matching between systems that use only 16 colors and images from servers that could be in 256 colors.

◆   Security Alerts—This is one of the most welcome options you can have in a browser. These allow you to be notified when a security environment is accessed, used, or mixed with others in such a way that it could open you up to problems like credit card fraud. There are more and more sites where you can carry out transactions online, and you must be mindful of possible security problems in such situations.

> **WARNING**
>
> Disabling the Submitting a Form Insecurely option when you're dealing with credit and money information could open the door to fraud. Keep this setting checked if you plan on making transactions online.

♦   Proxies—Most Web surfers will never use proxy servers, but Netscape allows them just in case. Proxies apply when you operate inside of a firewalled system and you need access to the Internet beyond the firewall. Firewalls are used to keep people from connecting to your server when they're not authorized. In Netscape, you may have to specify the proxy server for each action that you're doing. See your network administrator to see if you use proxy servers.

♦   Helper Applications—This is where you define the application to use when Netscape runs across documents and data files as you surf the Web. Some types Netscape handles on its own; others will require other applications. For instance, Winword handles rich text format (RTF) files, so I defined Winword as the application that will process RTF files. As you get into files more and more, you'll use this menu more to customize Netscape's handling of files.

Directory
Netscape's Home
What's New!
What's Cool!
Go to Newsgroups
Netscape Galleria
Internet Directory
Internet Search
Internet White Pages
About the Internet

The Directory Menu

The Directory menu has a set of menu options is nothing more than a set of links to the various functions that Netscape has in place to assist you in getting started in a variety of situations. You can find out what's new with Netscape, get to some news defined by your preferences, and more. It includes, for instance, the Internet White Pages directory service to help you find people and places on the Web.

The Help Menu

The Help menu has the following options:

Help

About Netscape...
Registration Information

Handbook
Release Notes
Frequently Asked Questions
On Security

How to Give Feedback
How to Get Support
How to Create Web Services

- ◆ About Netscape—Learn neat things about Netscape.
- ◆ Registration Information—Lets you register your copy of Netscape online! Quick and painless, too.
- ◆ Handbook—Provides access to the Netscape user's guide. It's always just a click away if you need help. Most folks never use this because Netscape is so easy to use.
- ◆ Release Notes—Gives you up-to-the-minute information on the product. Because it's online, Netscape can keep the manual up-to-date with the absolute latest information without having to reprint the manual each time the updates come out.
- ◆ Frequently Asked Questions—Leads to FAQs about the product itself.
- ◆ On Security—This leads to a paper on how and why Netscape developers handle security issues in Netscape, and what these issues mean for you. If you've 10 minutes, this is an intriguing paper to read.

The last three menu options, How to Give Feedback, How to Get support, and How to Create Web Services, all deal with support and services from Netscape as a company. You can use the feedback mechanism to send your thoughts, or ask why something doesn't work the way you thought it should, or just thank them for a fine product. Everyone wants to know they did a good job once in awhile!

Getting Started on the Web

Since we've spent the last dozen or more pages learning all about Netscape, I guess we should surf the Web with it to see how it really does, right? Why not—so let's work again on that vacation planning thing that we worked on with the Microsoft Internet Explorer.

But, Where Is the Beginning?

As always, we've conceived of the Web as starting at the point that we log on, or possibly at our home page. Well, the beginning of the Web, as far as we're concerned, is the point where we hope to find something. Not necessarily a home page, and not necessarily where we logged on. It's more of an idea and the realization of that idea as documents, files, or additions into our bookmarks! Let's keep thinking of that vacation we're planning on taking and see what difference Netscape can make on our efforts, just as we did with the Microsoft Internet Explorer.

One of the things we were looking for was a set of maps that could help us navigate around the country. Click on the top menu of Directory, then on Internet Search. You'll come to a Web page that brings together many of the same Web search tools that we found with the Microsoft Internet Explorer, but these are at

```
http://home.netscape.com/home/internet-search.html
```

Use the very first search platform, which is the InfoSeek search engine as shown in Figure 7-7.

Search Infoseek by using the keywords "travel maps," and look at the list of results. If you want to try the search directly without running it by the menu, try typing in

```
http://www2.infoseek.com/Titles?qt=travel+maps
```

which will run the search through the InfoSeek server itself. We've

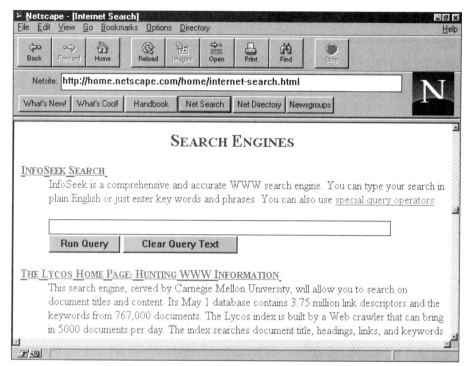

Figure 7-7
**Netscape's
Internet Search
Center**

found one item of interest for maps, and so let's add it to the list of bookmarks. Neat, it's a lot like the Microsoft Internet Explorer, but there's one important difference. In the Microsoft Internet Explorer, we could add bookmarks only one after the other, and as we saw, the list eventually scrolled off the screen as we hit the limit of 23. The others were in the folder for bookmarks but not on screen.

What Is a Bookmark?

A bookmark can be thought of as being just like the kind you might place between the pages of a book you read. It marks the place so that you can get back to it quickly. If you add too many bookmarks, getting back to one of them can be confusing and difficult. Netscape has a neat option under Bookmarks➤View Bookmarks that allows us to create a menu structure of bookmarks cataloged by topic. Let's give it a go and see how we can put this feature to work. With the Bookmarks List on screen and the list of bookmarks opened, click on the Edit button at the lower-right corner of the screen. The window enlarges to show a fuller set of options and functions, as in Figure 7-8.

To create menus within the Bookmarks menu, follow these steps after you've expanded the Editing menu:

1. On the left window pane, click once at the position you want the menu to be located. This moves the highlight to that location.

2. Click on New Header once.

3. The phrase "New Header" appears in the name field. Type the words **Travel Maps** and press (Enter).

4. The new menu name now appears with a dash to its left.

5. Repeat steps 1–4 as many times as necessary to add your menus.

Figure 7-8
Editing bookmarks and creating menus

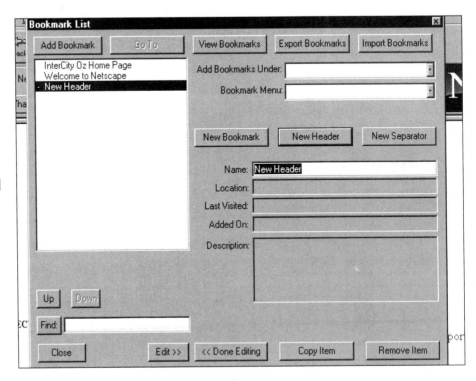

6. When you're finished, click on the Done Editing button to close the list.

What you've got now is a set of menus that can be used to store as many bookmarks as you have disk space for because you can now store sites under menus and not only at the top level. I found the process a bit tricky at first, but it's easy once you get the hang of it. After creating the Travel Maps, Campgrounds, and the Hotels submenus, I added the home page of my Internet provider as a test. The result was to place the newly added bookmark to the main screen list that you see in Figure 7-9 instead of under the Hotels submenu where I wanted it to go.

So what's the deal? Why didn't it put the bookmark in the proper place? Well, Netscape isn't that automatic or a mind reader, so you've got to tell it into which submenu to add these bookmarks. You do that by selecting Bookmarks➤View Bookmarks➤Edit➤ and the Add

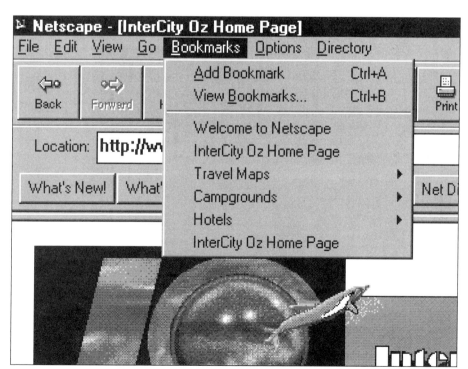

Figure 7-9
Adding a bookmark to a new submenu

Bookmarks under scroll box. You also need to tell the program, at the same Edit screen, to use the Hotels bookmark menu by selecting the Bookmark menu submenu. Now, and until you physically change this, all newly added bookmarks will be added under the Hotels menu. If you were to re-add the bookmark now, it would go into the correct location (Figure 7-10).

The Home Page

The home page is perhaps the most crucial element in a Web site. It's the one where you get your first impression of the site, and it provides the access points for the rest of the site. If the home page doesn't just jump right out at you and cause you to just say *Wow!* it may not be enough to get you to come back. Look for the home page to be the key element that guides and directs you around the Web.

Figure 7-10
Final appearance of the bookmarks

I say that because when you start adding bookmarks, your bookmarks can get rather large and your menu structures can get that way as well. Over time, it's not unreasonable to have one or two hundred bookmarks in your lists. Before I quit using NCSA Mosaic, I actively used around 60 in the normal course of surfing the Web. I used the same hierarchical presentation to manage my sites.

Jumps to Other Sites

Now that you've made it here after configuring Netscape, we can use the program a little more to plan more of that vacation we've been talking about. I saved the travel maps that I found earlier, so let's go back to them. The URL is

```
http://www2.infoseek.com/Titles?qt=travel+maps
```

in case you didn't write it down or save the URL. Go there and look at the selections we have! One site is at

```
http://nwlink.com/~travelbk
```

and appears to be what we've been looking for in terms of travel maps.

Let's return to InfoSeek by clicking on the Back button on the top left of the Button toolbar. In the campground search, I found several helpful references in the InfoSeek database by using the keyword "campground." Obviously, these searches are a bit better at solving our needs than were those we made with the Microsoft Internet Explorer. Does that mean that the Microsoft Internet Explorer is all bad? Of course not, it just means that Netscape's top-level menus are geared to different search engines than what we found earlier. Now that we've found the InfoSeek search engine, we could add that one to the Microsoft Internet Explorer's Favorites and use it there as well.

Frequented Locations— Bookmarks

The bookmarks that we've been adding and manipulating have served as our starting point as we've sought to use the data to the fullest. We'll next look at the bookmarks for our list of favorite places and see what we can do with them next. Add the Campground search to your bookmarks if you've not already done so.

CAUTION

If you forget which is the default menu where you added the new sites, your bookmark listing will not be as you desired.

If the undesirable condition of misplaced bookmarks occurs, not to fret. There's a way to fix it easy and cheap. The folks at Netscape had this in mind when they created the little buttons called Up and Down that appear when you click on Bookmarks➤View Bookmarks, and look at the bottom of the screen. Note that the site that is highlighted is the one that is moved up and down, so remember to cross the site by mouse first before moving anything!

Favorite Places

Let's go back to the InfoSeek search engine and not forget to change our default menu to the top level. If you added this site to your favorite places (which I keep referring the bookmarks to), just pull down the Bookmarks menu and click on it. As a matter of note, I created a submenu called Favorite Places just so I could have such a menu. I then moved the InfoSeek search engine so that it's under my Favorite Places. Since we're going to be looking at a few more search engines here, I made my Favorite Places the default menu. Now I can add these frequented places to my long list of favored sweet spots!

Getting back to the Internet Search home page, note that there are plenty of other search engines available. If you go to the bottom of the page, there's the CUSI search engine (Figure 7-11). Clicking on that page takes you to another fine Web resource.

If you set your default menu to the top level for the bookmarks, click on Bookmarks➤View Bookmarks➤Edit and then click on Add Bookmarks Under, choosing the place you want to keep the search engines; also do the same for the Bookmark menu. If you recall, the Bookmark menu sets the default menu that you'll see when you click on the Bookmarks top-level menu in Netscape. You can continue to build this listing to its fullest as you press onward.

Back and Forth——the Button Bar

Let's not forget about our old friend the Button bar, which holds the Back and Forward buttons. Remember those? They allow you to go one

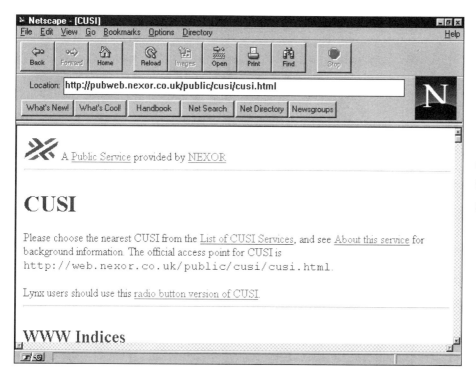

Figure 7-11
CUSI Web search engine

site back or forward from your present position if you've visited sites before or after the current one. If you click on the Go menu, what you see are the 10 most recently visited sites; the check is placed at the one you're at right now. Also notice the placement of the check—if it's between the 0 and the 9, then you can go both backward and forward to sites. If you're at the 0, then you're at the most current site and can only go backwards to sites visited in the past. This is one form of favorite places that I keep referring to, but it's not a permanent listing. When you exit Netscape, this list goes away and you start over as far as this history log is concerned.

Multiple Menus

The last subject for this section is the menus that you can build in the Bookmarks. Treat this as a serious venture. When you create these menus, think of them as you would a filing cabinet. What do you want to put into this cabinet? Do you think there'll be a lot of this kind of data? Are there logical divisions in this kind of data, such as specific kinds of Web sites? You can freely make menus within menus to your heart's content, but the process can quickly get out of hand and very complicated if you don't really think about these menus. It's well worth sitting down with a pencil and paper planning this part of your Web crawling.

Here's a suggested starting menu structure that I've developed and used for a few years:

Top Level
Favorite Sites
    Web Search Engines
    FAQs
    NCSA Home Page
    Gopher at Univ. of Minnesota
FTP Sites
    SunSite at UNC (`ftp://sunsite.unc.edu`)

NCSA Home site (`ftp://ftp.ncsa.uiuc.edu`)
InterNIC (`ftp.internic.net`)

and the list could go on, but it'd take several pages. The gist of it is that you ought to think out the structure of your menus before creating them. It'll save you immensely in not having to move all of those saved sites later. If there is a downside to Netscape, the ease with which you can create tons of menus is it, but I'll live with it.

Accessory Applications

Previously, we talked about the many helper applications that you could use while surfing the Web and getting into more trouble. Well, let's take a look at some of those and how Netscape will use them, and how to set them up. For this discussion, we're going to get an HTML viewer, configure helper applications to handle ZIP archives, and also deal with rich text format documents.

Where to Get Those Applications

Fire up Netscape, and let's head off to get the viewer for HTML documents. First, however, we need the unzip program if you've not gotten one by now. We'll use Netscape to navigate to the

```
ftp://nic.switch.ch/mirror/win3/util
```

location, where we'll download the file called HTMLED10.ZIP to whatever directory you've specified. That done, let's configure your unzipper in Netscape to handle this newly downloaded archive. I'm assuming that by now you've either acquired an unzip utility or are ready to go download one. Go to the

```
gopher://gopher.tc.umn.edu
```

site with Netscape and use Archie. This will be a good test for you if you don't have the unzip program. PKUNZIP can be found all over the Internet.

Setup and Use

With this acquisition of the files required, let's configure the first thing that we'll need, and that's the unzip program. If you downloaded the PKUNZIP self-extracting archive, extract it and place it to wherever you want. On my system, it's in the C:\DOS\UTILS directory as PKUNZIP.EXE. To set this up, click on Options➤Preferences, click on the scroll box, and choose Helper Applications. Scroll downward until you find the Extensions listing for "application/x-zip-compressed" and click on that item once (Figure 7-12). Next, click on the Launch Application radio button in the Action section. If you don't know the fully qualified

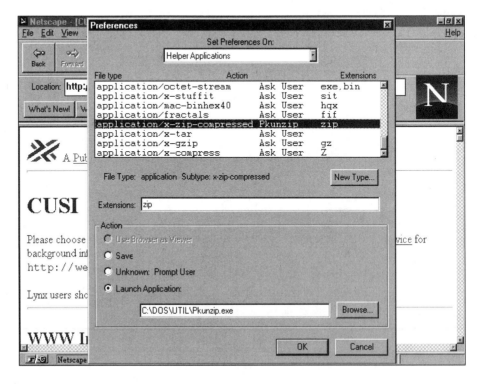

Figure 7-12
Adding a helper application

path for the unzip program, then use the Browse feature to find the program and click it into the field.

With this unzip application in place, when Netscape gets a ZIP archive you can unzip it seamlessly in place and have it working very shortly as you'll see. Now, we'll go get the HTML viewer I promised. Use the URL

```
ftp://nic.switch.ch/mirror/win3/util
```

and look for the file we mentioned earlier, `HTMLED10.ZIP`. When this application downloads, Netscape sees that it's a ZIP file and activates my copy of PKUNZIP, automatically unzipping the program to the location specified in my Preferences for the temporary directory. With that done, move the extracted files to a more permanent location and repeat the above steps we did for the ZIP program, but this time look in the extensions section of the Helper Applications part for the HTML, MTDL, and HTM extensions and specify the HTMLED executable. Viola! You can now view the Web pages source code and see how the gurus of the Web do it.

The last thing we'll configure is a resident application to look at rich text format files; I use Microsoft Word for Windows. However, if you don't use it or AMI Pro or any of the other word processors that support RTF files, take heart in that Windows 95 has a small program called Wordpad that supports RTF files just as Winword does. It's not as full-featured as Winword obviously, but it's a welcome addition to Windows 95. It's part way between the Notepad applet and Winword in functionality. Let's repeat the same process once more to add a helper application, but this time look for the RTF file extension—now you'll most definitely have to use the Browse function to find the application. You could just use Wordpad by going to the drive where Windows 95 is installed and look first in the Program Files directory and then in Accessories for the file called `WORDPAD.EXE`. It should be about 179K bytes.

Summary

This chapter concludes our most direct use of the Web, and of the utilities and browsers that make access to the Web what is and what it can be to us. We've seen how a full-featured and functional Web browser like Netscape can make our lives easier and simpler on the Web. As you begin wandering around cyberspace, talk to those around you and find out what browser they're using, and why. You'll get a good comparison across the board of the functions they use, and why and how much they use them. Compare this to what you've done in this and Chapter 6, and you'll get a better feel for what you really want out of the Web and how Netscape stacks up to other browsers as well. In Chapter 8, we'll explore parts of the Microsoft Internet Connection and the Microsoft Network as the two services relate to our online activities, and see how they can serve us on the Web. See you in Chapter 8!

The Microsoft Network and Its Own Internet Goodies

We've spent a goodly amount of time in this book talking about the Microsoft Internet Explorer and how we can use it along with a few more Internet and Web tools to peak efficiency to plunder the depths of cyberspace. We set up MSN and the Microsoft Internet Explorer along with everything else we could think of, and now it's time to backtrack just a little bit to where it all started, and that's with the Microsoft Network itself along with its related Internet services.

In this chapter, you'll learn all about:

- ◆ E-mail and the Microsoft Network
- ◆ Internet Newsgroups and the Microsoft Network
- ◆ MSN's Online Internet Resources

E-Mail and MSN

When you installed Windows 95 and subsequently installed the Microsoft Network, you installed the baseline software required for electronic mail, or e-mail for short, for both the MSN system and the Internet as a whole. This section will deal exclusively with setting up the Microsoft Network, your Internet e-mail account and needs if any, and other e-mail services such as the CompuServe Information Service (CIS for short). We'll include a section on using and setting up your address book, MS Exchange client, and more.

Your Address

Your address is just as unique as you are, and as your home street address is as well. There can never be two of the same address, and there can never be two for the same account as well. There's been plenty of talk on MSN about the possibility of having four users sharing the resources of a single account. MSN designers purposely declined to provide for such accounts as they believed them to be unfeasible in the long run.

You see, MSN doesn't differentiate between users—it has one set of user data files for each installation account, accessible through the personal address book (Figure 8-1). These files aren't a big problem to

Figure 8-1
Your personal address book and data

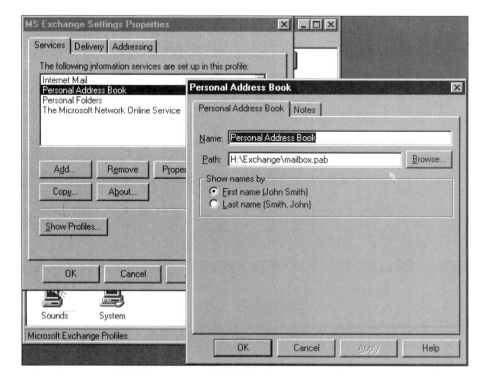

create and maintain; in fact, Windows 95's Exchange client has all the tools handy to do just that. The repercussions come from the legal and financial arena.

When you log on to MSN and don't exchange sets of data files, all the data for everyone who uses your computer are mixed into the same data files (which we'll look at in more detail later). The most important fact about shared accounts is that the owner of the account, meaning the person who created the account, is wholly and completely responsible for the financial and legal issues of the account. Even though you can specify different address books and data file sets, the user that created the account has his or her name attached to it directly. If someone using the account goes online and starts flaming or verbally abusing someone, guess who is held responsible for the actions? Yes, *you!*—the owner of the account.

WARNING

The primary owner of the account is totally responsible for the account and those that may use it. Be careful about who you let use it, and change your password every 30 days at a minimum! You can change it by going on-line, clicking on Tools and then on Password, and following the instructions.

It's for these and other ancillary reasons that MSN sanctions the one-account-per-user system of membership. Forget about the membership fee, if any will be levied, and think about these issues. It's worth it in the long run to give everyone separate accounts. As Figure 8-2 shows, you can easily log on under any user name and password you choose, even from a single PC with Windows 95.

All you have to do is change the user name and password when you go to connect. If several MSN members are going to use the same physical computer, *do not* check the Remember My Password radio

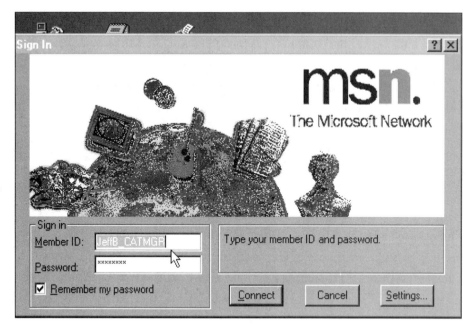

Figure 8-2
Logging in as a different user than the default

button. Not doing so prevents each user from attempting to log on with his or her user ID and your password, which won't work at all. It'll force each user to enter in his or her user ID and password each time.

Your Address Book

Your address book is a real work of art, courtesy of Microsoft. This one beats them all as far as I can see! Take a look at Figure 8-3, and we'll go over a few things about it. Remember, though, that it's geared to the thinking of the normal address book user, with a generous dose of Microsoft's planning in mind. Access your address book by going online to MSN and starting e-mail. At the Inbox, click on Tools, then on Address Book (Ctrl+Shift+B), and last on Show names from the scroll box so you can select an address book. It could be the main MSN address book or your personal one. With that name highlighted, right click on (yes, the right mouse button really does something!) the name and choose the Properties tab to get the screen shown in Figure 8-3.

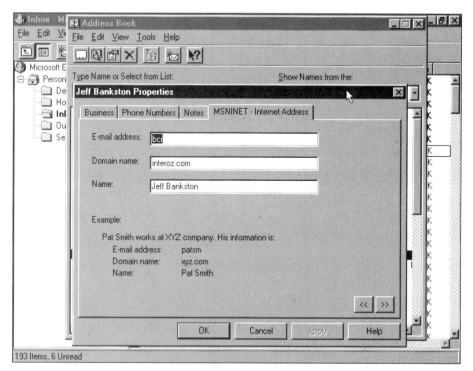

Figure 8-3
**Properties of
your personal
address book
entries**

Most address books have your service's online ID, of course, along with perhaps a few other details about your account. But, look at this one! There's a Properties tab for truly personal items, a place for online interests, a rather large place to keep notes under the Notes tab, and three separate entries for your MSN goodies. Very much a welcome relief to say the least!

The MS Exchange and E-Mail

All of this and more is controlled through a new feature in Windows 95 called the Exchange client. Exchange is the central control for e-mail connectivity between you and several sources. On the back end of MSN, there are several network servers dedicated to the task of getting your e-mail from here to there in one piece, and in time and not lost in someone's trash can. I've watched Exchange mature all through the beta process, and it's a pleasure to watch Microsoft work a piece of clay into a pottery object of functionality and beauty.

The end result is a technology tool set that enables you to exchange mail with various systems seamlessly so that you'll never be aware of the underlying differences between the services. After all, you've got to select a service to deliver the mail no matter what kind of mail you send, paper or electronic. To see the flexibility I'm speaking of, go to Start➤Control Panel➤Mail and Fax, and also look at Figure 8-4 to see how I've got my system configured for multiple mail accounts.

It's here that you can see the centralization of the Exchange client. In my case, I have the Internet Mail and my own MSN E-mail configured. It's here that I could add my CompuServe account if I wanted to, but I don't have room to do so.

Configuring the Exchange

Looking at the same figure as a reference point, single-click on Personal Address Book and then click on Properties to look at your address book

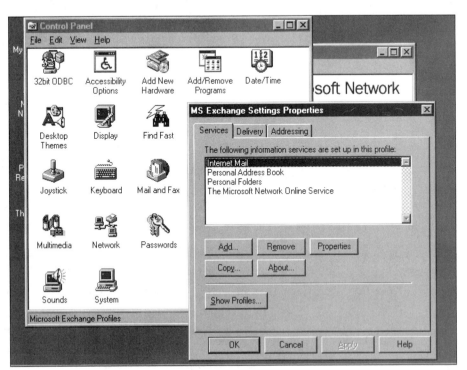

Figure 8-4
Basic Exchange functions

for a minute (Figure 8-5). This is where you can modify your personal data files, change their location, and add a ton of notes to any of them to describe what it's about.

Neat, yes? I think so! And I'm sure that when you start using it, you'll agree. You can use any of the other tabs to personalize your e-mail and Exchange settings to suit almost any need. Go back to the Exchange Inbox, and then click on Tools≻Options, click on the General tab, and look at the third information section down titled When Starting Microsoft Exchange. There's a radio button that says Always use this profile. Click on this if you've added a profile as I've done, and you'll see how you can use different connection settings for different occasions! Another really neat trick of the new Microsoft Exchange client brought to you by Microsoft Corporation and the Microsoft Network. What a winning combination! If I had another hundred pages, I could show you some neat things about MSN and the Exchange, but another fine Prima

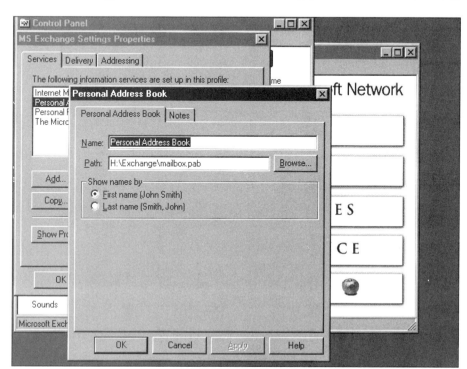

Figure 8-5
Properties of your personal address book

book will cover that aspect of MSN, so for the moment let's send a sample e-mail message to someone to demonstrate the power and flexibility of the Exchange client in Windows 95.

All the way back to the top of MSN, click on the E-mail banner and it'll take you to the Inbox—Microsoft Exchange where you'll see something closely resembling Figure 8-6.

It's here that all e-mail functions are carried out. Notice the personal folders at the upper-left corner of the screen. They are typical for an e-mail system:

◆ **Deleted Items**—Keeps a copy of every message that I've deleted just in case.

◆ **Inbox**—Just that, where my new incoming mail is stored for me until I can get to it. Unread messages are placed there in bold text to differentiate them from old stuff.

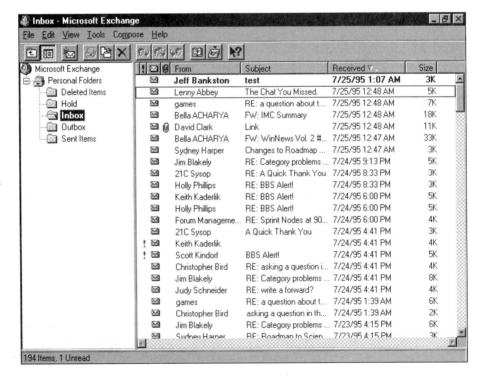

Figure 8-6
The Exchange's Inbox

◆   **Outbox**—Holds all of my e-mail ready to send out until I can log on and send it. If I'm already online, there's an option that says to queue up all mail until I'm ready to send it out.

◆   **Sent Items**—Where I store a copy of everything I send out for my own records. Currently at 483 messages for this month.

To send out a new e-mail message, follow these steps:

1.   Click on Compose.
2.   Click on New Message ($\boxed{\text{Ctrl}}$+$\boxed{\text{N}}$).
3.   You'll get a very detailed screen as in Figure 8-7.
4.   The cursor is flashing in the data field for the To: block awaiting a recipient's address. Click on the To: button.
5.   Your personal address book is displayed ready for you to select an address. Scroll down or begin typing a name. If the name is not in the personal address book, then click on the scroll box in the upper-right corner to bring up the Microsoft Network address book to select names.
6.   If you're not sure about the name in the address book, highlight the name and then click on Properties to see if this is the person you're looking for.

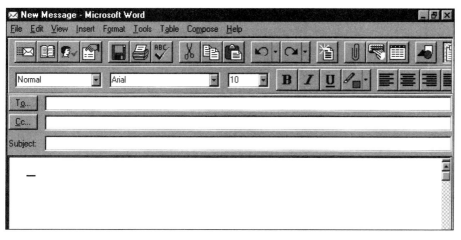

Figure 8-7
Composing a new e-mail message

7. Select the To: (primary recipient) plus the Cc: (any others) if you have any.

8. Click on the Subject field and enter the subject of the message.

9. Tab down to the body of the message and compose it.

10. Click on the yellow envelope button to send it.

What could be easier? As you're looking at that screen composing the e-mail, keep in mind that all of the options and preferences and toolbars that you see constitute a miniature word processor in itself. If you've ever used Word for Windows, you'd swear it had some striking resemblance to it! I'll leave that for you to decide.

A Little More about Newsgroups

Let's take one final look at the newsgroups and how we can use them in the Microsoft Network. During the beta phase of the project, newsgroups on MSN were a read-only function in which the MSN member could only see what was there and could not reply to a Usenet post. Another issue with newsgroups were the ever-present groups in which adult content was present. Microsoft has taken a credible step toward adult content and dealing with minors getting their hands on such matter. This section will address this and other concerns that newsgroups bring to light.

So You Want to Participate?

Do you remember back when you had the opportunity to participate in your first school play, or spelling bee? It was a bit scary, wasn't it? Sure it was, as you've never done such a thing before. You were never sure if you'd say the right thing at the right moment lest you look the part of a fool. The same thing probably occurred when you went out on your first date. What do you say, or do, or how do you act?

Newsgroups can have the same overall effect, but worse in that your post on a newsgroup goes before *millions* of readers. Yes, I said *millions* of people. It's estimated that as many as 40 million people make use of one aspect or another of the Internet, and one fourth of these people read some kind of news to catch up on events, gossip, or just to relax with their favorite group.

Let's take a look at some of the newsgroups that are available on MSN. Start your connection to MSN, if you're not already on it, and go to the top level of MSN as you normally do, but this time select Categories. For this discussion, let's head off to the Home and Family category, where we'll check up on the newsgroups. Look at the top of Home and Family, and you'll see a folder for the topic of Related Internet Newsgroups. Double-click on that and you'll get to the newsgroups that deal with some aspect of Home and Family topics (Figure 8-8).

There's one icon that you should pay particular attention to, and that's the one titled Newsgroups and Full Access Information. This is an

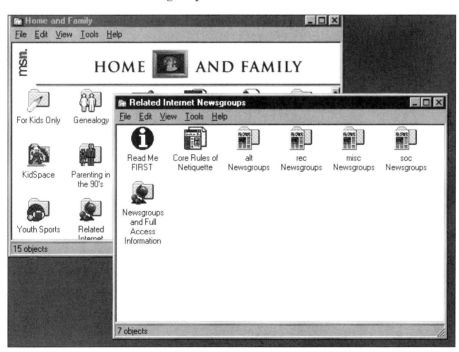

Figure 8-8
Home and Family newsgroups

electronic form, or *e-form* for short, that you'll have to fill out to get full access to all of the newsgroups, including the adult content areas. MSN believes in free speech, but that the younger members shouldn't get their hands on the wrong messages before their time. MSN also prohibits sleazy pictures or pornographic material of any type or origin from the service. Since MSN can't regulate what's on the newsgroups, and they don't want to do that anyhow, the adult e-form access request is the best option.

Don't get the idea that MSN administrators ever want to be in that position of censor, because I suspect they don't, but they accept that some material is best left out of the hands of minors until they come of age or their parents say otherwise. The e-form allows you to attest that you are over 18 and are aware of the kind of content that may appear in the newsgroups (Figure 8-9). We spoke of questions of etiquette and language back in Chapter 3, and we'll return to the topic soon, but next let's look at the news feed itself.

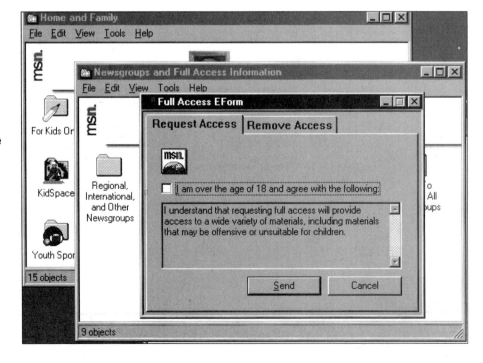

Figure 8-9
Completing the e-form to request full newsgroups access

Direct Access to News Feeds

Remember back when we were using the Microsoft Internet Explorer and Netscape, and we accessed the newsgroups? We had to specify a server for our newsgroups reader (we used WinVN once) and then subscribe to the newsgroups. Update the news headers, update the subscription list, and there we were online with the news not only from the raw news servers themselves but also from sources such as Gopher at the University of Minnesota. On MSN, no such configurations are required.

If you double-click on the `rec.scouting` group that we saw in the Home and Family newsgroups access screen, you get the full news feed as seen in Figure 8-10:

Isn't this neat? Sure it is, but with one minor problem—it's a read-only newsgroup! So how are we supposed to reply to a message now that we've gotten up the nerve to reply to one? I was informed that MSN will have full newsgroups access enabled by launch time so that you can

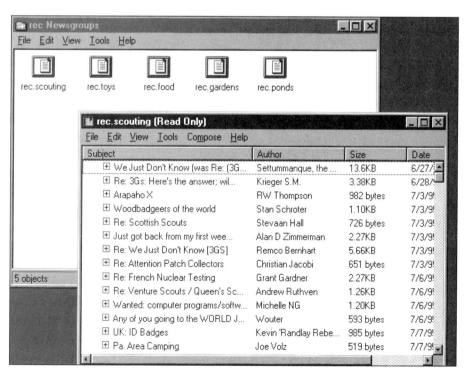

Figure 8-10
Full news access to rec.scouting

carry on regular news access just as we did on the Web newsreader in the last chapter.

TIP

Newsgroups here at the forum level and all across MSN are the exact same groups that you've seen when we were surfing the Web in previous chapters. If, for some reason, news here doesn't work just right, you can always use the Microsoft Internet Explorer to go back to the Internet and get the news.

This news that you've seen here is nearly exactly the same as the newsgroups that you saw on the Internet in its pure form with WinVN news reader, except that here on MSN it's a bit better formatted than on the Internet.

Adult Tokens and Protection

Okay, so we've finally gotten to this question of the adult tokens and what they're all about. A *token* is a rite of passage. In the networking world, everything in a multiuser computing environment consists of rights and privileges afforded the users by the network administrator commensurate with what they need to do or have the need to see. Tokens are a way to grant access to, or deny access from, users or groups of users for the purpose of system control. Your PC, for instance, has a system of controls called file attributes. They include *system*, *read-only*, *hidden*, and *archive*. In the networking world, add such attributes as those in Table 8-1.

Table 8-1
File Attributes in a Networking Environment

Attribute	Purpose
Sharable	Shares files, directories, or drives
Transactional	Pertains to online billing purposes
Searchable	Allows searching of the drive or directory
World	Gives access to everyone
Modifiable	Can be changed

These are but a few of the many types of file attributes in any given network system. By giving permissions, or tokens, to any one user or a group of users, the network administrator can partially or completely grant or deny access to any part of a network. This is no less true for MSN. With the newsgroups blocked off by default, you have to request access to the, ah, more sensitive areas of the Internet. MSN isn't being a censor at all, just protecting its membership from less than desirable material that some find offensive. Just as easily as you request and get access, you can remove access by using the same e-form.

MSN's Online Internet Resources

This last aspect of Internet life with MSN will show you all about how MSN itself supports its users with its own online resources of a wide variety. You've seen the newsgroups above, so let's explore the possibilities with third-party resources and with MSN's own resources.

The Core Rules of Netiquette

Among the most prevalent of the Internet's problems to date are the constant culture clashes, Usenet flame wars, and mail floods that occur from time to time. These problems frequently are the result of differences in opinion or miscommunication arising from the limitations of the medium. It's easy to mistake the written word for something that it's not intended to be.

For this and other reasons, a system of signals called *emoticons*, or emotional icons, came into being a very long time ago. A long list of these can be found in many places, but I want to cite a few for you. When you look at these, turn your head so your left ear is down to the floor and you're looking at the page sideways:

`: -)`	A smiley face
`8 -)`	A smiley face, but with glasses
`: -(`	A frown.
`<g>`	A grin
`<vbg>`	A very big grin!
`ROF,L`	Rolling on the floor, laughing
`tes^h^h^H^g6fting`	Heckling someone

These are a few examples. I once saw a list of over three pages of such laughables. Matters can get downright ridiculous, with examples like "roflafootc," which translates to "rolling on the floor laughing after falling out of the chair." The cause of this one was probably some world-class tomfoolery.

Although you may be able to express yourself clearly, try using an emoticon here and there to underscore your touch of irony or humor. When that's not possible, or you just don't want to, take some time to study an MSN document called "The Core Rules of Netiquette." This includes a basic set of 10 rules that you can enhance your online activities by following. Take off to the Internet Center from the Categories main screen and then click on something called *The Core Rules of Netiquette*, which is an excerpt from a fine book by Virginia Shea and Albion Press that talks a lot about how to behave on the Internet. We talked about that subject a bit in Chapter 3, but take a look at the opening screen shown in Figure 8-11 and read each of these *rules* (not formal rules, but commonsense rules) carefully.

When you're actually online, you can click on the gray buttons to the left side of any rule to get a more detailed presentation of that rule and what it's about. Very worthwhile reading.

The Albion Press on MSN

One of the online presences on the Internet and MSN for books is Albion Press, reached via the go word **Netiquette** on MSN (Figure 8-12). The center includes the Albion Channel, where you'll find several books that you can order bound and printed or read online on MSN. There are an Online Bookfair, a Newbees forum, and the Doors to CyberSpace, where

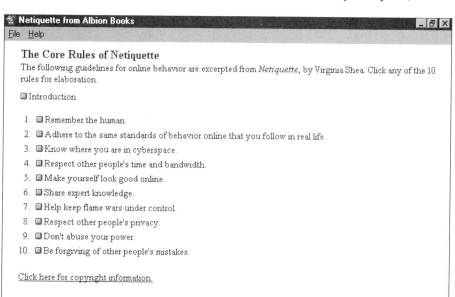

Figure 8-11
The Core Rules of Netiquette (Screen shot with permission of Albion Press, copyright Albion Press, all rights reserved.)

you're sure to get more information about Albion and MSN. You can also get to the Netiquette Center by going to The Internet Center, clicking on *The Core Rules of Netiquette*, and then going to the bottom of the set of rules. Clicking in the little gray box in the lower left corner takes you to the Netiquette Center, as shown in Figure 8-12.

The Internet Center

The last three sections of this chapter deal with the Internet Center on MSN (Figure 8-13). This is where you can get support on all kinds of Internet and MSN issues. The center includes chat rooms, file libraries, the Internet Café, where you can hang out with Internet types, another copy of the Core Rules of Netiquette, a suggestion box, means to request full newsgroup access, and more. From the main MSN sign-on screen, click on Categories➤The Internet Center, and you're there.

Figure 8-12
**The Netiquette
Center**

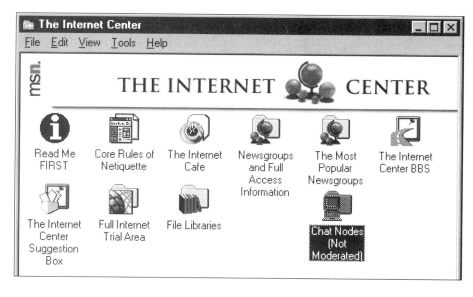

Figure 8-13
The Internet Center

NOTE

If you start using the Internet and find it tough going, always remember that you've got the Internet Café and the Internet Suggestion Box on MSN. These two functions provide the user with a wealth of information and assistance to get you going.

Access to Newsgroups

Head off to the Newsgroups and Full Access Information folder, where I want you to look at the Regional, Int'l and Other Newsgroups folder. When you open it, stand back! A the time of this writing, there are 154 newsgroup categories listed (Figure 8-14 includes a sample). These range from U.S. domestic to international flavors reflecting European and Asian interests. Do try to remember that MSN is an international service with all kinds of topics and sights to see. Please try to be open-minded as you breeze through MSN.

Opening one of these newsgroups will get you the news in that country's native dialect, or the closest possible. It's kind of nice to be able

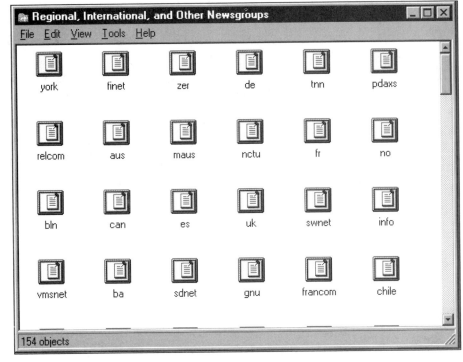

Figure 8-14
Massive numbers of newsgroups on MSN

to sample so much of the world around us at the touch of a mouse button, wouldn't you agree?

The Internet Café

Let's take off back to the top of the Internet Support Center and go to the Internet Café to see what's hopping. It could be general discussion, or a talk hosted by the forum manager, or just a free-for-all loose chat (Figure 8-15). You'll notice the names of the visitors in the right-hand windowpane, and you can send your messages by way of the compose windowpane at the bottom of the screen. If you look in the lower-right corner, you'll see just how many people are in this chat right now.

Each chat room has a limit of users, with most being set to 50. During special events, it's not unreasonable to have 250 guests online in the chat room at once. During one special phase of the MSN beta, one chat room had around 400 users in it before it broke and caused all sorts

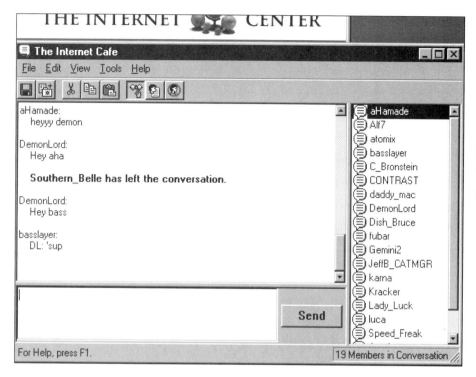

**Figure 8-15
The Internet
Café chat room**

of problems. At the time that we went into the Internet Café, there was no host. You'll recognize hosts by the gavel they carry just like a judge's gavel. The purpose of the gavel is to allow the host to silence the loudmouth or unruly chat visitor. They're silenced by virtue of having the shades put on them so that they can only look on at what's transpiring and can't talk until the host removes the shades or they leave and come back. At that time, the host can see if they're going to behave or boink them again!

The Chat Nodes

The next places to chat we can visit are the unmoderated rooms that are tables for two, three, or four persons (Figure 8-16). These are small chats where you and a few friends can huddle up and have at it much like at the old soda fountain store with its small booths. When I say unmoderated, I mean that there's no host present to run the show and

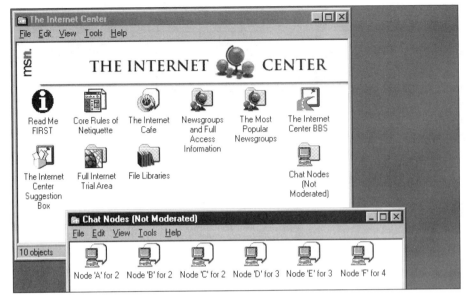

Figure 8-16
Chat rooms for small numbers, unmoderated

keep law and order. If someone gets out of hand, your only recourse is to fight back, calm him down, or leave.

The Internet Center File Libraries

The last thing I'd like to discuss about the Internet Center is the File Libraries, where you can download a few of the same files that we obtained earlier via the Microsoft Internet Explorer. Although the selection of files is limited as of this writing, it may be substantial by the time you read this. From the Internet Center, click on the File Libraries to begin this last part of our journey for this chapter (Figure 8-17).

You'll notice there's a place to *upload* your files, and a place to *download* files. You upload files to MSN for others to use, and you download files to your machine to use yourself. Click on the Upload Library first so you can see how to submit files. You can submit a file by following the following steps from there (Figure 8-18):

1.   Compose a new message just as you would for e-mail. Make the message a very concise description of what the file does.

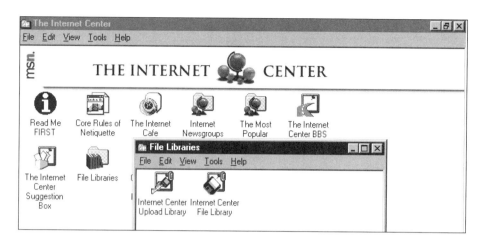

Figure 8-17
**The Internet
Center File
Libraries**

2.   When you've finished composing the message, click on the paper
clip on the right side of the toolbar. This brings up the Insert File
search menu. Navigate and find the file you wish to upload, and
click on Okay. Click on the little yellow envelope on the far left
of the toolbar to send the message and upload the file.

Downloading a file is just like reading a message; the only difference
is that the message has a file attached to it. Exit the Upload Library,
and go to the Download Library, which is read-only (Figure 8-19).
Double-click on any of the messages listed. Notice the paper clip
signifying an attached file to the message.

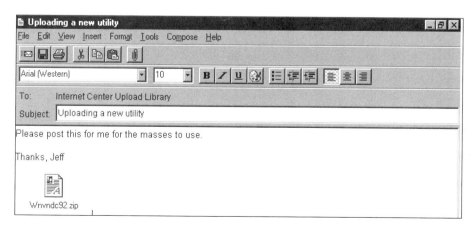

Figure 8-18
Uploading a file

Double-click on the attached file icon and choose to either just download the file or download and open it. Opening a file downloads as well as extracts it if you have an extractor handy. That's all there is to it. Just look in your Program Files>Transferred Files for the newly downloaded file.

Summary

This chapter has extended your Internet and Web surfing prowess as you had fun exploring and learning a new tool along with its helper applications. We've learned a little about the Microsoft Exchange, though not enough to be really dangerous. We've learned that it's a central tool set for messaging between systems. We saw how we can participate in newsgroups directly on MSN. Last, we found out that MSN has an Internet Center that serves us, the users, in getting the most for our dollar on MSN and the Internet. In Chapter 9, we'll learn a great deal about MSN itself, the whys and wherefores of the service, and how it's laid out to benefit us the most. See you there!

Figure 8-19
Downloading a file

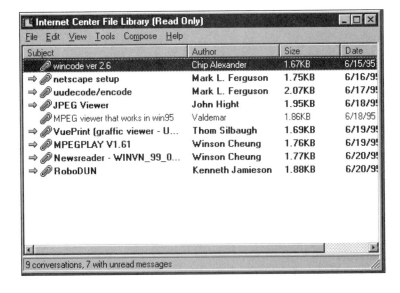

A Broader View of The Microsoft Network

In this final chapter of the MSN Saga, we'll take a minute to take in a more general view of the Microsoft Network. We're not going to get really deep in theory or thought; we'll just bounce a few ideas and topics around.

In this chapter, you'll gain some further general background on MSN and learn about:

- Working at home
- Something for the kids
- Research and reference materials
- One more aspect of chats
- Special events
- A word about words

The Basic Philosophy

The basic philosophy of the Microsoft Network lies in building the MSN community, sharing information, and looking to the overall education of the members. Each member has a unique set of interests and expectations of what to see and find from MSN, and what he or she can give in return to others around them on the service. Let's look at a few of these areas of interest, and see how they may contribute to navigation of MSN.

A Compelling Reason

One of the reasons, if not the biggest reason, that members will like MSN is that you can *point-and-shoot* your way to almost everything on the service. It's a piece of cake to get around MSN, and while doing so you'll see some of the most interesting aspects of online connectivity that have ever been around. As you may know, CompuServe, Prodigy, and America Online all have Windows-based navigational programs that make getting around these services easy as well. One thing about MSN that differentiates it from the other services is that you can connect to MSN and take advantage of all these features in one logon:

- Complete e-mail to MSN and the Internet
- Constant chat sessions, special events daily and weekly, and group auditoriums
- Interesting and vital material relevant to almost every aspect of computing and personal life
- Point-and-shoot access to the system; you don't have to remember any textual commands to get anywhere!
- Multimedia presentations and viewers
- Online MSN staff whom you can reach almost 100 percent of the time
- Multifunction system operation; you can have as many chats, e-mail messages, or forums on your screen as you have screen space and processing horsepower

Most of the current services have many of these features and functions now, with many of the rest in testing and soon to be fully operational. The point is that MSN has these things now, and it's actively awaiting your beck and call. The last bulleted item is a very important one: At times while testing the service, I've thought of how I could test my own computer to see what kind of a workload it is capable of in conjunction with a system like this. Well, Figure 9-1 shows exactly what you can do!—at least on a 486DX2/66 with 16MB of RAM and a 14.4K baud modem. Response time was about five seconds from MSN task to MSN task as I was moving around the screens and doing other things in between MSN requests.

Look carefully at how many screens of MSN content that I have open at once, and note that each is doing something and not just sitting idle. The chats are running while I'm checking e-mail and looking at two BBSs at the same time. Well, not simultaneously, but all are active on my PC at once. Because each is in a separate window, I can carry on as many or as few conversations as I desire with the click of a mouse button. Truly a compelling reason.

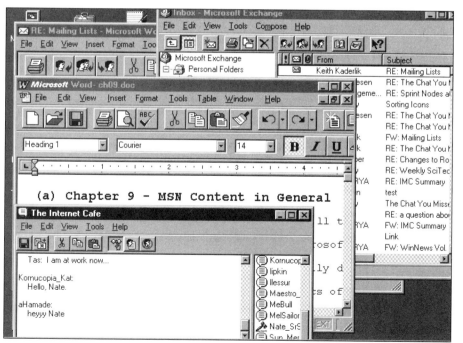

Figure 9-1
Pushing MSN to the upper limits

The GUI Connection

As I said before, the graphical user interface (GUI) element of the service is a positive and moving experience for those folks who have never really used it or come to appreciate the nature of the beast. "Graphical" means that you don't need to know, or care about, the underlying aspects of MSN unless you just want to. Take a look at Figure 9-2 and ask yourself "How does this thing work?" The next thing you can do for yourself is ask "Does it matter?"

Notice the change of the mouse arrow that signifies that you've positioned it over a hotspot in the document. This is your sign that you can click on the location and bring up that topic, as in Figure 9-3. When you click on it, you'll get a message that informs you that the online viewer process is starting. MSN has a multimedia viewer that enables this kind of compelling content to be presented to the member.

Favorite Places

One of my favorite places is Favorite Places. When you start up MSN, the main screen comes to life, letting you pick from five options:

Figure 9-2
Starting the
MSN Today
viewer

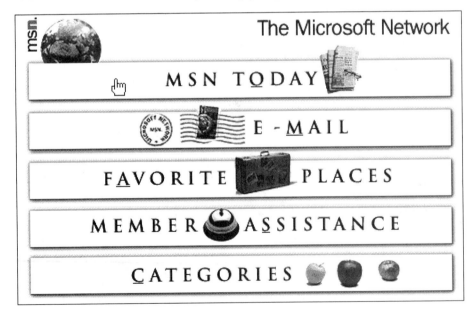

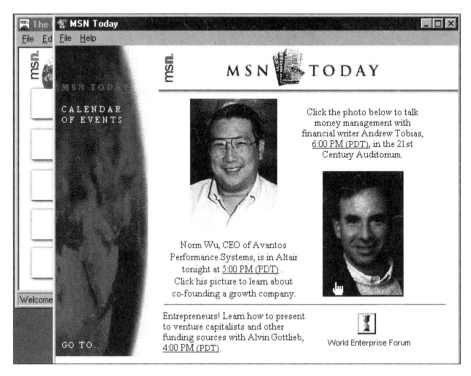

Figure 9-3
Starting the
multimedia
viewer

◆　**MSN Today**—Learn about the most current events.

◆　**E-mail**—Well, it handles your e-mail!

◆　**Favorite Places**—Save your most frequently visited places.

◆　**Member Assistance**—Get help when you need it.

◆　**Categories**—This is the gateway to the interest areas.

If you move your mouse to position it over the Favorite Places banner, notice how the mouse turns into a little hand pointing to the subject. It's MSN's way of saying "Hey, click on me!" to get there. Click on Favorite Places, and you'll see a screen like Figure 9-4, which shows you my icons of favored and most frequently visited topics.

As we get farther into this chapter, I'll show you how to add content here, and then how to refer to it.

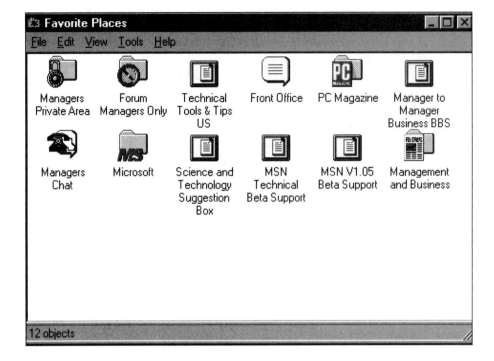

Hotspots and Viewers

I mentioned the hotspot earlier for Favorite Places and how to recognize it. As you go through the rest of MSN, you'll likely cross paths with many other such links, but with a different flair. Adding a topic to the Favorite Places folder works about 99 percent of the time, but the other one percent where it doesn't will place you in an interesting situation. Instead of something being added to Favorite Places, it'll have to be placed upon your desktop! A link for Favorite Places couldn't be created because of special conditions, such as *download and run* documents in which you download the document just as you would any other file, but in this case the document's associated application is executed to see the contents of the document. Some of these types of situations can't be placed into Favorite Places but rather must be located on the desktop itself.

Member Assistance——How to Get Help

Getting help is one of the most essential elements of any online service, and MSN is no exception. There are going to be the usual issues about billing, general account information, deleting accounts, and exactly what a member can do at times. There are several methods of delivery that members can use to get the help that they need. One of these is the 800 number for MSN Customer Service, 1-800-386-5550 during normal hours. If you can get online, use the MSN Member Assistance area (Figure 9-5), which is reached via the fourth item from the top at the main MSN sign-on screen. Clicking on the Member Assistance banner takes you to the designated support center. Notice the cute little bell on the banner for the top level of MSN. This area is the first place you should visit if you have concerns or problems with your account, or if you just need basic help.

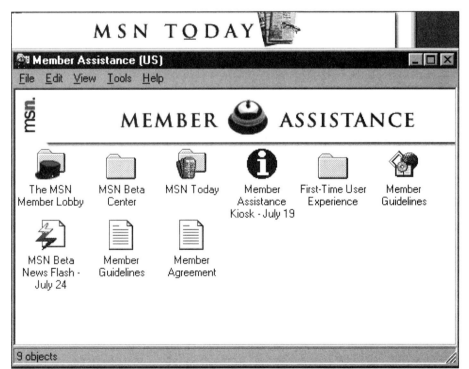

Figure 9-5
The MSN
Member
Assistance
Center

Home and Family

There's a growing trend across the country for folks to work at home. To that end, the need for additional support and services is growing faster than some experts originally had anticipated. MSN addresses that need by providing a unique forum called Home and Family, which we'll look at next.

Working at Home

As you explore the forum (Figure 9-6), take a look at some of the topics in the second row here, which will give you an idea of what this topic is all about. Especially notable are the two BBSs titled Work-At-Home Dads and Working Mothers that address issues usually approached the other way around. It used to be Dad at the office and Mom at home working, but these roles have been steadily reversing in magnitude in the recent years. These two areas are very popular lately with the middle-aged work force as many companies scale down and workers find themselves laid off with no way to be retrained to the degree required for a new career at age 40.

Figure 9-6
The Home and Family category

The Small Office/Home Office forum goes hand in hand with the Home and Family Forum. Click on Places of Interest and then on the SOHO forum. If you plan on working at home, or are currently doing so, this is the place for you! Follow the trail to the SOHO area and look at the topics that that are covered (Figure 9-7). Just about every aspect of working at home is covered here.

Speaking more of business in general, you may want to visit the Business and Finance category (Figure 9-8) which, as its name implies, deals with the many aspects of money. There are a few forums there that delve into working at home; they include Venture and Entrepreneur, which is a really neat place to learn about investment money, your business, and how you may be able to bring them together.

Telecomputing

Hand in hand with the SOHO paradigm is the fact that you'll need to be connected to perform many of your tasks. As a very active online user myself, I use four phone lines on a daily basis to perform my own work-

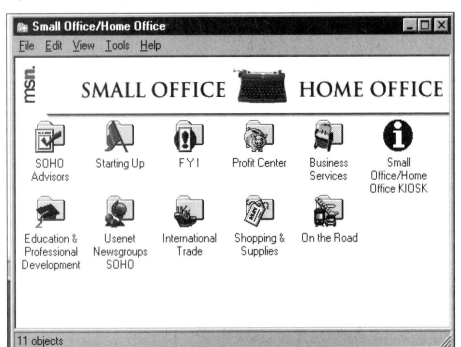

**Figure 9-7
The Small
Office/Home
Office forum**

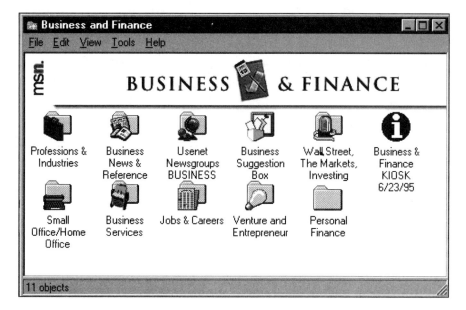

Figure 9-8
The Business and Finance category

at-home tasks. One line is for our regular house phone, the second, for the business phone, the third, for the dedicated data modem, and the fourth, for the fax/modem. (What's a business without a fax?) In a pinch, I can route any of my calls, data or voice, to any of the phone lines to ensure that I stay connected unless our local telco gets out of hand again. (Figure 9-9 suggests how.) The key to simplicity here is using standard phone jacks and phone cords with modular plugs at each end.

To handle these needs, hop over to the Computer Telephony forum, which can be found under the Computers and Software category, and then go to the Networks and Communications subcategory. As MSN matures more and more, these interesting topics will become more prolific. Related topics such as the Electronics and the Engineering forums that can be found under the Science & Technology category (described later in this chapter) will assist you in your quest for good phone lines.

Share and Share Alike

Once again, I'd like to reiterate one of the prime objectives of MSN, and that's building the MSN online community through whatever means possible to make membership both comfortable and productive. Perhaps the greatest gift that one member can bestow upon another is the kindness and understanding of an experienced member helping a novice user and showing that user how to do something. It's a fine thing to do, and it helps for folks to understand that computing isn't that difficult or as bad as it may seem.

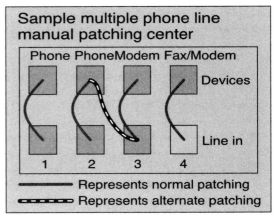

In reality, to share expertise and care for a newbie is perhaps the ultimate in showing online gratitude and is one of the Core Rules of Netiquette that we looked at earlier. Go to the Member Assistance forum

Figure 9-9
A sample telephone switching center, manual style

from the top level of MSN, and take a minute to look over the screen and its contents. The MSN Beta Center will be gone by the time this book hits the streets as it was a support area for the MSN beta, but look at the MSN Lobby, which is a support area for users that was mentioned earlier.

Kids and School

We've talked about the services and features of MSN and the Internet, but what have we done for the rest of the gang? Not much up until now, so let's show the rest of our people what MSN is about.

A Place for Us, A Place for Them

To address the younger crowd, go back to the Home and Family category and really take notice of the forums represented there. There's a KidSpace (which we'll talk about next), a Teen Forum devoted to the not-a-kid-anymore-but-not-yet-an-adult segment of our society, Youth Sports, and Parenting in the '90s for folks like myself who are juggling two careers, a family, three cats, two kids, one puppy, and a computer in the networking tree. Then head off to the Places of Interest forum and take a look there (Figure 9-10).

This is very interesting in that not only is there a place for the SOHO we visited earlier, but look at the ones for Splash Kids and Theme Parks, which are tailored to having fun and sharing experiences.

Do Your Homework, Kids

Here at this same location, the kids can enjoy the use of the Microsoft Encarta and the Microsoft Bookshelf online editions. Figure 9-11 was taken in the beta period, but this aspect of online life should go public when MSN does. It's a welcome edition to school life, and there's a CD-ROM version that you can purchase from Microsoft or your local retail computer store. This is one investment that I have made now and use all the time. You can also take off to the Education and Reference category, which is a growing source of information concerning the educational system in its various aspects.

**Figure 9-10
The Places of
Interest forum**

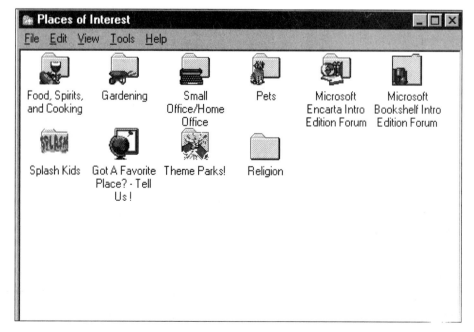

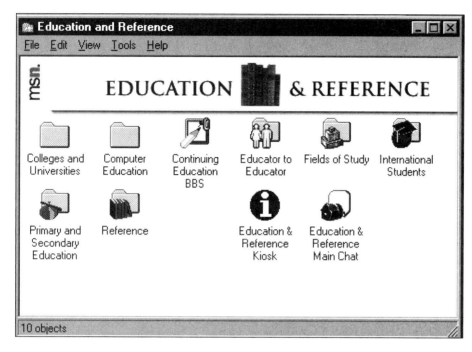

Figure 9-11
The Education and Reference category

Playing Hookie!

Let's face it—we all get tired of school, work, and the other varied ways to wear our lives down, and we need an outlet. Got to have some relief, to be sure, or you'll turn into a book and wind up on someone's shelf for the rest of your life. From the top level of MSN, click on the Arts & Entertainment category (Figure 9-12). This category is one of the really fun ones that enlighten you, amuse you, and provide some of that relief you seek. There are forums for writing, theater, movies, and much more than I could do it justice here. The best I can say is, pay them a visit when you want a change. Wonderful place.

Another interesting place to visit is the Comedy Connection, which can be found in the Arts & Entertainment category under the Comedy and Humor subcategory (Figure 9-13). This is a lively place just to unwind, relax, and kick your shoes off for as long as you want. This place was once referred to as MSN's Virtual Nightclub because you can find virtually any kind of comedy for all ages of kids and adults.

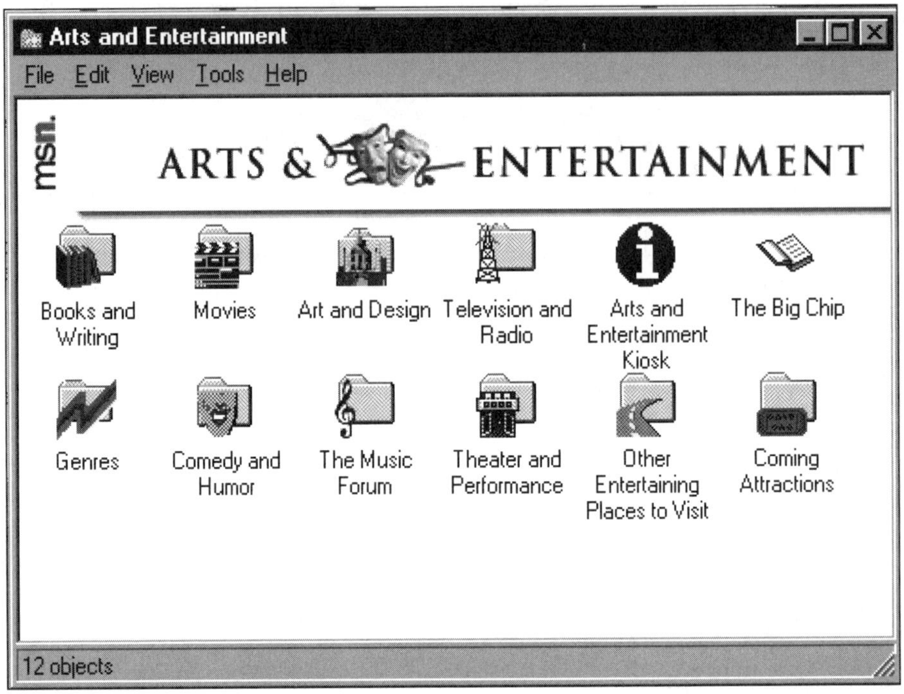

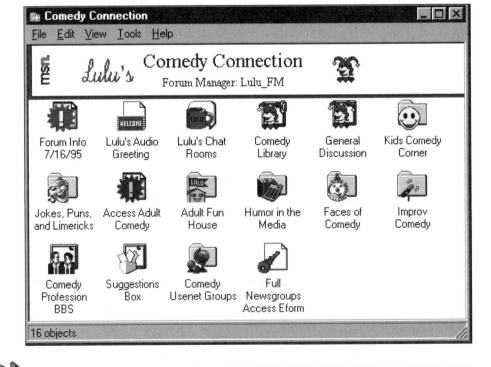

Figure 9-12
The Arts &
Entertainment
category

Figure 9-13
The Comedy
Connection

There are other places you can relax, such as the Interests, Leisure, & Hobbies category (Figure 9-14). This is a really fun and exciting place where you can check out a host of hobbies, playing with finger painting, pottery, and the martial arts to name a few. It's a place where you can tell the manager of the Alien Encounters and UFOs forum where you last saw the spacecraft zooming about your town!

Just as diversified as our online world is the makeup of our society as a whole. That's why you should take a break from it all and check out the People and Communities category, where you'll learn about the many aspects of other cultures and worlds. Just as we all come from different backgrounds, so do we bring different attitudes toward religion and the things sacred to us. The Religion forum, which is linked in all across the forums, is an excellent starting place to find out how others view religion, how they worship, what they worship, and how we as people in general can learn to be more tolerant of others' feelings and attitudes.

Ever want to learn a little bit about how our political system works as seen from the perspective of the newspapers and other information

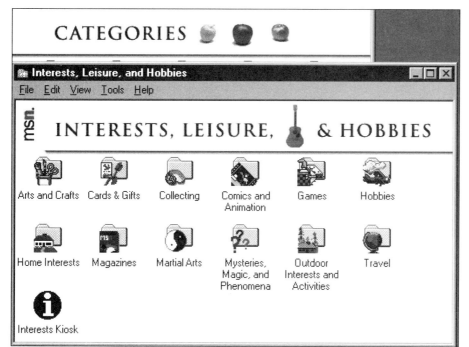

Figure 9-14
The Interests, Leisure, & Hobbies category

systems? Take off to the Public Affairs category and look at its selection of informational services (Figure 9-15). For those of you who have never served in the armed forces, you may want to examine the Armed Forces section and listen to the veterans of the services both here and abroad to see how they did it. Some folks never went to war, others have been in several of these horrendous events. But what it all boils down to is sharing the experience so that others may learn from the dastardly deeds that have been done. War was once described as man's inhumanity to man, and I really believe it. As a twelve-year veteran of our Air Forces, I've seen preparations for war (and steps toward recovery from the same) that I never had to actually use—thankfully. I am more thankful to those who have served and have came back, and to those who were left behind. *Lest we forget our missing few.*

Last and surely not least is an area made just for the sports nut in your home, the Sports, Health, & Fitness category (Figure 9-16). There's

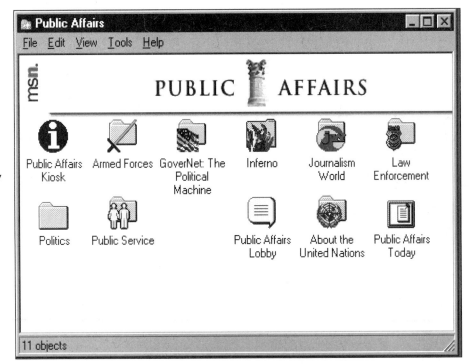

Figure 9-15
The Public
Affairs category

car racing, motorcycle racing, speedboats, powerboats, all other kinds of water sports, and more. You can check on your health and how to better it, run a virtual five kilometer race, talk with the real racers, and keep abreast of the latest happenings of the outdoors. For those of you desiring the colder side of life, there's a whole subcategory dealing with nothing but winter sports.

Research

Okay, so you're in the middle of a project, a monster problem came up, and you simply have to have it fixed before you can turn the project in to your science teacher tomorrow or complete those special plans for the boss at work. What was that all about? A computer network, new software from someone that you've never heard of, and it's got to be done by morning?

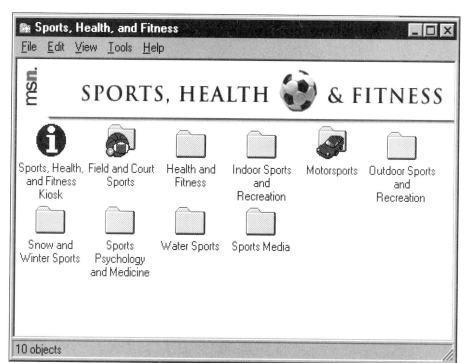

Figure 9-16
The Sports, Health, & Fitness category

Where and When

The Computers and Software category, from the MSN top level, is a fine starting place for anything computer-related (Figure 9-17). It heads up a group of topics as diversified as computing itself. Naturally, there are the hardware and software that make up the systems we use, but look at the rest of it. You'll find software development, training issues, computer publications such as *PC Magazine*, and more.

Science and Technology

If things get down and dirty beyond the normal bounds of computer life, then head off to the Science & Technology category to look at the many scientific and technical aspects of our lives (Figure 9-18). There's the Engineering Forum, Communications Technology, Computer Technology, Electronics, Math, and most of the usual aspects of the academic world.

Check out, for instance, NASA's space program by looking at the Astronomy and Space Forum located in the Science & Technology

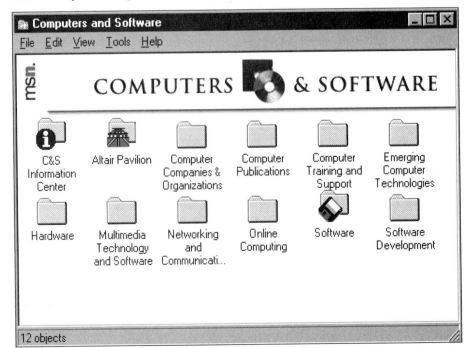

Figure 9-17
The Computers and Software category

Figure 9-18
The Science and Technology category

category. This forum is dedicated to the worlds nearest and farthest beyond us and everything in between.

Special Events

Special events held on MSN are a real treat. These functions are scheduled as often as possible and are held in many of the categories. Look in the MSN Today menu to see when the next scheduled hot event is to be held, or you can go to the Special Events category shown in Figure 9-19 and see the whole topic covered.

Auditoriums

Auditoriums are where all of the action happens (you can participate in the MSN version of an auditorium via Special Events, as shown in Figure 9-20), the central nervous system, to be sure. Have you ever been to a speaking engagement, either as a speaker or a listener, and got the jitters? Same

Figure 9-19
The Special
Events category

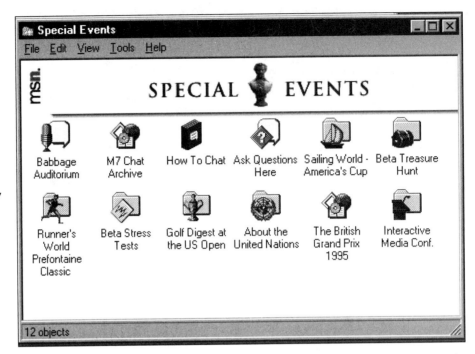

here, except that you're at a keyboard and the audience members are in their chairs as well watching you type out your answers to their questions.

An auditorium is very close to what a normal chat session is, with one important difference. Each speaking engagement is hosted by the forum manager, the category manager, or some other functional manager of the service area. This manager or one of the ICPs (independent content providers) has asked a guest to speak in their auditorium to a group of people at a specific date and time. Not too far from what real speakers do, right?

Close, but in this case a speaking engagement goes something like this (refer to Figure 9-19, the Special Events category): You'll notice that there's a chat room titled Ask Questions Here off to the side of the Babbage Auditorium itself. Everyone is in the auditorium with the guest and the host, but only the guest and the host can talk. Notice the *sunshades* on all of the other folks there (Figure 9-21). If you are shaded, you can't speak but can listen. This is what is known as a *moderated chat*, meaning that it's being held under controlled circumstances.

Figure 9-20
**The Babbage
Auditorium**

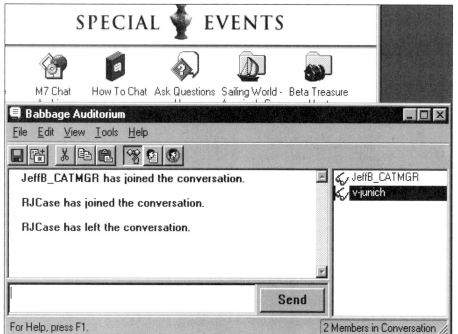

Figure 9-21
**A chat with
everyone in
shades**

In other chat rooms, if participants have become unruly, the host can *give them the shades* to shut them up and restore order. In this situation, however, it's a controlled strike of the gavel that maintains order. Any person desiring to ask a question of the guest has to go to the Ask Questions Here chat room, where someone working with the host will repost the question to the guest as the guest has completed answering the previous question.

Depending on how much time a guest has, the chat may rely on questions that have been asked days in advance to improve order and expedite the discussions. Before coming to a moderated chat, if you plan on asking questions, consider following a few simple guidelines:

- Ask only pertinent questions. If the chat is on heart attacks, don't ask a question about ankle problems.
- Think your questions through so you can keep them as close to the topic as possible.
- Be patient. Ask your question and then give matters time. In really active chats, your question can easily be 15 or 20 questions behind the current one.
- Give others a chance. Normal events usually have 25 to 50 participants, and some are constantly asking questions without giving way to others.

NOTE

If you're constantly asking questions, your chances of getting answers may actually decrease!

Be considerate, and allow others to ask a question or two. Being overbearing is a sure way to be noticed and known as a problem member. You don't want that to happen. You'll never be able to get rid of the onus, either, unless you quit the service or create another account.

Jam Sessions and Brainstorms

In most cases, the auditoriums across MSN are closed during normal business times and are opened only during special events. There are times, however, when you may indeed see such a place open for general public usage. These are usually times when category-wide events are held to get more information from the members. The occasion could be a "What do you think about us" type of session, or a welcoming party for a new group on the service, or anything deemed worthy of opening the auditorium, which is a hefty resource consumer on the MSN servers. Such events don't happen all the time, but MSN is fully capable of supporting them.

Common Meeting Places

Think of these places as like the old watering hole back in the wild west. If you wanted to keep going, you stopped by and tanked up before riding off to your next destination. It's only natural that we look after our own interests at one point or another, and we can do that on MSN through these features.

Many of these places are located at the top level of each category, and although they have different names, all of them have one object: to help members make their trek across MSN as enjoyable as possible. Take a look at Figure 9-22. Here, the class of features we are describing takes the form of a Front Office that is used much the same as a company's information desk when you walk into its place of business.

Every area has its own way to offer support and services to the membership, and it's more often that not customized to that particular atmosphere.

Moderated or Not?

These chat areas and auditoriums are usually moderated so that there's a manager of the relevant part of the service available to support the

Figure 9-22
Science and
Technology's
Front Office

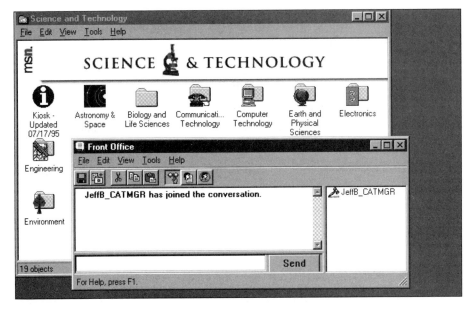

members online, keep order, and maintain proper guidance and direction for the forum. However, managers or their assistants can't always be online. When no one with authority is around, and this usually happens during the late night and early morning hours, things can get out of hand very quickly.

Loose Lips and Tight Fists

When these wild and woolly times strike, it's easy to let your temper get the best of you. Don't! Just back off and ignore the person who's getting your goat. In a chat, look at the right side of the chat screen, where you will see the names of the people in the chat. Move the mouse pointer to the name of the offending person and right-click the mouse. Then you can select the Ignore function, which blocks out that person's words to you (Figure 9-23). Instantly ignored!

At times, the offending person just keeps it up and won't stop. When this occurs, send e-mail to the manager of the forum, and try to keep copies of any mail that may transpire between you and the troublemaker. If the person is badgering you by way of e-mail, then send a message to the *MSN Sysop* explaining what happened, and also send copies of any relevant messages. MSN is very sensitive to the needs of the membership and won't put up with any kind of harassment.

Pushing the Limits

Oh, sure, you can fight back verbally and stand your ground, but please do so politely. Firmly and authoritatively, but politely. It'll keep you out of the hot seat if the other person insists on being an infernal pain in the behind. You should understand up front that personal attacks upon someone's character and persona will get you smacked faster than anything. It's fine to have a spirited discussion, but keep the language on a professional level, with none of those four-letter words of ill repute.

To Join or Not to Join

This last section of our endeavor is about being shy and quiet. Huh? Has the author gone wacko at the very end? Not really, but I just wanted to throw in a few parting words about being an active participant of any service, not just MSN. It's easy to understand people may have, by their very nature, been quiet and kept to themselves all of their lives and now are suddenly on a service that thousands see every day. When you're on stage at that speaking engagement, it's time for instant feedback. They

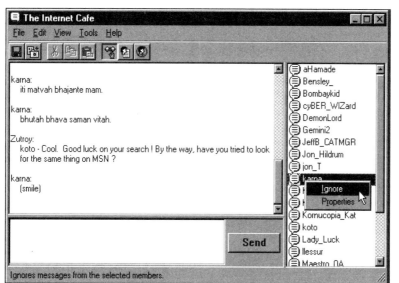

Figure 9-23
Ignoring a person in chat

can see you, and you can see them. The sweaty palm syndrome.

But, online life is a completely different ballgame. Sure, it's the same crowd, but in a different environment and with a different set of rules. You're shielded by the computer and screen, but your words become your facial expressions. This situation can be a bit tricky for someone not accustomed to typing in a clear and concise manner. Mess up one word, and the entire meaning can be misconstrued. Don't let that dissuade you from participating! As time goes on, you'll find out that the member *next* to you who is having the same problem you did last week could surely benefit from your idea for a bug fix. Share that data in your head, and be wiser for it. Help people help themselves, and you've taken yourself to the next plane of computer existence—that of a participant.

Summary

Wow! What more can I say other than how'd we manage to make it to the end? We've covered an entire service in one short book, hit the high points, covered a few different points from other services, and then traveled all across the Web and MSN to find virtually any piece of data possible. It's got to be one of the most fun things I've ever done—writing this book and taking you for a cruise with the Microsoft Internet Explorer, MSN, and the Web.

I surely hope that you've seen how much fun and use the Web can be for you. While it's true that the Web is mainly a document storage and retrieval system, in general, you can access the many thousands of files and types of systems made possible through the efforts of those stalwart pioneers and trailblazers of yesteryear. Their goals, fears, and heartaches paved the way for our smooth sailing and surfing so that we can share the knowledge and power we've gained from the experience.

As you close the back cover and put this book back on your shelf, remember all of the bookmarks in your mind that have assisted you in navigating some of the rough waters we did, and pass that bookmark file on to a friend. Share in the experience, share in the pain, and share in the gain so that future surfers don't get beached before they launch.

Commonly Used Terms

Alias

A substitute name for the real entity. A nickname that generally refers to the actual device; "INTEROZ.COM" is the alias to the IP address 204.49.131.201.

Analog

Said of an electrical voltage or current used to cause physical devices to perform a set task. Your modem is connected to an analog phone line.

ANSI

American National Standards Institute. The ruling body that formulates and oversees the standards for nearly all aspects of computer life including hardware and software.

ARPANET

The Advanced Research Projects Agency Network. The forerunner to the Internet, which is now often referred to as "The Information Superhighway."

ASCII

American Standard Code for Information Interchange. A standard in which letters, numbers, punctuation, and control characters are in a common format for the most basic character set.

Bandwidth

The volumetric capacity of a device. In computerese, this refers to the maximum capacity of a communications device such as telephone lines for a modem or a fiber optics cable for networking information. T-1 communications channels have the bandwidth to carry data to and from up to 56 of the now-common 28.8K baud modems at one time.

Baud Rate

A relative measurement of the speed with which a modem transfers data. Closely approximates the true throughput of the device.

BPS

Bits per second. This is the true rate of speed at which a modem transmits data.

Cache

A temporary holding area for data. Disk drives and processors each have a cache to store the most recently used data. Caches greatly speed the performance of devices.

Carrier

The signal on the telephone line used to carry your modem data as an analog signal.

CERN

The European High Speed Particle Physics Laboratory where the World Wide Web was born.

Client

The software installed on your computer used to access the site to which you're connected.

Client/Server

The computing model in which your computer (the client) requests information or services from the network computer (the server) and the server returns the results of the request.

CM

Category Manager. The middle tier of managers for the Microsoft Network, responsible for overall daily operations of one MSN category.

Core Memory

Iron oxide–coated electronics devices used to accept and retain binary computer data. Core memory was the 1960s forerunner to the random-access memory chips in your PC.

CPS

Characters per second. Another relative measure of the amount and speed at which data are transferred in a modem.

CSLIP

Compressed Serial Line Interface Protocol. An advanced form of an Internet SLIP connection that allows for faster transmission of data.

DARPA

Defense Advanced Research Projects Agency. This is the research arm of the U.S. government that originally promoted and built the Internet as a means to connect many government and research agencies.

Digital

Of the form of data that computers use, which takes the form of either a binary 1 or a binary 0. Modems convert analog telephone signals to a digital form that computers can use.

DNS

Domain Name System. A methodology by which Internet servers can resolve an alias to the actual IP address.

DNS Resolution

The process of resolving an *alias*. This involves a data file in which the alias is matched to the numerical equivalent.

Domain

A *territorial* region of ownership of a set of computing devices. Think of a tiger that has a set amount of land that he rules, which is the tiger's *domain*.

E-Mail

Electronic mail. The computerized version of a letter written on paper. E-mail accounts for nearly 50 percent of Internet traffic.

Emoticons

Emotional icons. Graphical key board symbols that represent feelings. 8-) is a smiley face with glasses.

FAQ

Frequently asked questions. A text file in which the user can get answers to the most often asked questions about a given service or other subject.

Firewall

A software function on a server that limits or regulates access to and from a network server. A firewall prevents unauthorized access to Web sites.

Flame Mail

Vocally abusive e-mail in which the participants exchange heated and often vile language. This is the written equivalent of a street fight!

FM

Forum Manager. The frontline manager of the Microsoft Network's online service. The FM is responsible for daily operations and functions of one forum or group of forum topics.

FTP

File Transfer Protocol. The standard by which computers transfer files across the Internet.

GIF

Graphical Information File. A graphics file format owned by CompuServe, Inc., commonly used for pictures on the Internet.

Go Word

The short alphabetical representation of a longer forum or topic name. For example, the Science and Technology Suggestion Box on MSN has a go word of **st_sugg**.

GUI

Graphical User Interface. A means of interacting with a computer through the means of windows, menus, icons, and other graphic devices.

Hop Count

The number of times your data must traverse a router, server, or bridge to get to the destination.

HTTP

HyperText Transfer Protocol. The standard that defines how data are moved between Web sites and your client PC.

HTML

HyperText Markup Language. The standard that defines how Web pages are created and presented.

ICP

Independent Content Provider. This term characterizes service providers on MSN such as PC Magazine, Seagate Technologies, and IBM that sell their company's products or services on MSN. ICPs pay to be on MSN. Forum managers and category managers, by contrast, are both contracted by MSN for support and services.

Internet

The term *Internet* is used to represent a myriad of networks connected together in such a way as to provide global access to data.

InterNIC

The Network Information Center for the Internet. InterNIC is a clearing house where IP addresses, domains, and related matters are cleared and registered. If you establish a Web server, you should register it with the NIC to ensure that no one else duplicates your name and that the Internet users know that you're out there.

IP Address

The numerical representation of the Internet site or user. My provider's IP address is 204.49.131.201. See alias.

ISDN

Integrated Services Digital Network. This is the format of high-speed data transmissions in which voice and data are mixed together into one data stream. ISDN is capable of up to 128K baud.

JPEG

Joint Photographic Experts Group. A group of scientists who have defined a graphics format for computers.

Keyword

A word that serves as the focal point of a topic.

LAN

Local Area Network. The entity that is composed of a network server and several client workstations that communicate with the server.

Mainframe Computer

A computing device capable of performing high-speed multiple tasks along with multiple users simultaneously. The term is generally used to refer to computers that historically operated entire companies and financial centers.

Microcomputer

A personal computer normally found on the average desktop.

MIE

The Microsoft Internet Explorer.

Minicomputer

A powerful computing system not quite as big as a mainframe but larger than a personal computer.

MIS

Management Information System. This is the term most often used to refer to the corporate data centers and their managers.

MPEG

Motion Picture Experts Group. A group of industry representatives that have defined a standard for compressible file formats for movies.

NASA

National Aeronautics and Space Administration. An arm of the Department of Defense that runs the nation's space program and was one of the original agencies involved in the creation of the Internet.

Newsgroups

The Usenet groups (also available through MSN and the Web) used to disseminate information between users just like a note board in an office.

NSF

National Science Foundation. The body of individuals that operate a research arm of the Internet.

POP

Point of Presence. A network node to your actual service provider available to you via a local telephone call.

PPP

Point to Point Protocol. One method of connecting a personal computer to the Internet by way of a modem. It's generally more stable than a SLIP connection.

Proxy Server

When firewalls are used, a proxy server lets an authorized Internet user send requests to the Web site and get answers back without the actual server being infiltrated by undesirable outside users.

Remote Access

Said of Internet users that are not connected to a site directly through the server's network. Most of us are connecting via modems and could be called remote users.

Server

The hardware and software combination that provides multiuser and multitasking functionality for users. Web sites are servers and respond to client actions.

Senior Sysop

One of the upper-level managers of MSN who form the nucleus of its online managerial capabilities. Seniors who are contracted are highly experienced managers.

SLIP

Serial Line Interface Protocol. The original method of connecting to an Internet provider by way of a modem attached to a serial port on a computer.

SMTP
Simple Mail Transport Protocol. A standard that defines how different mail applications on different types of servers can transparently exchange mail.

TCP/IP
Transmission Control Protocol/Internet Protocol. The standard that defines how computing systems can communicate with each other regardless of the type of hardware used by each.

Telco
Telephone Company—your local phone provider.

Telnet
An Internet function used to make a rudimentary connection from a PC to a server.

Tokens
Access rights used to grant or revoke access to different parts of MSN, or to grant or revoke various privileges on MSN.

Usenet
The User Network—the newsgroups collectively.

URL
Uniform Resource Locator. The standard definition of how to connect to various Web functions.

v.32
The standard transmission rate for current day modems, 14.4K baud.

v.34
The new standard for high-speed modem connectivity that defines standard transmission rates of 28.8K baud and compressed rates of up to 115,000 baud.

WAIS
Wide Area Information Server. One source of informational documents gathered from many Web servers. WAIS serves as a central repository for many sites.

Web
An Internet service used to create graphical hypertext links among documents on many sites.

Web Browser
A software program used to link the client computer (you) to the Web site (server) to allow informational exchanges.

WebMaster
The site administrator for a Web site.

Winsock
The Microsoft Windows Applications Programming Interface that defines how PCs connect to Internet resources.

Worm
An Internet function that crawls through Web sites in search of information.

X-Windows
A graphics-based software application and operating system that runs on 32-bit computers commonly running UNIX or Sun Solaris.

The Structure of MSN

Appendix B is designed to provide an overall picture of The Microsoft Network. It does this by listing the primary parts of the service and then breaking each down into its principal elements. This perspective on MSN was created three weeks before the service was due to go live, and should change only minor amounts during the initial 60 days after MSN's launch date. While this appendix includes all of MSN, breaking down each of the forums here would've been prohibitively large for you to read; therefore, I've kept it on a shallow level.

The Overall Structure of MSN

MSN is broken down into five primary functions. The last of these functions, called "Categories" in the Main menu, consists of a set of subject categories under which you'll find MSN's various forums. These categories and constituent forums are listed at the end of this appendix.

NOTE

The forums listed are those in existence as this book is being written, at an early stage of MSN's development. Forums are bound to come and go over time.

- MSN Today
- Electronic Mail
- Favorite Places
- Member Assistance
- The Categories

We'll start from the top, at MSN's Main screen, shown in Figure B-1.

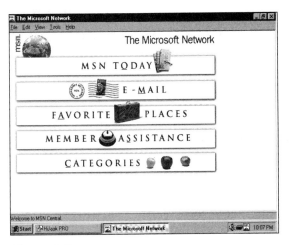

Figure B-1
MSN's Main screen

MSN Today

MSN Today displays hot topics and highlights of coming events, and it offers direct links to them.

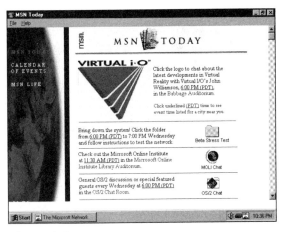

Figure B-2
MSN Today

E-Mail

MSN provides its own e-mail system and also offers access to other mail systems via MS Exchange for the Internet. As you can see in Figure B-3, MSN provides the usual member tools such as an address book, an inbox, an outbox, a special box that holds your deleted mail in case you want to recover something, and functions for creating more folders to handle special mail needs. You can send, receive, and forward mail, and you can transfer files as attachments to e-mail.

Favorite Places

Favorite Places can save you a lot of time getting to your most frequently visited

Figure B-3
E-mail on MSN

placcs. When you go to one of your MSN activities, single-click on the right mouse button and tell the program to Add to Favorite Places. This creates a shortcut to the topic and places it in your Favorite Places (Figure B-4). The next time you want to go to one of these gems, open this folder and away you go! You don't have to remember any levels of the MSN structure once you've saved it.

Member Assistance

This area, shown in Figure B-5, is your primary location for support and services on MSN. Almost any condition can be handled here except that you can't get connected. In that case, call 1-800-386-5550 for support. If you can get online, however, Member Assistance should be your first destination.

Figure B-4
Favorite Places

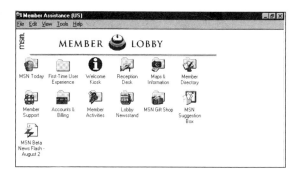

Figure B-5
Member Lobby

The Categories

This is where you'll find the main contents of MSN. I'll break down each category into its principle parts, list the forums, and tell you briefly about each one.

NOTE

As you traverse the category tree, you may see the same forum name listed in two or more areas. These are multiple links to individual forums placed so that members can jump between related forums under whatever general rubric caught their attention. This format is a great time-saver that converts to money savings for you!

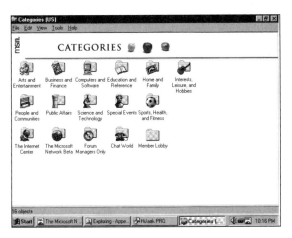

Figure B-6
The Categories

Arts and Entertainment

This list names the forums reached through the Arts and Entertainment category screen, shown in Figure B-7.

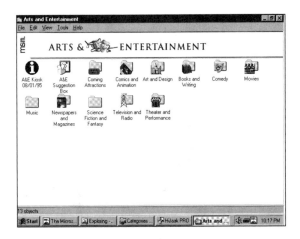

Figure B-7
Arts and Entertainment

- ◆ A&E Information Kiosk
- ◆ A&E Suggestion Box
- ◆ Coming Attractions
- ◆ Art and Design
- ◆ Books and Writing
- ◆ Comedy
- ◆ Movies
- ◆ Music
- ◆ Newspapers and Magazines
- ◆ Science Fiction and Fantasy
- ◆ Television and Radio
- ◆ Theater and Performance

Business and Finance

This list names the forums reached through the Business and Finance category screen, shown in Figure B-8.

- ◆ Professions and Industries
- ◆ Business News and References
- ◆ Usenet Newsgroups for Business
- ◆ Business and Finance Suggestion Box
- ◆ Wall Street, the Markets, and Investing
- ◆ Business and Finance Information Kiosk
- ◆ Small Office/Home Office
- ◆ Business Services
- ◆ Jobs and Careers
- ◆ Venture and Entrepreneurs
- ◆ Personal Finance

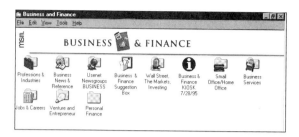

Figure B-8
Business and Finance

Chat World

This list names the forums reached through the Chat World category screen, shown in Figure B-9.

- ◆ Atrium Restaurant
- ◆ Chat Garden
- ◆ Chat World Elevator
- ◆ Chat World Front Desk
- ◆ Chat World Lobby
- ◆ Concierge Information Kiosk
- ◆ Games and Casinos
- ◆ Lobby Photo Gallery
- ◆ Pool and Spa
- ◆ Concierge

Figure B-9
Chat World

Computers and Software

This list names the forums reached through the Computers and Software category screen, shown in Figure B-10.

- ◆ C&S Information Kiosk
- ◆ Altair Pavilion
- ◆ Computer Companies & Organizations
- ◆ Computer Publications
- ◆ Computer Training and Support
- ◆ Emerging Computer Technologies
- ◆ Hardware
- ◆ Multimedia Technology and Software
- ◆ Networking and Communications
- ◆ Online Computing
- ◆ Software
- ◆ Software Development

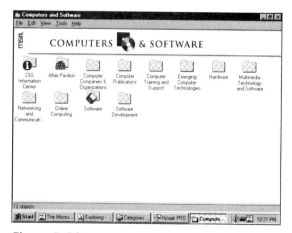

Figure B-10
Computers and Software

Education and Reference

This list names the forums reached through the Education and Reference category screen, shown in Figure B-11.

- Colleges and Universities
- Computer Education
- Educator to Educator
- Fields of Study
- International Students
- Primary and Secondary Education
- Reference
- Education and Reference Kiosk
- Education and Reference Main Chat

Home and Family

This list names the forums reached through the Home and Family category screen, shown in Figure B-12.

- For Kids Only
- Home Improvement
- KidSpace
- Parenting in the '90s
- Teen Forum
- Work-at-Home Dads
- Working Mothers
- Youth Sports
- Other Places of Interest
- Related Internet Newsgroups
- Home and Family Town Hall
- Home and Family Library
- Help and Information Center

Interests, Leisure, and Hobbies

This list names the forums reached through the Interests, Leisure, and Hobbies category screen, shown in Figure B-13.

- Interests Information Center
- Arts and Crafts
- Automotive Interests

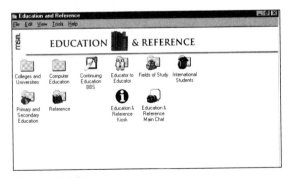

Figure B-11
Education and Reference

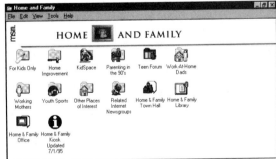

Figure B-12
Home and Family

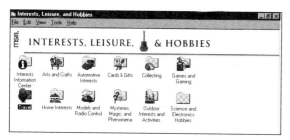

Figure B-13
Interests, Leisure, and Hobbies

- Cards and Gifts
- Collecting
- Games and Gaming
- Home Interests
- Models and Radio Control
- Mysteries, Magic, and Phenomena
- Outdoor Interests and Activities
- Science and Electronics Hobbies
- Travel

Member Lobby

This list names the forums reached through the Member Lobby category screen, shown in Figure B-14.

- Welcome Kiosk
- Reception Desk
- Maps & Information
- Member Directory
- Member Support
- Accounts and Billing
- Member Activities
- Lobby Newsstand
- MSN Gift Shop

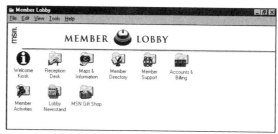

Figure B-14
Member Lobby

People and Communities

This list names the forums reached through the People and Communities category screen, shown in Figure B-15.

- Cultures
- Advice and Support
- Religion
- People to People
- Women Online
- Men Online
- Cards and Gifts
- People and Communities Kiosk
- People and Communities Suggestion Box

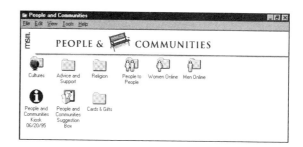

Figure B-15
People and Communities

Public Affairs

This list names the forums reached through the Public Affairs category screen, shown in Figure B-16.

- Public Affairs Information Kiosk
- Armed Forces
- GoverNet: The Political Machine
- The Inferno
- Journalism World
- Law Enforcement
- Politics
- Public Service
- About the United Nations
- Public Affairs Today
- Public Affairs Lobby

Science and Technology

This list names the forums reached through the Science and Technology category screen, shown in Figure B-17.

- S&T Information Center
- Edison Pavilion
- Astronomy and Space
- Biology and Life Sciences
- Chemistry
- Communications Technology
- Computers and Electronics
- Geology and Geography
- Engineering
- Environment
- Math
- Medicine
- Physics
- Transportation
- Front Office
- Science and Technology Suggestion Box

Special Events

This category is dedicated to events of all kinds and covering all sorts of topics (Figure

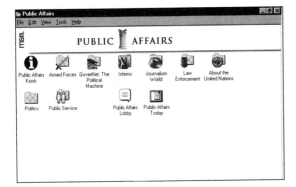

Figure B-16
Public Affairs

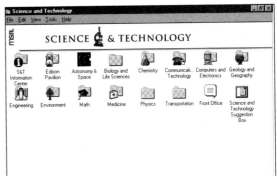

Figure B-17
Science and Technology

B-18). By the time you get this book, these subjects and events may have changed, but the theory is the same. If you want to know what's coming up soon, tune in here.

- ◆ Babbage Auditorium
- ◆ How to Chat
- ◆ Ask Questions Here
- ◆ Sailing World— America's Cup
- ◆ Runner's World Prefontaine Classic
- ◆ Golf Digest at the US Open
- ◆ About the United Nations
- ◆ The British Grand Prix 1995
- ◆ Interactive Media Conference
- ◆ Tekno*Comix Forum

Sports, Health, and Fitness

This list names the forums reached through the Sports, Health, and Fitness category screen, shown in Figure B-19.

Figure B-18
Special Events

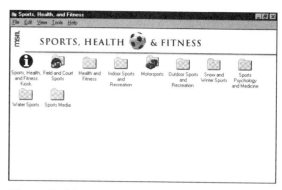

Figure B-19
Sports, Health, and Fitness

- ◆ Sports, Health, and Fitness Kiosk
- ◆ Field and Court Sports
- ◆ Health and Fitness
- ◆ Indoor Sports and Recreation
- ◆ Motorsports
- ◆ Outdoor Sports and Recreation
- ◆ Snow and Winter Sports
- ◆ Sports Psychology and Medicine
- ◆ Water Sports
- ◆ Sports Media

The Internet Center

This list names the forums reached through the Internet Center category screen, shown in Figure B-20.

- ◆ Read Me First Kiosk
- ◆ Core Rules of Netiquette
- ◆ The Internet Café
- ◆ Internet Newsgroups

- ◆ The Most Popular Newsgroups
- ◆ The Internet Center BBS
- ◆ The Internet Center Suggestion Box
- ◆ File Libraries
- ◆ Chat Nodes (Not moderated)
- ◆ Full Internet Trial Area

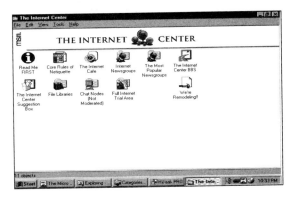

Figure B-20
The Internet Center

Index

Available Now!

Build a Web Site: The Programmer's Guide to Creating, Building, and Maintaining a Web Presence	$34.95
The CD-ROM Revolution	$24.95
CompuServe Information Manager for Windows: The Complete Membership Kit & Handbook (with two 3½-inch disks)	$29.95
Computers Don't Byte	$ 7.95
Computer Gamer's Survival Guide	$19.95
Create Wealth with Quicken, Second Edition	$19.95
Cruising America Online: The Visual Learning Guide	$19.95
Free Electronic Networks	$24.95
Interactive Internet: The Insider's Guide to MUDs, MOOs, and IRC	$19.95
Internet After Hours	$19.95
Internet for Windows—America Online Edition: The Visual Learning Guide	$19.95
The Internet Warp Book: Your Complete Guide to Getting Online with OS/2	$21.95
KidWare: The Parent's Guide to Software for Children	$14.95
A Parent's Guide to Video Games	$12.95
PROCOMM PLUS for Windows: The Visual Learning Guide	$19.95
The Slightly Skewed Computer Dictionary	$ 8.95
Software: What's Hot! What's Not!	$16.95
Sound Blaster: Making WAVes with Multimedia	$19.95
Stacker Multimedia: The Joy of Crash-Free Computing	$19.95
Thom Duncan's Guide to NetWare Shareware (with 3½-inch disk)	$29.95
UnInstaller 3: Uncluttering Your PC	$19.95
The USENET Navigator Kit (with 3½-inch disk)	$29.95
WinComm Pro: The Visual Learning Guide	$19.95
Windows 3.1: The Visual Learning Guide	$19.95
Windows 95: The Visual Learning Guide	$19.95
Windows 95: A to Z	$34.95
Windows 95: Easy Installation Guide	$12.95
The Windows 95 Book: Your Definitive guide to Installing and Using Windows 95	$24.95
WinFax PRO 4: The Visual Learning Guide	$19.95

To Order Books

Please send me the following items:

Quantity	Title	Unit Price	
_____	_____	$ _____	$ _____
_____	_____	$ _____	$ _____
_____	_____	$ _____	$ _____
_____	_____	$ _____	$ _____
_____	_____	$ _____	$ _____
_____	_____	$ _____	$ _____

Subtotal	$ _____
7.25% Sales Tax (CA only)	$ _____
8.25% Sales Tax (TN only)	$ _____
5.0% Sales Tax (MD only)	$ _____
7.0% G.S.T. Canadian Orders	$ _____
Shipping and Handling*	$ _____
Total Order	$ _____

> * $4.00 shipping and handling charge for the first book and $1 for each additional book.

By Telephone: With MC or Visa, call (916) 632-4400. Mon-Fri, 9-4 PST
By Mail: Just fill out the information below and send with your remittance to:

Prima Publishing
P.O. Box 1260BK
Rocklin, CA 95677

Satisfaction unconditionally guaranteed.

Name _____

Address _____

City _____ State _____ ZIP _____

MC/Visa# _____ Exp. _____

Signature _____